Gender and Families

THE GENDER LENS:
A Sage Publications / Pine Forge Press Series

Series Editors

Judith A. Howard
University of Washington

Barbara Risman
North Carolina State University

Mary Romero
Arizona State University

Joey Sprague
University of Kansas

Books in the Series

Yen Le Espiritu, *Asian American Women and Men: Labor, Laws, and Love*

Judith A. Howard and Jocelyn A. Hollander, *Gendered Situations, Gendered Selves: A Gender Lens on Social Psychology*

Michael A. Messner, *Politics of Masculinities: Men in Movements*

Judith Lorber, *Gender and the Social Construction of Illness*

Scott Coltrane, *Gender and Families*

Pepper Schwartz and Virginia Rutter, *The Gender of Sexuality*

Books Forthcoming

Francesca Cancian and Stacy Oliker, *A Gendered View of Care*

Patricia Yancey Martin and David Collinson, *The Gendered Organization*

Gender and Families

Scott Coltrane
University of Southern California

PINE FORGE PRESS

Thousand Oaks ■ London ■ New Delhi

For information:

Pine Forge Press
A Sage Publications Company
2455 Teller Road
Thousand Oaks, California 91320
E-mail: sales@pfp.sagepub.com
(805) 499-4224

SAGE Publications Ltd.
6 Bonhill Street
London EC2A 4PU
United Kingdom

SAGE Publications India Pvt. Ltd.
M-32 Market
Greater Kailash I
New Delhi 110 048 India

Printed in the United States of America

Library of Congress Cataloging-in-Publication Data

Coltrane, Scott.
    Gender and families / by Scott Coltrane.
        p. cm. — (The gender lens)
    Includes bibliographical references (p.   ) and index.
    ISBN 0-8039-9036-7 (pbk.)
    1. Family—United States. 2. Sex role—United States. 3. Gender
identity—United States. I. Title. II. Series.
HQ536.C718 1997
306.85'0973--dc21   97-4878

98 99 00 01 02 03 10 9 8 7 6 5 4 3 2 1

Production Editor: Diana E. Axelsen
Production Assistant: Karen Wiley
Typesetter: Christina M. Hill
Indexer: Trish Wittenstein
Print Buyer: Anna Chin

CONTENTS

CHAPTER 3

Paid Work and Family Life 53

CHAPTER 4

Mothers, Fathers, and Family Care 75

CHAPTER 5

Engendering Children 107

CHAPTER 6

Regulating Families and Gender 132

CHAPTER 7

Where Do We Go From Here? 160

It is now over 20 years since feminist sociologists identified gender as an important analytic dimension in sociology. In the intervening two decades, theory and research on gender have grown exponentially. With this series, we intend to further this scholarship, as well as ensure that theory and research on gender become fully integrated into the discipline as a whole.

Beth Hess and Myra Marx Ferree, in *Analyzing Gender* (1988), identified three stages in the study of women and men since 1970. Initially, the emphasis was on sex differences and the extent to which such differences might be based in biological properties of individuals. In the second stage, the focus shifted to individual-level sex roles and socialization, exposing gender as the product of specific social arrangements, although still conceptualizing it as an individual trait. The hallmark of the third stage is the recognition of the centrality of gender as an organizing principle in all social systems, including work, politics, everyday interaction, families, economic development, law, education, and a host of other social domains. As our understanding of gender has become more social, so has our awareness that gender is experienced and organized in race- and class-specific ways.

In the summer of 1992, the American Sociological Association funded a small conference, organized by Barbara Risman and Joey Sprague, to discuss the evolution of gender in these distinctly sociological frameworks. The conference brought together a sampling of gender scholars working in a wide range of substantive areas with a diversity of methods to focus on gender as a principle of social organization. The discussions of the state of feminist scholarship made it clear that gender is pervasive in society and operates at multiple levels. Gender shapes identities and perception, interactional practices, and the very forms of social institutions, and it does so in race- and class-specific ways. If we did not see gender in social phenomena, we were not seeing clearly.

The participants in this ASA-sponsored seminar recognized that although these developing ideas about gender were widely accepted by feminist sociologists and many others who study social inequalities, they were relatively unfamiliar to many who work within other sociological paradigms. This book series was conceived at that conference as a means to introduce these ideas to sociological colleagues and students, and to help further develop gender scholarship.

As series editors, we feel it is time for gender scholars to speak to our colleagues and to the general education of students. There are many sociologists and scholars in other social sciences who want to incorporate scholarship on gender and its intersections with race, class, and sexuality in their teaching and research, but who lack the tools to do so. For those who have not worked in this area, the prospect of the bibliographic research necessary to develop supplementary units, or to transform their own teaching and scholarship, is daunting. Moreover, the publications necessary to penetrate a curriculum resistant to change and encumbered by inertia have simply not been available. We conceptualize this book series as a way of meeting the needs of these scholars, and thereby also encouraging the development of the sociological understanding of gender by offering a "gender lens."

What do we mean by a "gender lens"? It means working to make gender visible in social phenomena, asking if, how, and why social processes, standards, and opportunities differ systematically for women and men. It also means recognizing that gender inequality is inextricably braided with other systems of inequity. Looking at the world through a gendered lens thus implies two seemingly contradictory tasks. First, it means unpacking the taken-for-granted assumptions about gender that pervade sociological research, and social life more generally. At the same time, looking through a gender lens means showing just how central assumptions about gender continue to be to the organization of the social world, regardless of their empirical reality. We show how our often unquestioned ideas about gender affect the worlds we see, the questions we ask, the answers we can envision. The *Gender Lens* series is committed to social change directed toward eradicating these inequalities. Our goals are consistent with initiatives at colleges and universities across the United States that are encouraging the development of more diverse scholarship and teaching.

The books in the *Gender Lens* series are aimed at different audiences and have been written for a variety of uses, from assigned readings in introductory undergraduate course to graduate seminars, and as professional resources for our colleagues. The series includes several different styles of books that address these goals in distinct ways. We are excited about this series and anticipate that it will have an enduring impact on the direction of both pedagogy and scholarship in sociology and other related social sciences. We invite you, the reader, to join us in thinking through these difficult but exciting issues by offering feedback or developing your own project and proposing it to us for the series.

About This Volume

In *Gender and Families*, Scott Coltrane shows how popular culture and everyday family life reflect and perpetuate patterns of gender inequality. Coltrane persuasively argues that families and gender are inseparably linked. He demonstrates how it is impossible to understand families without reference to the meanings assigned to manhood and womanhood in any culture. Reviewing decades of research in the social sciences, *Gender and Families* shows how gender relations and family life are so intertwined that it is impossible to understand one without paying attention to the other. Coltrane combines a social construction and a social structural approach to show how gender and family relations have changed in the past and how they will continue to change in the future. He shows how families and gender are shaped by economic and institutional forces. Topics covered include family rituals, romance and marriage, paid work and housework, family care, child rearing, family policy, and prospects for the future. Coltrane draws on many sources: personal stories, letters, diaries, questionnaires, interviews, demographics, historical records, court proceedings, and media imagery. He describes the lives of diverse families, white families, ethnic minority families, and nontraditional families. Questions of power and control are especially salient throughout the book, because gender, ethnicity, and family structure all help to grant or deny access to privileges and comforts.

Gender and Families is appropriate for use in any class concerned with family structure, family interaction, work-family linkages, parenting, child development, inequality, gender, or social change. The insights generated from reading *Gender and Families* will benefit those who work in various human service fields, including counseling, social work, education, child development, and health services, as well as those who are working toward degrees in sociology, psychology, women's studies, family studies, or other social sciences. *Gender and Families* is the first book-length analysis of the intersection between gender and families, providing a valuable resource for teachers of both beginning and advanced college classes.

CHAPTER 1

The Social Construction of Gender and Families

Most people think of gender and family as two separate things, but they are tied together like the proverbial chicken and egg. Asking which one comes first ignores that we cannot understand one without reference to the other. It may not always be obvious, but when we talk about *family* values—such as whether children need two parents—we are also talking about *gender* values, because a "yes" answer implies that only women with husbands should have children. In the same way, when we talk about *gender* issues—such as whether men should be paid higher wages than women—we are also talking about *family* issues, because a "yes" answer implies that husbands should be the family breadwinner.

Conservatives avoid talking about women's rights when they claim that America's problems are the result of a breakdown in family values. Liberals avoid talking about family values when they claim that women's problems are the result of job discrimination. Most political and religious rhetoric carries messages about both, even if it seems to focus on just one. Adding to the false division between gender and family, most academic researchers study one or the other, rarely focusing on both simultaneously. Similarly, college classes tend to be divided into those focusing on families and those focusing on gender or women's studies. In contrast, this book gives equal weight to both, highlighting the many connections between them. As the following chapters will show, gender relations and family life are so intertwined that it is impossible to understand one without paying attention to the other.

A Social Constructionist Approach

I use a social constructionist approach in this book. The basic idea behind this theoretical approach is that "reality" is not as real as it seems. Depending on personal histories, individual characteristics, social experiences, environmental contexts, and many other factors, people tend to "see" the world differently. For example, children growing up near the Arctic Circle learn many different names for *snow* and can recognize subtle distinctions among them. In contrast, children growing up in a rain forest near the equator who see snow for the first time might call it *rain* or perhaps not know what to call it at all. The rain forest children would see the snow differently from the Arctic children because the cognitive framework and language for making sense of it would be missing. Naming physical objects (such as snow) encourages people to think and talk about them in specific ways, which, in turn, helps individuals perceive them in culturally appropriate ways.

If we change the focus from physical objects to social customs, we need to pay even more attention to possible differences in meaning. Take, for example, the complex set of expectations called *manners* or *etiquette*. Rules dictating what is polite or rude are much more plentiful among the privileged upper classes of modern industrial societies, but even among the poorest segments of modern societies or in the most remote of tribal villages, there are explicit rules and taken-for-granted customs about how to act in various social circumstances. Without knowing quite a bit about the specific culture, it is impossible to know what behavior is acceptable for which occasion. In our society, a loud belch at the dinner table is seen as offensive (unless you are involved in a raucous drinking and burping contest—a ritual custom rumored to have occurred in some college fraternity houses). In past times and in other cultures, however, that same belching could be interpreted as an expression of appreciation for a meal that was well prepared. In those settings, *not* burping would be considered rude and impolite.

Proper behavior is always defined both in the broader cultural context and in the more specific social setting in which it occurs. The little rules and expectations that govern people's everyday actions are learned through years of interaction with others in various social settings. The ways that we interpret our own or other people's thoughts, feelings, and behaviors similarly depend on a shared understanding of what is going on. This is true even when we are alone and thinking about what happened yesterday—or about what you want to do when you finish reading this page. In a general sense, then, people everywhere must continually construct a shared sense of reality, and this is accomplished primarily through interacting with other people.

Things such as ethnic identity, masculinity, and even sexiness are socially constructed, insofar as they depend on a shared understanding of what they mean in certain social settings. Although the social world seems relatively fixed and outside us, we are constantly engaged in re-creating social meanings simply by following our normal daily routines. When we encounter something that does not fit with our social expectations, we either find a way to make "normal" sense of it, or we forge a new understanding of it by checking in with the people around us. If we burp after a meal but also compliment the cook, then others at the table can reinterpret the burp as a relatively minor transgression or, depending on the cultural context and our persuasiveness, as an appreciative compliment. In these small ways, we maintain old meanings, subtly shift expectations, and contribute to the perpetuation of shared cultural understandings. This social constructionist approach to studying people, culture, and society has a long and varied history within philosophy, sociology, anthropology, and social psychology (see, for example, Berger & Luckmann, 1966; Blumer, 1969; Garfinkel, 1967; Geertz, 1973; Goffman, 1967; Mead, 1934/1967; Schutz, 1970).

As this book will show, using a social constructionist approach to study gender and families allows us to see how they have changed and continue to change. Combining a social *constructionist* approach with a sociological, or social *structural*, approach allows us to see that people's lives are also shaped by economic and institutional forces. Only by looking at the structural constraints people face—such as access to education or jobs—can we understand how cultural definitions and practices governing gender and families have developed. And only by combining a social constructionist approach with a social structural approach can we evaluate the prospects for people's actions and perceptions changing in the future.

What Is Family?

Although most people take for granted what *family* means, it is not a term with a fixed meaning (Gubrium & Holstein, 1990; Levin & Trost, 1992; Settles, 1987; Stacey, 1996; Trost, 1990). The U.S. Bureau of the Census (1990) defines a family as "two or more persons who are related by birth, marriage, or adoption who live together as one household." This definition does capture something important about the legal institutions of marriage and parenthood and makes it easier to count people in population surveys. But most of us use the word *family* to refer to much more than this. Sometimes, it refers to people: long dead ancestors, distant cousins one never sees, siblings or other blood relations, divorced people who live apart, friends who are so close that they have become honorary family members, and so on. Sometimes, the word *family* refers to children, as in "Do you have a family?" and "She's in a family way." Other times, *family* implies a specific feeling, usually a special type of love and caring, although it can also refer to negative emotions or interactions, as when a potential romantic partner is invited to dinner and is told, "Don't pay attention to all the teasing, it's a weird family thing." Often, people use *family* to refer to ownership, as in "a family heirloom" and "the family car," but it is also frequently used to imply shared knowledge or practices, as in "a family secret," "family talk," and "a family tradition." The word *family* is also increasingly used in political rhetoric to claim the moral high ground, for example, when someone who thinks homosexuality is wrong says that two gay men who want to get married are denigrating "family values" or when a divorced mother and an unmarried mother who have been raising their three children together for six years say, "We're more than roommates, we're a family."

The word *family* can mean many things to many people, and those meanings can change. This is especially true today because there are so many types of families, and people are increasingly likely to experience changes in their own family and household structures. For example, because of high levels of cohabitation, divorce, and nonmarital childbirth, fewer than 60% of children in the United States lived with both biological parents in the early 1990s. But almost all children continue to live in households that call themselves families.

FIGURE 1.1

The Composition of U.S. Households Has Changed
SOURCE: DeVita, 1996, Figure 12; U.S. Bureau of the Census (1994b).

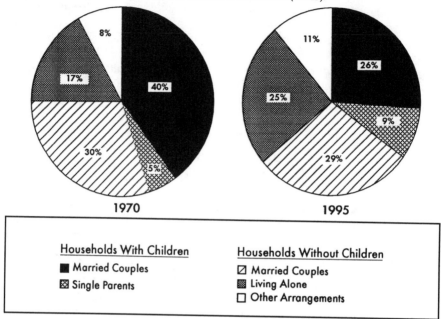

Figure 1.1 shows how the composition of U.S. households has changed since 1970. The biggest changes include fewer households with children, more people living alone, fewer married couples with children, and more single-parent households. The proportion of households containing married couples with no children living in the home has not changed much in the past few decades. Despite large changes in the structure of households from 1970 to 1990, since then the mix of different household types has changed relatively little (DeVita, 1996).

People in different types of households adjust their definition of *family* to accommodate changes in their marital status, living arrangements, amount of contact with spouse or parent, and concomitant emotional attachments. For example, children living with stepfathers are much more likely to say that their stepfathers are members of their families than they are to include their nonresident biological fathers as family members (Furstenberg & Nord, 1985). When parents remarry after divorce, the stepparents do not replace the children's nonresident parents but add to the stepchildren's stock of potential kin. Because there is so much variability in the amount of contact that biological parents, stepparents, and other adults have with children, it is difficult to predict how family will be defined—or redefined—when things change. In one recent study of inner-city African American families, a common distinction was made between "fathers" (the biological parents) and "daddies" (those men who assumed responsibility for the children; Furstenberg, Sherwood, & Sullivan, 1992). In other words, different versions of fatherhood, parenthood, and other family relationships are not necessarily accorded by birth or marriage. Kinship must be earned by making regular connections with people—seeing them regularly, writing or phoning them, or giving or receiving help (Cherlin & Furstenberg, 1994; Seltzer, 1994).

In addition, we can never be quite sure what *family* means unless we can understand the context in which it is used. People use the idea of family in their talk, and they indicate what they mean by family when they are interacting with each other. In this sense, the meaning of family is constructed through talking or *discourse*. We can find out what people mean only by paying attention to how they use the term in everyday life (Gubrium & Holstein, 1990). To simplify matters, we can say that the term *family* describes a set of interpersonal relationships, alerts us to the social meaning of those relationships, and suggests ways to think and act as we go about our daily lives.

Multiple meanings of family are evident today, but it gets even more confusing when we look back in history or across cultures to see how the word *family* (or its equivalent) has meant different things in different times and places. In ancient Greece, *family* (*oikos*) referred to the household economy—including the land, house, and servants. In medieval Europe, peasants who lived on feudal estates were considered part of the lord's family, and he was called their father (*pater*) even though they were not related to him by blood (Collins, 1986). In many countries, such as Mexico, godparents (*compadres*) are treated as family members and act as coparents toward the children, disciplining them and providing financial or emotional support, although they have no direct biological relationship to them (Griswold del Castillo, 1984). Similarly, in contemporary Native American (Indian) families, the terms used to describe family relationships are more encompassing than narrow English use implies: A "grandmother" may actually be a child's aunt or grandaunt, and "cousin" may have variable meanings not necessarily based on birth and marriage (Yellowbird & Snipp, 1994). To understand families and the specific social relations they represent, we must therefore recognize that the term and the idea are socially constructed, that is, the meaning of family changes in response to a wide variety of social, economic, political, cultural, and personal conditions.

One of the most important reasons for paying attention to the different meanings of family is the increasing ethnic diversity of our society. In 1995, nearly 70 million people in the United States were classified by the Census Bureau as minorities. African Americans constituted the largest segment—32 million people, or roughly 12% of the total U.S. population (see Figure 1.2). People classified as of Hispanic origin (Mexican, Puerto Rican, Cuban, and South and Central American, etc.) numbered 27 million, or 10% of the population. Asians and Pacific Islanders constituted 3% of the total, and Native Americans about 1%. Because of interracial and interethnic marriages, immigration, and births, the minority population is increasing. By the year 2020, 118 million Americans are projected to be of minority backgrounds.

Most people think of race and ethnicity as things with fixed and stable meanings, but just as for the term *family*, these terms are socially constructed and

FIGURE 1.2

The U.S. Population Will Become More Diverse
SOURCE: DeVita, 1996, Figure 4; U.S. Bureau of the Census (1993b).

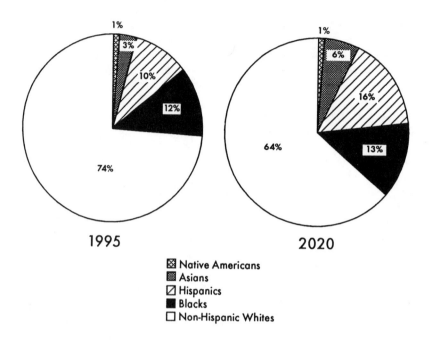

1995   2020

⊠ Native Americans
▩ Asians
◨ Hispanics
■ Blacks
☐ Non-Hispanic Whites

subject to change. Federal agencies did not even regularly collect data on race until the 1964 Civil Rights Act and the 1965 Voting Rights Act were passed in an attempt to reduce racial discrimination. The four official census categories for race (white, black, Asian/Pacific Islander and American Indian/Alaska Native), and the two for ethnicity (Hispanic, Non-Hispanic) were not developed until 1977 (DeVita, 1996). Note that racial identity is distinct from ethnic identity, so Hispanics can be of any race.

People change the way they classify their race or ethnicity depending on the social meanings of the terms. For example, although the census ethnic category *Hispanic* includes many groups, people tend to identify themselves more specifically, often depending on the country from which their ancestors came (e.g., Mexican, Puerto Rican, and Cuban). Relatively few people in the southwestern United States call themselves *Hispanic:* Some use the inclusive term *Latino,* some use *Chicano* (originally referring to the people of Spanish/Mexican descent who lived in the region before it was part of the United States), and others use present-day country designations (Mexican American, Guatemalan, Salvadoran, Colombian, etc.). This flexibility is confusing for census survey takers who would like to have simple and fixed racial/ethnic categories, but it reminds us that people have some control over the ways they see and talk about things.

What Is Gender?

Just as there is no stable definition of *family* or *ethnicity*, the definition of *gender* is also variable (Connell, 1987; Kimmel & Messner, 1992; Lorber, 1994; West & Zimmerman, 1987). Gender refers to what it means to be a man or a woman in a specific time and place. Although most people assume that *masculinity* and *femininity* have set meanings, what is desirable in a man or a woman changes significantly from era to era and from culture to culture. People often equate males with masculinity and females with femininity, but they don't automatically go together. It is a bit unsettling to think about it this way, but gender is not a direct result of biological sex.

The term *sex* is used to refer to relatively distinct biological differences between males and females such as genitals, hormones, and chromosomes. Sex also refers to erotic behavior, or sexuality, as when people say "we had sex." Gender, on the other hand, is social and refers to how we think someone should look, act, or feel. Gender describes how, in a particular culture, the typical man is supposed to present himself (as masculine) and how the typical woman is supposed to present herself (as feminine). In everyday life, we also usually assume that the person "is" the gender that corresponds to his or her sex: Males are masculine, and females are feminine.

But we all probably know women who are aggressive—a supposed masculine trait—or men who are sensitive—a supposed feminine trait. This suggests that gender and sex are not the same thing. We will see in later chapters that biology does not predetermine the specific tasks that men are supposed to perform nor dictate that women must act or feel a certain way. Instead, as the social constructionist approach suggests, ideas about gender are created by men and women as they go about living their daily lives and interacting with other people.

In different historical periods and in different cultural contexts, gender has had widely divergent meanings. For example, among noblemen in 17th-century France, it was manly to wear perfume, curly wigs, high-heeled shoes, and blouses with frilly lace cuffs. Today, the same attire would be considered unmanly or effeminate. According to historians and sociologists, traits that affirm one's masculinity (or femininity) in one social context can undermine it in another (Connell, 1993; Kimmel & Messner, 1992; Lorber, 1994). Because the meaning of gender changes in response to differing cultural and historical contexts, it is socially constructed.

Gender and Social Reproduction

Calling gender socially constructed leads to focusing on the social conditions that promote different versions of gender and implies that people can change it. But we should be careful about what this means. It does *not* mean that gender does not seem "real," that it is unimportant, or that people can avoid it. There is a patterned structure to gender that is virtually impossible to ignore. Nevertheless, people have more control over defining gender than they usually assume. This is especially evident when we look at everyday language use.

The ways people use or transform gender-linked terms can have important consequences. Take, for instance, the gender-neutral term *significant other* (surely one of the most cumbersome labels ever invented to stand for boyfriend/girlfriend/companion/lover/mate/partner/wife/husband/etc.). Forty years ago, the term was unheard of, but as social norms surrounding marriage and dating changed, *significant other* gained wider acceptance. Other terms for the same thing have not disappeared, but among some groups of (mostly younger) people, labels such as *significant other* now compete with older labels such as *fiancée* and *sweetheart*. As discussed in the next chapter, older terms and concepts continue to shape our perceptions of romantic relationships. At the same time, however, individuals are adopting new terms, transforming courtship practices, and subtly changing the meaning of gender.

Sociologists Candace West and Donald Zimmerman (1987) suggest that to be considered competent members of a society, we are all required to "do" gender. We accomplish this by acting in a manly or womanly fashion, or at least close enough to it to be considered a man or woman, boy or girl. According to West and Zimmerman, doing gender is not a choice: We cannot avoid being labeled, or labeling others, as fitting (or not fitting) socially accepted gender categories, even if we recognize that these categories are inappropriate or changing (see also Cahill, 1986; Kessler & McKenna, 1985). In a similar way, we are also required to make sense of family relations and "do" family by defining our actions with regard to our family relationships (or lack thereof; Gubrium & Holstein, 1990).

This book is about the intersection between these two forms of constructing social reality: doing gender and doing family. The book is also about how definitions of family and gender can change and about how some definitions become more important or influential than others. It is also about how taken-for-granted understandings reflect and perpetuate various structural conditions—such as opportunities for education, jobs, and housing. Gendered cultural meanings and identities result from men's and women's actions under historically specific conditions. These actions shape, and are shaped by, social reproduction—the maintenance of life on a daily basis and, ultimately, across many generations (Laslett & Brenner, 1989).

We all develop unique understandings of gender and family depending on our ethnic background, social class, place of residence, and personal experiences. In the United States, immigration patterns, spatial segregation, and job discrimination have limited the life chances of many ethnic groups, as well as contributing to a strong tradition of ethnic and racial differences in patterns of family life (Mindel, Habenstein, & Wright, 1988). At the same time, most of us have been exposed to similar dominant cultural images (often quite unrealistic) of what a family should be, how women should feel, and how men should act. By focusing on some common overarching stereotypes about gender, marriage, and child rearing, I hope to expose some of the taken-for-granted assumptions about the "typical" American family. I will show how various ideals and practices have allowed family members to provide love and care to one another but also how families have created gender differences and perpetuated inequality. By describing some families that do not fit the normative pattern, I will also highlight the diversity of experience that has always been a part of American life.

Understanding Gender and Families

Using Gender as a Lens

Throughout the book, I use gender as a type of lens or looking glass. As a biologist uses a microscope to analyze cells, and an astronomer uses a telescope to bring distant planets into view, I use gender to bring certain aspects of family life into focus. I do this by repeatedly asking what difference it makes that a man or a woman does things that a husband/wife, father/mother, son/daughter should do. It is a little like those laser dot pictures that are sometimes displayed in shopping malls. Until you figure out how to look at them, you don't see the hidden three-dimensional images. I hope that you will discover that a gender lens brings hidden dimensions of family life into view.

Any lens or way of seeing necessarily highlights some things at the expense of others. The family practices that a gender lens brings into focus are not the same ones that a biological lens, an artistic lens, or a religious lens would emphasize. Nevertheless, without the insights generated from using a gender lens, we would not be able to understand overall patterns of marriage and family life. Gender illuminates family practices that are so taken for granted that most researchers have ignored them in the past. Using a gender lens, however, allows us to see more clearly what family members do, why they do it, and what impact gender has on people in different times and places. Perhaps most important, using gender as a lens will help us understand some of the stresses and strains faced by families today and can help us predict what families will look like in the future.

Thinking for Yourself

Public leaders, scholars, and professional experts have been studying families and telling people what to do for centuries, even though people have not always followed their advice. The critical study of gender is more recent, although one can find provocative questions about men's and women's roles as far back as the beginning of written records. Recent studies of families and gender lead to contradictory conclusions, but accumulating evidence now points to some surprising assessments of the ways that families and gender are linked. This book is about those linkages. There are few easy answers, however, and most of the important questions are still open to debate.

Studying families is a tricky business because it is impossible to be completely objective. I have strong feelings about many of the issues in this book, and I am sure that you have some strong feelings about them, too. I am considered an expert because I have a Ph.D. in sociology and have spent years studying families, reading about gender, and thinking about how they fit together. But you have some knowledge about these things, too, because you grew up in a family and have your own ideas about gender. Keep your personal experiences in mind as you read the material in the book, but try to avoid making generalizations from just your own life or from just those who live in circumstances similar to your own. To help you see how your own experiences might be unique, I have used examples from people living in different settings and drawn from history to describe family life in past times. I challenge you to compare the evidence in the book with your own experiences, to consider the experiences of people unlike yourself, to ask difficult questions about personal issues, and, I hope, to conduct some further research into family and gender issues on your own. Ultimately, it is up to you to forge your own understandings and to draw your own conclusions about what is important.

As I tell my students when I teach classes on the family and gender, if you don't get offended by something I say, then you are probably not paying enough attention. It is my job as a sociologist to question the obvious, to look for patterns of power and domination, and to challenge conventional wisdom. This may make you feel uncomfortable. It is supposed to. It makes me uncomfortable. But discomfort should not stop you from thinking and talking about these important issues. This book is thus a deliberate attempt to stimulate discussion and debate. It is your job to read and reflect (and if you are a student, to remember enough to pass the class!). I hope it also becomes your job to challenge and transform these ideas because only when you develop your own perspective on gender and families will you be able to feel in control of your life. And only by learning from the past will you be able to build a more just and equitable future.

Using Popular Culture

You may be reading this book because you selected it from a bookstore shelf, but most of you are reading it because it was assigned in a college class. I need to warn you, however, that this book is different from most textbooks. To begin with, it is much shorter than a conventional textbook. The chapters are designed to introduce some important gender and family topics to you, rather than to cover completely all the research in any specific area. In addition, the style of presentation may be different from what you are used to. Instead of presenting abstract theories about gender and families and then summarizing empirical studies, I include popular portrayals of family life in every chapter—movie excerpts, advice columns, want ads, nursery rhymes, news clippings, and so on. Instead of starting the chapters with definitions of important terms and then explaining the correct way to use them, I offer some common cultural stereotypes and ask you to think about their possible meanings. Theories, definitions, and scientific studies can help shape your thinking about families, but popular cultural images can also bring some important questions about families and gender into focus.

The chapters in this book are about common family practices: getting married, earning money, cleaning house, and raising children. The chapters are also about common feelings and processes that lie just beneath the surface of family interactions: love, joy, belonging, and survival but also fear, power, control, and resistance.

In describing these practices and feelings, I draw on observations and reports of family life from many sources: personal stories, letters, diaries, questionnaire studies, interviews, demographic data, historical records, journalistic sources, government reports, court records, popular media, and various scholarly publications. I describe the lives of stereotypical white middle-class families, working-class families, single-parent families, ethnic minority families, and nontraditional families. For the most part, I focus on families in the United States, but occasionally I use information about families from other times and places to show how family and marriage practices can be different. Not everyone's family experiences will be captured here because there are as many experiences as there are families. Nevertheless, the situations and popular images I describe provide a glimpse into some of the tensions and contradictions embedded in family life.

Family dramas, love affairs, and power struggles have provided material for countless books and plays through the years. From *Hamlet* to *War and Peace,* many of the most enduring and popular dramatic stories in Western literature have focused on families, and most have included subplots about sex and gender. More recently, family problems and gender issues have been the focus of innumerable novels, movies, and television shows. Media depictions of family life cannot be taken as reflections of actual practices in American families, but our preoccupation with them suggests that they carry profound public and private significance.

Since the 1950s, family sitcoms (short for situation comedies) have been a staple of television programming in North America. In the 1950s, shows such as *Leave It to Beaver, Father Knows Best,* and *Ozzie & Harriet* celebrated the supposedly typical suburban white middle-class family. Like the majority of family sitcoms that followed in the 1960s, 1970s, and 1980s, these programs usually included a kind and benevolent father with a loving housewife who was called on to solve a minor dilemma and dispense pearls of wisdom at the conclusion of each show. In the 1980s, *The Cosby Show* and *The Jeffersons* demonstrated that black middle-class families could be idealized (and trivialized) just as white families had been. But family sitcoms have not always been about living in the suburbs. Even in the 1950s, popular shows such as *I Love Lucy* portrayed interethnic urban marriages and poked fun at conventional notions of middle-class American housewives.

White working-class families have also been present on television from the 1950s up to the present. Before the 1990s, they were less common than their middle-class counterparts, and their domestic arrangements were typically shown in a less favorable, if somewhat more realistic, light. Ralph Cramden on *The Honeymooners* and Archie Bunker on *All in the Family* were more likely to be the brunt of a joke than to provide any meaningful advice or leadership. More recent shows in this tradition of male incompetence, such as *Coach* and *Home Improvement,* show men who are unlikely successes in their "manly" jobs but who need plenty of help at home to figure out the simplest problem. Similarly, working-class men on animated family shows such as *The Flintstones* and *The Simpsons* are bumbling idiots whose wives must rescue them from their own ineptitude. Most working-class wives on family sitcoms have been more rough and assertive than the mild-mannered, beautiful, and somewhat vacant middle-class moms of television, but both have routinely solved problems using cleverness and trickery. Almost inevitably, the women demonstrate their superior family skills at the same time that they salvage their husbands' fragile self-esteem (Cantor, 1990).

American television comedies about family life have been enormously successful during their initial runs, and many have made even more money in syndicated reruns. Few programs have enjoyed as much lasting popularity as family shows such as *I Love Lucy, Leave It to Beaver, All in the Family, The Brady Bunch, Family Ties, Cosby, Full House,* and *Roseanne* (although few have received the critical acclaim that television comedies of similar popularity enjoy). In addition to comedies, some of the most popular television westerns have been built around families (from *Bonanza* to *Dr. Quinn, Medicine Woman*), as have many popular prime-time dramas (from *Dallas* to *Picket Fences*). Every fall, the major networks premiere a few new family shows that look remarkably like the old shows but with a little more diversity. More of the shows now include people of color, single parents, and stepfamilies, and some comedies (most notably *Married With Children*) portray all family members, not just the fathers, as idiots. Other family shows now even include controversial topics that used to be taboo on television, such as teenage sex, abortion, same-sex marriage, religious devotion, and drugs.

Why are television programs about families so successful, and why do viewers continue to think they are funny? In the typical sitcom, family members are expected to do conventional things, encounter unanticipated problems, bungle the situation, get tangled up in unsuccessful attempts to hide their inadequacies, and eventually admit their ineptitude to their loved ones. Viewers see this as funny because they feel similar normative expectations, know what "should" happen, foresee the characters' inability to meet the ideal, and laugh at the inherent contradictions and ensuing exposure of human frailty. In most cases, a minor personal trauma or family problem is solved through the thoughtful intervention of Mom. We are left with the message that love can conquer all and, not incidentally, that family matters are best left to women. There are several variations on this theme, including one in which family problems are solved by comic but competent single men who have little need for women, for example, *Bachelor Father, My Three Sons, Who's the Boss, Full House,* and *Mr. Belvedere* (Cantor, 1990; Coltrane & Allan, 1994).

Real life is less scripted and more diverse than seen in television comedies, and real problems are not solved as easily with humor, trickery, and good intentions. Unlike television comedies, in real life there are many more poor families than affluent ones, and many more single mothers than single fathers raising children. Adults and older children know that life on television is not real, but somehow the stereotyped images still get into our heads and influence our thinking. The classic story lines that get repeated over and over take on a reality of their own and provide a backdrop for the ways that we think about our own lives. Even when we don't want to, we sometimes end up comparing our own experiences with those of the fictitious characters we see on the screen. As Chapter 2 will show, many of us carry around images of a modern-day Prince Charming (perhaps looking like Richard Gere, Mel Gibson, Brad Pitt, Keanu Reeves, Wesley Snipes, Denzel Washington, etc.) or a modern-day Cinderella (perhaps looking like Halle

Berry, Sandra Bullock, Whitney Houston, Julia Ormond, Julia Roberts, Meg Ryan, etc.).

The images of romance, marriage, and family life that we see on television and in the movies are not made up from scratch. Rather, they reflect a specific framing of events that are part of the culture in which we live. Along with family experiences, personal memories, and many other sources of information, people rely on media-generated frames to simplify and make sense of the world (Entman, 1993; Gamson, Croteau, Hoynes, & Sasson, 1992). The repeated framing of events in specific ways contributes to the perception that what we are observing is "natural" and inevitable. Popular media, including music, novels, television, and film, invoke certain frames to elicit specific feelings and create expectations in the audience. Setting up one set of expectations and then switching frames to reveal another "reality" is a common technique of both mysteries and comedies. Switching frames in the interest of suspense or humor, however, usually does not challenge the original cultural stereotype. We refer to such instances as "exceptions that prove the rule." For example, although we see more Mr. Moms on television, bumbling husbands who are comically inept at doing laundry confirm our belief that men are not good at housework. Similarly, television images of ambitious professional women who ruthlessly trample their colleagues on their way to the top can be seen as cautionary tales about what happens to women who forsake their feminine wifely duties.

Television shows tend to reflect and reproduce conventional gender stereotypes, in part because they are designed to sell us products. By invoking the warm, fuzzy feelings associated with Mom and apple pie, or the sexual desires aroused by lifeguards in skimpy bathing suits, television programs deliver eager consumers to advertisers who tell us we will be happy if we buy more stuff (Baran, Mok, Land, & Kang, 1989; Barthel, 1988). It is therefore not surprising that television sitcoms offer up stereotyped and relatively unrealistic images of families (Cantor & Cantor, 1992; Lichter, Lichter, & Rothman, 1994; Taylor, 1989).

What about the "big screen"—the movies? Here at least is a medium with supposedly higher artistic and dramatic standards than television. Critics have both celebrated and derided Hollywood for its portrayals of family life, and the issue periodically enters into political debates (Byars, 1991; Cavell, 1981; Rapping, 1994; Traube, 1992). In this short chapter, I cannot address the question of what the relationship between film, popular culture, and family life can or should be. I can, however, use film to introduce an important and provocative topic: How do popular family rituals contribute to our ideals about what families should be and what roles men and women should play within them?

Family Rituals and the Construction of Reality

Home for the Holidays

In the Jodie Foster film *Home for the Holidays*, Claudia (played by Holly Hunter) is a single mother who takes a trip to her parents' house for Thanksgiving. After getting fired from her job at a Chicago museum, Claudia gets a ride to the airport from her teenage daughter. As Claudia grabs her bags and leans over to say good-bye, her daughter tells her that she is planning to have sex with her boyfriend over the weekend. Thus begins a humorous look at one of the most popular family rituals in America—the Thanksgiving holiday feast.

This movie, like television sitcoms, shows what is expected of a "typical" American family at holiday time and simultaneously illustrates some departures from the "normal." Suffering from a cold, lamenting her job loss, worrying about her daughter, and fretting about the upcoming visit, Claudia picks up the airplane telephone and calls her brother in Boston. When he doesn't answer, she frantically recounts her tales of woe for the answering machine and pleads with him to join her at their parents' house for the holiday. (This little performance leaves her feeling even more stupid and foolish than she felt before.)

Arriving at her parents' house, Claudia is forced to answer probing questions from her mother (played by Anne Bancroft) about why her daughter did not come with her. Her mother immediately intuits that Claudia was fired from her job, despite Claudia's saying only that she is thinking about a change, whereon her mother closes the door and admonishes her not to tell her father. When Claudia's gay brother, Tommy (played by Robert Downey Jr.), arrives with a handsome friend in tow, Claudia mistakenly assumes that he is her brother's new lover. Later in the movie, we learn that Tommy and his longtime lover, Jack, had a marriage ceremony on a Massachusetts beach some months before. Among the immediate family, only Claudia seems ready to accept Tommy's being gay, and in the beginning, only she accepts Jack as an important part of Tommy's life.

The plot thickens as Claudia and Tommy's high-strung sister shows up with her uptight husband and two bratty children. For some unstated reason, and with much tension, the sister brings in her own turkey and several other Thanksgiving dishes. The women (and daughter) migrate to the kitchen to finish the meal preparations, while the men (and son) sit in the living room. As the feast begins, the women recruit men to carve the turkeys, with obnoxious Tommy reluctantly hacking away at his mother's bird. Unintentionally, but with little remorse, Tommy ends up dumping the entire greasy turkey onto the lap of his uptight sister, who freaks out and flies into a rage. Aunt Gladie, eccentric and senile, has too much to drink and tells everyone how wonderful it was to kiss her brother-in-law some 30 years before. With the tension high and decorum broken, Claudia asks Tommy to field a question about how *her* life is going. To her surprise and amusement, he reveals that she was fired from her job, kissed her 60-year-old boss, and is expecting her daughter to have sex with her boyfriend that evening (which doesn't actually happen after all). Obviously flustered and angry, the mother storms out of the room, retreating to the pantry for a cigarette. Claudia catches up to her and tries to console her, followed by Tommy, who ends up eating with Claudia in the kitchen while the others finish the feast in the dining room.

After the meal, the women go to the kitchen to clean up, and the men go outside to play football. Tommy gets into a fistfight with his sister's husband, and the father, who is washing the sister's car, turns the hose on the "boys," creating even more havoc and leading to a swift departure of the daughter's family. Claudia cannot patch things up with the sister, has both harsh and tender words with her mother, shares a beer watching football with her father, resists having sex with Tommy's amorous friend, and in the end is surprised and delighted to find him joining her on the airplane for a romantic flight back to Chicago.

Making Sense of the Thanksgiving Ritual

This movie version of a Thanksgiving holiday ritual is a good place to begin exploring how families and gender are socially constructed. Many of today's families look different from this one, and holidays are celebrated differently, depending on family composition, geographical location, ethnicity, income, and family traditions. But we can use this Eastern, white, suburban middle-class family Thanksgiving, with all its quirks and comic relief, to see how family rituals work and why they are important.

Family rituals such as Thanksgiving appear timeless to many people and invoke nostalgic images of "the good old days" and "old-fashioned family values." As historians point out, however, most family rituals looked different in the past, and most holiday rituals such as Thanksgiving and Christmas were not the isolated family-centered emotional events that they have become during the 20th century. Prior to the 1900s, civic festivals and Fourth of July parades in America were much more important occasions for celebration and strong emotion than family holidays. Only in the 20th century did the family come to be the center of festive attention and emotional intensity (Coontz, 1992, p. 17; Skolnick, 1991).

Celebrating family holidays such as Thanksgiving has become more common during the past century, and holidays have increasingly taken on special emotional significance. Why do many American families go through some version of this feast year after year, and what purpose does it serve? Sociologists and anthropologists suggest that celebrating holidays such as Thanksgiving and sharing special meals is one way that families create and reaffirm a sense of themselves. As noted above, families do not have an automatic meaning or definition. That is, they tend to have fuzzy boundaries and need some shared activities to give them shape (Gubrium & Holstein, 1990). Although our culture provides us with an overarching sense of what a family should be, we need to learn what it means to be in a particular family through direct experience and learning, and we need to re-create a sense of belonging over and over again. As described below, periodic family rituals such as birthdays and holiday feasts, along with other activities, actually construct family boundaries and teach us who we are as family members. Who is in, who is out, and what it means to be part of a particular family are literally created and re-created through these routine ceremonial events (see, for example, Berger & Kellner, 1964; Gubrium & Holstein, 1990; Imber-Black, Roberts, & Whiting, 1988). Routine rituals help create family scripts—mental representations of ordered events that guide people's actions within and across family settings (Byng-Hall, 1988; Stack & Burton, 1994).

More important for the purposes of this book, these ceremonial occasions—along with countless other routine family practices—combine to create a sense of ourselves as gendered beings: as mothers or fathers, wives or husbands, daughters or sons, women or men, boys or girls. Ideals from the larger society contribute to these gender ideals, but routine family practices give personal meaning to the larger social definitions and provide us with interpersonal scripts to follow. Ritual family events such as Thanksgiving reinforce conventional expectations about what it is to be a man or a woman, and these messages are then generalized to other social settings.

In Claudia's family's Thanksgiving, as in most American families, the women orchestrated the ritual event. They prepared and served the meal, as well as cleaned up afterward, and we can assume that they also planned the menus, bought the food, and began preparing it well in advance of Thanksgiving Day. The holiday was organized around the feast, and it was the women who made it happen. This was a common pattern in the past and is still typical in many contemporary American families, although things are changing in some families (Coltrane, 1996; DeVault, 1991; diLeonardo, 1987; Fenstermaker-Berk, 1985; Luxton, 1980; Thompson & Walker, 1989). Why aren't men more involved in meal preparation? Why don't boys get asked to set the table or help out with cooking as much as girls? As future chapters will show, this gender-based division of labor has important implications for the development of different feelings of competence and entitlement in girls and boys, men and women (Hochschild, 1989; Pyke & Coltrane, 1996).

Throughout history, family work—such as cooking and preparing food—and productive work—such as growing and harvesting food—have been closely tied together. Only relatively recently have housework and paid work seemed like separate things, although they are still closely intertwined. Without being fed, clothed, and housed, workers could not stay on the job. Without the resources that come from jobs, people could not maintain households. Recent research shows how paid and unpaid work continue to be linked in modern American families. Studies by economists and sociologists demonstrate that men's ability to get higher-paying jobs allows them to avoid housework (Becker, 1981; Coltrane, 1996; Delphy, 1984; Hartmann, 1981; Shelton, 1992). Because most employers have assumed that wives will perform family work, women's wages and chances for job promotion have been limited (Baxter, 1993; Hochschild, 1989; Luxton, 1980). Opportunities in the job market thus affect decisions about family work at the same time that assumptions about family work affect the structure of the job market (Reskin & Padavic, 1994). What happens in individual families has profound effects on our assumptions about which type of work is appropriate for men and which is appropriate for women (Coltrane, 1989; West & Fenstermaker, 1993).

What makes something women's work or men's work? As discussed in Chapters 3 and 4, the tasks performed by one gender or the other are subject to change as historical circumstances change and people's needs are evaluated differently. It seems as if men are supposed to carve turkeys only because people have been exposed to it year after year in family rituals such as Thanksgiving. In *Home for the Holidays*, the father is physically unable to carve the turkey (or at least his wife insists that he is), so Tommy is recruited to perform the task, even though he makes a mockery of it and drops the greasy bird in his horrified sister's lap.

Why didn't Claudia or one of the other women assume the task of carving the turkey?

A look back across different civilizations shows that divisions of labor are not the same everywhere. In one society, men might be the only ones to set up the dwellings, whereas in another, this might be a woman's job. In the United States, men are rarely asked to cook but are expected to barbecue hamburgers and carve turkeys. Why should it be "feminine" to stuff and bake the turkey but "masculine" to cut it up? Why are the top professional bakers and chefs virtually always men, although women do most of these tasks in the vast majority of American homes? These questions cannot be answered without looking at issues of power and control in families, topics discussed throughout this book (see also Blumberg & Coleman, 1989; Ferree, 1990; Komter, 1989; Thompson & Walker, 1989; Thorne, 1992; Vannoy-Hiller, 1984).

As shown in *Home for the Holidays*, watching or playing football is also a Thanksgiving tradition in some American families—or more accurately, it is a tradition for some men. While women cook or clean up, men congregate in the living room to watch football on television or go outside to throw the ball around. Although not often acknowledged, this ritual teaches boys that they are entitled to special privileges. They get to play games while the girls are expected to help with the meal preparation, cleanup, and child care. Of course, this does not happen in every family, but for many American men, Thanksgiving is a relaxing event. For most women, it entails work. This does not mean that women do not also find such events to be fun and rewarding. It is mostly women who initiate, plan, and conduct them year after year. But it is clear that ceremonial meals are primarily downtime for men, whereas for women they include work as well as pleasure. This is another example of what sociologist Arlie Hochschild (1989) calls the "leisure gap"—men's greater opportunities for relaxation at home. The leisure gap is narrowing in some families, but it is still likely that at Thanksgiving gatherings in homes across America, the women are waiting on the men.

Another gender division in many families revolves around caring for others and talking about emotions. In *Home for the Holidays*, Claudia and her mother check in with other family members to see how they are doing and initiate conversations about their feelings. They show their concern by talking. Tommy, in contrast, is joking most of the time, and although he is expressive and playful, his teasing is often at others' expense. His father shows his affection for his wife by saying "come 'ere, gorgeous" and dancing with her, but when things get tense around the dinner table, he gets quiet. He demonstrates his concern for his daughter by going outside and washing her car.

In most American families, women consider it their duty to worry about family members and to take care of their everyday needs. They derive great satisfaction from doing so. Often, mothers (and sometimes fathers) focus on making sure that everyone is well fed. Preparing and serving food are thus more than just work because they represent love and care that are given to family members. Women also stereotypically show their love by talking about feelings and trying to help everyone get along. In *Home for the Holidays*, as the women cooked and served, they chatted about the food but also about people and relationships. When the conversation turned argumentative and offensive at the dinner table, Claudia's mother tried, in vain, to make it "nicer," and Claudia eventually took responsibility for letting things get out of hand. The men, in contrast, talked less and focused their conversation on things: work, investments, and football. The tone and style of talk differed as well. The men argued and teased one another, talked louder, changed topics more frequently, and interrupted the women and each other. These conversational patterns reflect gender differences that are common in many American families (Pearson, West, & Turner, 1995; West & Zimmerman, 1987; Wood, 1996).

Rituals Reaffirm Family Ties

Home for the Holidays showed an atypical Thanksgiving feast, insofar as the usual tensions and disagreements were contentiously and comically revealed, rather than staying submerged. More typically, people at family gatherings get along a little better, downplay their disagreements and hostilities, and pretend that everything is OK. Acting as if everything is OK (even when it isn't) is one way to normalize the situation and maintain a sense of family unity and continuity. Ritual celebrations such as Thanksgiving allow families to do this on a regular basis.

In a more general way, rituals help construct group identity and create a shared sense of reality. Historically, most rituals started out as community affairs, whereby people got together on special occasions to reaffirm their commitment to some common purpose—an alliance with another clan, a shared religion, a new community settlement, or allegiance to a king or other ruler. These ceremonial gatherings brought people together in face-to-face interaction; focused their attention on some common symbols; heightened their emotions through a group activity such as singing, chanting, and dancing; and linked those emotions to the symbols and to the common purposes of the group (Collins, 1988; Durkheim, 1915/1957; Goffman, 1967). These rituals served many purposes but, most important, gave people a sense of belonging to the group and reaffirmed everyone's commitment to its purposes and symbols.

Although times have changed, we still have many rituals, and they still give people a sense of belonging. Increasingly, modern rituals—at least the face-to-face ones—are centered on family activities. In the past, many public rituals and celebrations were also family based because wealthy families sponsored them, and they tended to solidify alliances between families. Today, family alliances are still important, but they are no longer the central basis of marriages, politics, business, and warfare as they once were. As public displays of family alliances have become less important, family rituals have become more focused on the personal relationships within them. Like earlier rituals, modern family celebrations and activities continue to provide family members with an important sense of place and reinforce feelings of joint membership. These rituals are sometimes linked to national holidays, such as Thanksgiving, but everyday routines, such as eating meals together and watching television together, can serve the ritual function of solidifying family bonds.

Various types of rituals create families, insofar as the family has no fixed definition, and ritualized practices are needed to define and reinforce the meaning of family. If we did not have family rituals such as weddings, anniversaries, and birthdays and holiday get-togethers, we would have a weaker sense of what it means to be a family member. If we did not have more mundane family rituals such as eating together, going on outings, and sharing inside jokes, family would seem less real. Periodic holidays and everyday rituals thus combine to create a shared sense of the family and reinforce our connections to other family members.

In the past, families had many more connections that gave a strong sense of belonging. Most people lived on farms, and family members and relatives contributed on a regular basis to the needs of everyday life. Young adults were dependent on parents and other relatives to learn skills and get jobs. Most people had frequent contact with their parents and grandparents (if they were still alive) because they relied on them for a place to live and for their means of survival. In those days, changes in family membership shaped one's access to resources, and a family member's marriage or death could significantly change the allocation of wealth in the family. The ritual of a wedding symbolically joined the fates of two families, and the ritual of a funeral reaffirmed the living family members' commitments to each other and to the larger family.

Family Rituals Reproduce Gender

Families are now smaller and have less control over the jobs and future life chances of their members, so it is no surprise that family rituals have become more individualized. People still put great emphasis on things such as weddings and funerals, but they are likely to be smaller and to satisfy the needs of immediate family members rather than those of the entire community. Instead of forging cross-family links and defining political alliances, rituals now define a more narrow sense of family—what it means to be in a specific "McLaughlin," "Rodriguez," "Davis," "Parducci," or "Nguyen" family. Because society now has fewer outward mechanisms for regulating gender, family rituals and other family practices have become central carriers for the meaning of gender. Family and gender have always been linked, but family rituals and family celebrations probably carry even more significance for individual gender identity than they did in the past.

Most family practices include hidden messages about gender, especially rituals marking transitions between different family statuses. Consider the venerable institution of marriage and the rituals associated with it. It is not just the wedding ceremony that marks this transition: Engagement parties, showers, bachelor parties, wedding receptions, and honeymoons are all rituals that define two individuals as a married couple and redefine their relations with other friends and family members. Equally important, marriage-related rituals reflect a gender-segregated pattern that serves to create the very differences they are supposed to express. For example, bachelor parties encourage raucous behavior in men, and baby showers encourage women to focus their energies on infants. Only recently, and usually unofficially, have public rituals begun to acknowledge that a woman might want a raucous party to celebrate the end of her single life or that an expectant father might be more concerned with changing diapers than with earning money. As the next chapters will discuss, the United States is in the midst of some major social changes surrounding love, marriage, and child rearing. Most of these changes move us away from strict definitions of separate spheres for men and women. But we are still bound by many family rituals that celebrate differences between men and women, and these rituals make those differences seem real.

Next time you go to a wedding ceremony, listen carefully for references to gender. Are the husband and wife agreeing to the same terms, or does the ritual foretell something about marriage being a different type of bargain for the wife than for the husband? Is there talk about the wife obeying and the husband protecting? Wedding rituals and marriage laws reflect some pretty sexist assumptions about the natural abilities and rightful duties of husbands and wives. For example, the modern American custom of the wife taking the husband's name at marriage is based on laws that stripped women of legal rights to earn money or enter into contracts on the same basis as men.

Wedding rituals mark the formation of new families, but most family rituals, such as birthdays and holiday feasts, mark the continuation of families and help reaffirm family members' commitment to each other. Even in the film *Home for the Holidays*, family members used the Thanksgiving ritual to come together periodically, to find out how other family members were doing, and, not incidentally, to redefine the group in the case of new arrivals or departures. Tommy's partner, Jack, did not get invited to the Thanksgiving feast (although Tommy's dad did talk to him on the phone and tell him that he was "all right"). In many families, inviting a boyfriend or girlfriend to a family holiday gathering indicates that one is getting "serious," and various relatives feel they have a right to question the new friend mercilessly. When someone gets divorced, family holidays provide an opportunity to redefine who is in and who is out. As in *Home for the Holidays*, when a family member chooses not to come to a gathering, people wonder what is happening and begin to question that person's commitment to the family.

People usually do not think about family gatherings as ceremonies with ritual significance, but one of their functions is to define family boundaries—to regulate who is in and who is out. As noted above, another function of family gatherings and rituals is to make sure people know their "proper" place in the family. As you may have already guessed, this is something that is increasingly subject to debate in modern American families, especially with regard to gender differences but also concerning the appropriate relations between children and their parents. Whether someone has a right to speak up, talk back, serve others, or get served during family gatherings helps create feelings of entitlement or obligation that carry over into future relationships.

Family rituals do not have to be ceremonial gatherings to reproduce the meaning of family and reinforce gender stereotypes. Daily routines as trivial as housework are just as consequential for defining what families are and what roles individuals should play within them. As future chapters will show, everyday rituals such as who takes the first shower in the morning, who puts the breakfast dishes away, and who makes the kids' lunches can tell us important things about family roles and family obligations. Similarly, we can learn from other little rituals of everyday family life, such as who sets the alarm clock, who reads the newspaper, who operates the TV remote, and who answers the telephone. Even the most mundane family activities can tell us something important about the patterning of love, entitlement, and gratitude in families.

Whether a family ritual seems small or is a big event such as a Thanksgiving feast, the interaction defines the family and gives people instructions about their places within it. Sometimes the messages are fairly direct, as when children are told they cannot sit at the head of the table because "that is Daddy's place." But often the messages are more subtle, as when a sidelong glance gives a hint that a particular topic is not suitable for dinner table conversation, or when no one comments on whether the food tastes good. Every family has its own rules for such things, although the family members themselves probably could not list many of them or would deny that they were really rules in the first place.

Most families develop habits, patterns, and rules that make interpersonal interactions and household tasks unthinking and habitual. This ensures that things get accomplished with minimal effort, little conflict, and scant attention to questions of individual intent or equity. Most family rules are unspoken and operate just below the surface. Because they are reinforced by countless little daily rituals, they seem natural and inevitable. We usually learn about the rules only when they are violated, and even then, taboos may forbid direct discussion of them (Handel, 1985; Henley, 1977; Laing, 1971; Schur, 1984).

Home for the Holidays revealed some of these unspoken rules, even as it showed more arguments and more direct discussion of taboo subjects than happen at most family gatherings. In most cases, even if adults harbor resentments, they tell each other how nice it was to have gotten together, collaborating in creating the impression of family unity and family harmony. Knowing that people are supposed to love and appreciate their parents, spouses, children, siblings, grandparents, and so on, people generally try to act that way. When we try to bring our emotions in line with social expectations, it is called *emotion work* (Hochschild, 1983). Family routines and rituals teach us about managing our emotions and, as the movie showed, challenge our ability to be honest and follow family rules at the same time.

Although most theories suggest that family rituals perpetuate solidarity, or feelings of harmony and belonging, families are not necessarily cooperative units that meet every family member's needs. All families have conflict, even when family members do not like to talk about it or try not to show it. On average, people follow other family members' expectations most of the time, but no one is a robot who automatically does what a parent, spouse, or sibling expects. As a consequence, the needs or wants of individual family members inevitably come into conflict. How families deal with this conflict is an important focus of concern for family counselors and clinicians. Family routines and rituals often promote feelings of love and belonging, but these same family practices can perpetuate feelings of resentment and alienation in some family members (Laing, 1971).

Whether we do what is expected of us, and whether we like it or not, family rituals and practices help define the terms of family membership and set up complex feelings of obligation and entitlement. Because we are dependent on the love of family members, we pay attention to what other family members want from us. We develop expectations and learn various meanings from family interactions that ultimately shape our feelings about ourselves and about our own future family relationships. What makes a good wife, husband, mother, father, son, daughter, brother, sister, aunt, uncle, cousin, and so forth? These expectations are initially set up in our families of origin.

Family Diversity

To move beyond our own narrow family experiences and to gain a broader understanding of how families work, we need to look at a range of different families in different social contexts. Because the population of the United States is becoming more diverse all the time (see Figure 1.2), it is especially important to understand and appreciate differences and similarities among different American families. For example, the family composition of households from different race/ ethnic groups tends to vary. About a sixth of black households and a quarter of white households are married couples with children, whereas more than a third of both Asian and Hispanic households are of this type (see Figure 1.3). Of Hispanic or Asian households, 1 in 6 is a person living alone, compared with 1 in 4 black or white single-person households. Fewer than 1 in 16 white or Asian households are single parents, whereas almost 1 in 4 black households are of this type.

The differences in household composition among different ethnic groups are a product of many historical and contemporary factors, including both economic and cultural forces (Taylor, 1994). For African Americans, the influence of slavery, persistent discrimination, spatial segregation, and other cultural and economic factors produced family patterns that are somewhat different from other groups (e.g., Gutman, 1976; McDaniel, 1994; Morgan, McDaniel, Miller, & Preston, 1993; Rolison, 1992; Ruggles, 1994; Wilson, 1987). There is substantial variation in household composition for African Americans, with one in four households being single-parent families (see Figure 1.3), and more than half of these living in poverty (see Chapter 4, Figure 4.4). Nevertheless, about a third of all African American households are married couples, and these families are much more likely to have middle-class incomes (Willie, 1981, 1985). The varied experiences of subgroups within the Asian and Latino subgroups have similarly led to a range of household types and patterns that are both distinct from, and overlapping with, those of majority whites. For Asian Americans and Latinos, cultural traditions, occupational opportunities, immigration patterns, and many other social and economic factors have combined to shape family structures and interaction patterns through the years (e.g., for Asian Americans—Espiritu, 1997; Kitano & Daniels, 1988; O'Hare & Felt, 1991; for Latinos—Starrels, Bould, & Nicholas, 1994; Valdivieso & Davis, 1988; Vega, 1991).

Although this book is focused more on gender than on race and ethnicity, it is important to remember that the meanings of gender and family vary depending on ethnicity and culture. Equally important, social class differences and access to

FIGURE 1.3

Household Composition Differs by Race/Ethnicity
SOURCE: DeVita, 1996, Figure 13; U.S. Bureau of the Census, Current Population Surveys for 1995.

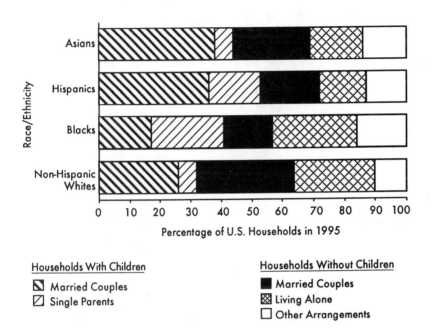

Percentage of U.S. Households in 1995

Households With Children

◩ Married Couples
▨ Single Parents

Households Without Children

■ Married Couples
▧ Living Alone
□ Other Arrangements

economic opportunities substantially affect the way that people experience family and gender, as well as influencing people's understanding of race and ethnicity. None of these can be understood adequately without reference to the other. (For more complete discussions of the intersection between race, class, gender, and family, see, for example, Anderson & Collins, 1995; Benería & Stimpson, 1987; Blumberg, 1991; Espiritu, 1997; Glenn, Chang, & Forcey, 1994; Higginbotham & Weber, 1992; Rubin, 1994; West & Fenstermaker, 1993; Zinn, 1989).

As noted above, in addition to varying according to race and class, families differ and can be analyzed according to their composition, past experiences, legal status, or special characteristics of their members. For instance, researchers can study nuclear families (married husband and wife with children), extended families (other relatives in household), cohabitors (living together but not married), single-parent households, only-child families, childless families, and so on. Researchers can also focus on various family types such as divorced mothers, single fathers, stepfamilies, adoptive families, gay couples, lesbian parents, families with disabled children, families with aging parents, and a wide variety of other classifications. All these family types are important, and most have been studied and written about, although relatively little is known about some of the newer and less prevalent types.

In this short book, I use gender as a lens to investigate processes that occur in all sorts of different families. So-called traditional families—married couples with children—are most often portrayed in the popular culture, and images of them influence perceptions of what "the American family" should be. Nevertheless, other household and family types are equally important. Researchers have spent less time figuring out how gender and family are related in nonnuclear households and in ethnic subgroups, making it harder to draw conclusions about them. Using gender as a lens in looking at both traditional families and other types of households can help us see why families have taken different forms and how they have benefited and constrained different family members. Focusing on gender and marriage can also help us understand some important recent changes and enable us to make some predictions about the future of family life in America.

Organization of the Book

The rest of the book focuses on the main themes raised in this first chapter: that gender and family are inseparably linked and that they are socially constructed. The following chapters also explore some marriage and family rituals but expand the analysis to focus on the ways that larger social, economic, and political structures shape both families and gender. This is accomplished with reference to more data from the past because historical variation is one of the best ways to show how our taken-for-granted ideals are products of particular circumstances. Issues of power and control are especially salient throughout the book because gender, ethnicity, and family structure help organize people into social hierarchies and grant or deny them access to privileges and comforts.

Chapter 2 explores where our love ideals came from and how they became associated with marriage. I investigate how and why men and women approach love differently and examine the meaning of sex in the courtship process. I introduce the concept of market exchange to understand patterns of falling in love and getting married. This sets the stage for looking at what happens after people get married and become parents.

In Chapter 3, I look at how paid work and family life are interrelated. By tracing patterns going back several hundred years, I examine how the transition from an agricultural economy to a market economy influenced family life. I follow the development of the ideal of separate spheres for men and women, with men becoming good providers and women becoming homemakers. For the modern era, I then summarize how paid work and housework are divided in American families today.

In Chapter 4, I turn to parenting and family caregiving. I summarize some important historical changes in images of children, fathers, and mothers. Children were transformed from duty-bound workers to emotionally precious objects as the economy shifted from home production to market capitalism. I also explore how the ideal of separate spheres limited fathers' involvement with their children and revered women for their nurturing capacities and moral purity. I trace the development of modern ideals of motherhood and fatherhood, describing what mothers and fathers have done for children since the 1950s. Finally, I show how the socially constructed meaning of parenthood continues to change up to this day.

In Chapter 5, I turn to the children, exploring how parents train boys and girls to become men and women, fathers and mothers. Drawing on theories and studies of child development and gender acquisition, I describe how families and parents encourage children to see the world as divided into two distinct and mutually exclusive categories. I focus on continuity and change in gender socialization and speculate about linkages between child rearing and gender in future generations.

In Chapter 6, I explore the institutional and political bases of marital and family relationships. I describe the history and evolution of laws and policies regulating family life. I pay particular attention to legal arrangements between husbands and wives, relating the laws to the social changes and power relations described in earlier chapters. I investigate recent changes in marriage, divorce, and child custody laws to illustrate how gender, family, and state power are interwoven.

In the last chapter, I review and summarize how family lives and gender meanings are mutually forged and inseparably linked. I offer some predictions about economic, social, demographic, and political trends to estimate what the future might hold. Using family change as a lens to examine potential changes in gender, I conclude with some surprisingly optimistic projections.

CHAPTER 2

Love, Sex, and Marriage

Americans are preoccupied with love and sex. Romance novels are best-sellers, hit movies have obligatory romantic subplots, and soap operas dominate daytime television. Sex scandals and the love affairs of movie stars continue to be mainstays of the tabloid newspapers, radio call-in shows about love and sex garner huge followings, and countless magazines at supermarket checkout stands offer advice on how to attract, impress, satisfy, keep, and even dump the mate of your choice. Americans did not invent this obsession with love and sex, but Hollywood-style romance featuring beautiful women and daring men has become one of our most influential and profitable cultural exports. Remarkably, each week *Baywatch* is seen by more viewers than any other television program in the world.

How did we get here, and what does it all mean? In this chapter, I begin to address these questions by looking at popular advice to would-be lovers from the 1930s, 1960s, and 1990s. I explore how men and women have been taught to approach love and marriage differently and how gendered patterns of courtship are changing—and *not* changing. Going even further back, I trace the historical roots of sentimental love to the erotic ideals of ancient Greece and the chivalrous flirtation of noble courts during the Middle Ages. Using cross-cultural and historical examples, I introduce the idea that sex and love can be seen as forms of property to be exchanged between families or individuals. Even today, romance occurs within the context of a marriage market, and I use modern examples to show how this works. I close the chapter with a brief discussion of how individual choices about love and marriage continue to be structured by age, race, gender, and social class.

Love Advice in the 20th Century

For most of this century, many Americans have turned to advice columns to get help with their love relationships (or to experience someone else's romantic feelings or problems vicariously). Today, teenage girls can read magazines such as *ym, Seventeen,* and *Teen* to find out how to attract boys or solve relationship problems. Women can turn to a huge array of magazines for such advice, from the often steamy *Cosmopolitan, Ebony, Moderna, Glamour,* and *Elle,* to the more staid *Redbook, Woman's Day,* and even *Working Woman.* The advice is directed not just to singles: Magazines such as *Family Circle, Good Housekeeping,* and *Parenting* regularly have articles and columns that tell mothers (but rarely fathers) how to keep love alive in their relationships.

"Dear Abby," "Ann Landers," and "Helpful Heloise" are examples of newspaper advice columns, but they are not the first of their type. "Dorothy Dix" was the "Dear Abby" of our great-grandmother's generation, yet her practical advice, excerpted below, could be mistaken for something out of the pages of one of the contemporary women's magazines. Similarly, excerpts from Helen Andelin's (1963) *Fascinating Womanhood* presented below have a timeless quality: They were inspired by booklets from the 1920s, were published in the early 1960s, resonate with advice from 1970s best-sellers such as Marabel Morgan's (1975) *The Total Woman,* and prefigure ideas from the best-selling relationship book of the 1990s, *Men Are From Mars, Women Are From Venus* (Gray, 1992). Finally, so you don't feel trapped in some bizarre time warp, I also draw on advice from a popular book about love and sex in the 1990s: *Hot and Bothered,* by Wendy Dennis (1992). Looking at these examples of love advice from across the 20th century will enable you to see what has stayed the same and what has changed and will also set the stage for talking about love and the marriage market.

Advice for the Lovelorn, 1900 to 1950

Dorothy Dix (whose real name was Elizabeth Meriwether Gilmer) was born in 1861 and married in 1882. After discovering that her husband would be ill for life, Dix began writing, won a prize in a newspaper short story contest, and became a journalist. In 1897, she was sent to cover Queen Victoria's Diamond Jubilee by the New Orleans *Picayune.* By 1901, she was writing for the *New York Journal.* She showed a remarkable ability to reply to readers seeking help with relationships, and her advice to the lovelorn column was syndicated and read by millions of people in the United States and throughout the world. When she died in 1951, at the age of 90, she had been counseling readers for more than half a century.

Dorothy Dix's advice about love and marriage both reflected and shaped Americans' attitudes toward romance in the early 20th century. In *Middletown,* a classic sociological study of family life in 1920s America, Robert and Helen Lynd (1929/1956) wrote that Dorothy Dix's column was "perhaps the most potent single agency of diffusion from without, shaping the habits of thought of Middletown in regard to marriage, and possibly represents Middletown's views more completely than any other available source" (quoted in Stein & Baxter, 1974, p. i). Her advice shows how women were coached to attract and "hook" men.

How to Win and Hold a Husband

The girl who wants to catch a man dangles before him the charms which he prefers and at which he is most likely to bite. Of course she makes herself as good-looking as nature and the style shops permit. Then she proceeds to make herself agreeable and to cultivate a line that will appeal to the particular man on whom she has an eye and she is bookish or golfish or musical or domestic, as the case calls for. Then she goes where the fish are plentiful, for she knows that there is no use in throwing a line and praying for luck in waters that have been fished out or from which the fish have fled to other pools.

Virtually any woman can get her man if she will just stalk him long enough. . . . And, of course, women sell themselves to men by feeding them and by flattering them and by listening to them talk about themselves. . . . The surest recipe for getting a husband is like that for making a rabbit pie. First catch your rabbit, and there is no hard-and-fast rule for doing this because men differ in temperament and a girl has to vary her technique to suit her subject. The line of attractions for which one man falls will leave another man cold.

If, for instance, the man you desire is very bashful and timid, your best play is a bold move. Don't wait for him to make the advances. Take the initiative yourself, but do it so quietly and unobtrusively that he never suspects that you are starting his feet along the path that leads to the altar. Otherwise you will scare him off. Ask favors of him. Make him feel that you depend on him. Ask his opinion and show him that you regard him as an oracle. No one on earth is so amenable to flattery as the shy man, and any woman who is a deft salve spreader can get him. But don't wait for him to propose. He will never summon up enough courage for that. Just casually remark someday, "John, don't you think the middle of next month would be a good time for us to get married?" And the wedding ring is yours!

On the other hand, if you have set your affections on a bold, bad lady-killer the best way to get your man is by flouting him. Be snooty. Show no interest in him whatever. Snub him. Break dates with him. Confide to some little cat who will purr it to him that you don't consider him so much of a much anyway and nothing to write home about. That will give him the shock of his life because he is used to having women kowtow before him, and he will get busy trying to find out what is the matter with your eyes that you can't see what a sheik he is. You will put him on his mettle to make a conquest of you, and the chances are that while he is doing this you will bowl him over. That type of man always hankers after the peach that hangs highest on the tree. He never wants the one that is ready to fall into his mouth. (Dix, 1939/1974, *How to Win and Hold a Husband,* pp. 65-69, © 1939 by Doubleday, a division of Bantam Doubleday Dell Publishing Group. Used by permission of Doubleday.)

Dorothy Dix's advice column was successful because she offered practical advice about how to catch a man. Rather than assuming that there was one right way to do this, Dix offered helpful hints about how to alter one's strategy depending on the man's temperament and preferences. Her analogy of fishing and catching a man suggests that the successful woman approaches courtship and marriage with shrewdness and clever calculation. She assumed that it was the woman's job to get the man, and her advice was intended to make that job easier.

Dix suggested that women use indirect tactics to get men's attention, such as positioning themselves nearby, wearing special clothes, smiling encouragingly, and playing up to them. This type of subtle flirting was more common among young women of past generations because it was one of the only resources they could use to try to win a mate. Passive techniques in courtship are still used much more frequently by women than by men (Cochran & Peplau, 1985; Wood, 1994a). Why is this so? Why don't women just walk up to men and say they want a relationship, rather than hanging back, trying to look pretty, and using trickery to get men's attention? In general, the reasons have to do with our taken-for-granted ideals of romantic love and with a topic elaborated later in the book—women's limited access to more direct means for obtaining wealth, power, and influence.

Dorothy Dix's advice also illustrates an interesting pattern of gender difference in initial emotional commitment. She coaches the women to make the men fall in love with them before the women commit. According to most studies, this is a pattern that still holds in many courtship rituals. Men report that they fall in love earlier in the relationship than women, and when national surveys are conducted, men are more likely than women to say that they believe in "love at first sight" (Brehm, 1992). As noted below, it used to be the case that men would be more likely than women to say that they based their decision to marry on having fallen in love with their spouse (Kephart, 1967; Safilios-Rothschild, 1977).

In addition, as Dix suggests, women often try to enhance their beauty to catch men. Even today, men are likely to say they are smitten by a potential mate's good looks: Since the 1960s, surveys have shown that men are more likely than women to choose a partner on the basis of physical attractiveness (Allgeier & Wiederman, 1991; Buss, 1989; Patzer, 1985; Smith, Waldorf, & Trembath, 1990). Just as in Dix's day, studies also show that women place more emphasis than men on a potential marriage partner's ambitiousness, industriousness, and financial prospects (Allgeier & Wiederman, 1991; Buss, 1989).

What's going on here? In a sense, men can afford the luxury of using "falling in love" or physical beauty to pick their marriage partners, whereas women have had to be more careful about the practical aspects of selecting someone to marry. Women do care about the emotional aspects of marriage and usually spend more time than men thinking about and talking about such things (Frazier & Esterly, 1990; Rubin, 1983; Thompson, 1993). But they tend to focus on the men's love for them, as much as, or even more than, their own feelings for men. Although both men and women worry about meeting the right person, it is still more typical for women to worry about getting men to notice them and fall in love with them than the other way around (Wood, 1996). Most studies show that women spend more time and effort than men on staying attractive to their love partners and keeping them interested in them (Rubin, 1983).

This extra effort in catching and keeping a man seems a bit old-fashioned to many young people, but there are reasons that this pattern persists. Although this particular gender difference in courtship is not as strong as it once was, it has definitely not disappeared. For the gender difference to go away completely, men and women would have to be equally dependent on marriage, and that it is still not the case today, as later chapters will show. Gender differences in courtship make sense in how men and women have had to use marriage differently. Because women have had to use marriage for financial security, they have had to be more cautious, calculating, and subservient in their approach to it.

"Fascinating Womanhood" in the 1960s and 1970s

As women's opportunities expanded in the 1960s and 1970s, some counter-movements arose to reassure women that their "proper" place was in the home pleasing men. Following her interpretation of biblical teachings, Helen Andelin (1963) led workshops for women during this era to help them become "ideal women" and to acknowledge their husbands' "leadership right." According to Andelin, it was not necessary for the man to do anything, because the woman was responsible for "awakening a man's love." Doing so was supposed to provide her with happiness in marriage because her actions would cause him to appreciate her and do things for her. In her book, *Fascinating Womanhood*, she suggests that a woman can find happiness and fulfill her feminine "nature" by yielding to her husband and admiring his manly qualities, thereby gaining his respect and protection.

The "Ideal Woman" From a Man's Point of View

> To understand the masculine viewpoint, we must learn to view the ideal woman through a man's eyes and realize that his ideas of feminine perfection are different from our own. . . . To become "The Ideal Woman" from a man's point of view, a woman must have Angelic qualities: [She] understands men, has deep inner happiness, has a worthy character, [and] is a domestic goddess. . . . The Angelic arouses in a man a feeling near worship, and brings him peace and happiness. We would do well to copy the manner in which children express emotions, especially the emotions of anger, hurt, disappointment, sympathy, tenderness and joy. I believe that by so doing, women can solve some of their most difficult marital problems. Truly fascinating women always remain somewhat little girls, regardless of their age. . . . Every woman can become childlike, for we all have this trait somewhere in our nature. It is part of being a woman. Remember that it was not long ago that you were a little girl when these traits were natural to you. . . . [I]f you are to be loved and treated like a woman, you must make him feel like a man. (Andelin, 1963, *Fascinating Womanhood*, pp. 17, 35, 263, 297)

Fascinating Womanhood assumed that women could get more emotional fulfillment from heterosexual relationships if they did not try to compete as equals with men. The message was that women were different from men, that wives should serve husbands, and that the woman's job was to keep the man interested in her. Research confirms that most American women value close emotional relationships more than men and therefore choose to spend more of their time and effort getting romances started and keeping them going (Cancian, 1987; Chodorow, 1978; Rubin, 1983; Thompson, 1993; Wood, 1994b). Not only have women generally worked to get men to notice them, but they have also taken the lead in talking about the relationship, have taught men how to talk about their feelings, and have sometimes given in to men's sexual advances from a sense of obligation. These actions relate to the larger gender balance of power in the society and show that women have traditionally been more dependent on marriage than men (Cancian, 1987; Rubin, Peplau, & Hill, 1981; Sattel, 1992). This dependence has encouraged women to emphasize relationships but to be less impulsive than men about falling in love or wanting to get married.

For example, in one study (Kephart, 1967), more than 1,000 college students were asked, "If someone had all the other qualities you desired, would you marry them if you were not in love with them?" Two of three men, but only one of four women, gave a definite "no" answer. A majority of the women in the study answered "maybe," leading Kephart to conclude that women exercised more control over their romantic feelings than men. The college students' answers indicate that women were more careful than men about falling in love, in part because they realized that their choice of a marriage partner would have profound implications for their economic futures (Cancian, 1994).

During this era, women were encouraged to subjugate their feelings and to focus on the supposed needs and desires of their male partners. "Fascinating womanhood," according to Andelin, included becoming a follower and learning how to influence men without challenging them. She offered checklists for women on how to do this:

How to Give Feminine Advice	*How to Be the Perfect Follower*
1. Ask leading questions.	1. Let go of the reins.
2. Use "insight" words, like "I feel."	2. Have a girlish trust in him.
3. Don't appear to know more than he does.	3. Be adjustable.
4. Don't be motherly.	4. Be obedient.
5. Don't talk man to man.	5. Support his plans and decisions.
6. Don't act braver than he is.	6. When you don't agree, support his right to decide.
7. Don't have unyielding opinions.	7. Present a United Front to the children.
	8. Assert yourself.

SOURCE: Andelin, 1963, *Fascinating Womanhood*, pp. 136-137, © 1963, Pacific Press.

Things have changed since the 1960s and early 1970s, when most advice books suggested that women give up independence to get a man. Evidence of this change is provided by follow-up studies to the Kephart research on whether people would consider marrying others if they had all the qualities they wanted in a mate. Researchers asked college students in 1976 and again in 1984 if they would consider marrying someone even if they were not "in love" with them (Simpson, Campbell, & Berscheid, 1986). In 1976, men were still more likely than women to say they would not marry without being in love (86% vs. 80%). In fewer than 10 years, however, the percentage of women saying "no" to the question more than tripled, and the percentage of men increased by more than 10%. By 1984, the college women's opinions had caught up to the men's, with about 85% of each reporting that they would not marry without being in love. The researchers concluded that the reason for the shrinking gender gap was that women had become more economically independent and were therefore less willing to settle for someone who was only a good provider (Simpson, Campbell, & Berscheid, 1986). In addition, the women's movement helped create an environment in which women were more willing to consider their own needs and less willing to make themselves subservient to men.

Romance in the 1990s

Things have continued to change. In the 1990s, when researchers asked the romantic love questions again, about 9 of 10 college men and women answered that being in love was essential to marrying (Allgeier & Wiederman, 1991). The gap between men and women had disappeared for that question, but the researchers discovered that, for other mate selection criteria, gender differences remained. For example, 1990s women ranked physical attractiveness and social skills as more important in a mate than had their sisters from an earlier era. As before, however, 1990s women ranked physical attractiveness much lower than did the men who constituted the pool of their potential mates. Studies show that women continue to be much more concerned than men about the future earning power of their prospective spouse. The gender gap in romantic love is thus shrinking, but there are still some differences in what men and women desire in a mate. In short, men are still valued more for providing and women more for their beauty (Allgeier & Wiederman, 1991; Buss, 1989). At the same time, these studies underscore the trend for both men and women to be increasingly committed to the idea that they must be in love before they get married.

Gender and Emotion Management

Because most women want to fall in love *and* find a good provider, how do they manage this? In part, women are able to align the two by consciously analyzing and discussing their feelings about their partners. In general, this allows them to fall in love less impulsively than men and makes it more likely that their love will develop incrementally or practically (Hendrick & Hendrick, 1989; Wood, 1994a). Of course, both men and women manage their emotions through countless personal adjustments and internal conversations. Compared with men, however, women more actively manage or regulate their emotions through talk, thought, and interaction with other people, usually ending up with a better fit between what they "want" and what they "feel" (Cancian, 1987; Hochschild, 1983; Sattel, 1992).

Hochschild (1983) uses the term *emotion work* to describe this process of aligning one's emotions with the dictates of the situation and finds that women tend to do more emotion work than men. For example, if a woman thinks a man is a good match, she is more likely to allow herself to be overwhelmed by her emotions. On the other hand, if she is attracted to a man who is unacceptable as a marriage partner, she is likely to deliberately work at falling out of love with him. Men do this type of emotion work too, but traditionally they have not been as focused on it as women have.

A woman's tendency to work on her emotions and to focus on getting the right man to love her is partly a matter of personal choice, but it also reflects women's historically weak bargaining position in the society and in the marriage market. Because women have been dependent on marriage for economic support, they end up paying more attention to initiating and maintaining love relationships and are more likely to adjust their feelings through emotion work, as recommended by the romance advice columns. Men, on the other hand, have been able to follow their impulsive feelings and let women pay attention to building intimacy. Traditionally, men have been quicker to be smitten by Cupid's arrow and to fall head over heels in love with a vision of their ideal mate.

These basic differences in the ways that men and women have approached romantic relationships do not hold for every person because they are just general tendencies that are subject to change (Hendrick & Hendrick, 1996). What happens to men sometimes happens to women, and vice versa, and the gender differences seem to be getting smaller as men's and women's lives become more similar. The ideals and practices of romantic love also differ according to ethnicity, religion, and the like, with enormous variation between different groups. Nevertheless, a consistent message that we get from the popular culture and hear from many people around us is that gender differences in courtship are natural, unchanging, and beneficial for both men and women. Most people concede that there are some general differences in women's and men's approach to romance, but increasingly, people are questioning whether they are necessary or helpful.

Contemporary Patterns of Flirting

Dennis's (1992) discussion of flirting in the 1990s shows how some of the older ideas about courtship are still with us:

> Most women realize that many men still find the notion of a sexually aggressive woman distasteful. . . . [D]espite all of their feminist rhetoric, many women are still waiting for Prince Charming to show up at their doors and sweep them off their feet. . . . [W]hile men appear to be the sexual aggressors . . . they are in fact responding to subtle signals. . . . Women draw men to them through flirtatious behavior: glint of eye, seductive posture, tone of voice, pressure of touch. . . . Predictably, men warm to a laugh, a smile or a touch. [W]hen a woman carelessly executes a hair flip, head toss, skirt hike or lip lick, the needle goes right off the attraction-meter and the guys are off and running. . . . [M]en respond to . . . the woman who flatters, compliments and sweet-talks them without being phony, who [is] coy without being coquettish, who seduces by appreciation, not aggression.
>
> . . . [One] man recalled fondly a woman he'd met who knew a thing or two about the fine art of flirting. "Within an hour of meeting we were flirting like mad. She was instigating it, for sure, but I found it utterly charming. We had a

mock fight in a subway station, and she touched me and the touching was pregnant with meaning. As she left, she sort of turned over her shoulder and asked in this curious, little-girl voice, 'Do men like anal sex?' God, it was erotic! It was the perfect combination of innocence and sleaze." (Dennis, 1992, *Hot and Bothered: Sex and Love in the Nineties,* pp. 92-95)

This 1990s advice to women carries some of the same gender assumptions as earlier advice columns, insofar as women are expected to flirt and indirectly entice men into paying attention to them. For women, this entails exuding just the right combination of "innocence and sleaze." This 1990s version of love advice is much more sexually explicit and also considerably more contradictory than advice from past decades. For example, Dennis (1992) begins her book with the observation, "In the sixties, when I discovered sex, there was no such thing as a politically correct blow job" (p. 1). Like much of love advice from contemporary sources, Dennis both appreciates the benefits of feminism and laments that women's gains have made romance more complicated. The old romantic and sexual scripts from the popular culture were never realistic for the majority of people, but today they are harder than ever to enact. According to Dennis, it is difficult for women in the 1990s to perform the delicate tightrope act that forces them to balance "dogma and desire, sexism and sexiness, feminism and femininity" (p. 268).

In the 1990s, men are also under pressure to figure out what women want and, according to Dennis, to offer women just the right combination of sensitivity and bravado. Although past sex advice to men usually portrayed good lovers as sensitive and responsive, the overriding emphasis in popular culture has been on tough loners who make women swoon and take what they want without having to express themselves. Marital advice, in contrast, has typically focused on men being good providers, protectors, and role models. In this context, Dennis's 1990s advice to men looks different because it expects men to do some of the same sorts of things in romance that women have done in the past.

Like men, women warm to seduction by appreciation. Courtship, they say, is a dance, not a duel. . . . Just as women love a lover with a gentle touch, so too do they cherish a gentle approach. An appreciative look scores big with women; a lurch, a paw, or a leer does not. . . . A great flirt always leaves a woman feeling good about herself. He knows how to compliment her on her charms without making her feel as if she is a piece of meat. He looks her in the eye, listens to what she is saying, jokes and spars with her in a delightful, engaging way. (pp. 94-96)

The flesh-and-blood New Man of the nineties who wishes to emulate the currently fashionable model of manhood certainly has his work cut out for him. . . . He has to be gentle but not weak, malleable but not limp, masterful but not macho, sensitive but not sappy and stylish but not shallow. He has to cook! He has to clean! He has to garden and decorate! If he's married, he has to chauffeur the kids and pontificate knowledgeably on the subject of fatherhood. In his leisure time, however, should he experience a moment of heaving desire, he has to radiate the animal magnetism of a Tom Cruise, do a me-Tarzan, you-Jane routine and (with her lusty consent, of course) pin Jane against the fridge, remove her panties and make the earth move for her. (Dennis, 1992, *Hot and Bothered: Sex and Love in the Nineties*, p. 69)

Popular Images of Romantic Love

For decades, Americans have been bombarded by media images of romantic love. Most of the images are unrealistic, and some are unpopular, but even when the images are unattainable or out-of-date, we still tend to carry them around in our heads. Turn on the radio and the first song we will hear is probably a love song—about the joys of falling in love or the sorrows of breaking up. If we happen to tune into a call-in radio talk show, the subject matter is as likely to be about sex and love as to be about politics. On the Internet, chat rooms are used for "cyber-romance" and "cybersex." Television talk shows are even more dominated by bizarre testimonials about romantic and sexual desires, practices, and disappointments. Movies and television shows, even when they focus on action, almost always contain a story line that includes heartthrobs or heartaches. Most of these stories are about conventional heterosexual loves, and most include some version of a strong male hero rescuing a beautiful and (at least partially) helpless woman and defeating the evil bad guys. But whether boy meets girl, girl meets boy, or some creative blending of the two, love imagery is rarely absent from the popular media.

This heavy emphasis on romance in popular culture provides us with a unique view of love. But it also sets us up for disappointment by creating unrealistic expectations. Some critics even suggest that romantic love is a type of trick because it recruits women into marriages in which they are expected to perform free domestic labor for their husbands (e.g., Rapp, 1992). Most of us don't like to think about love and marriage in these terms because our romantic ideals tell us that love transcends worldly matters. But marriage has always been mixed up with issues of power and control and has always been shaped by a variety of practical concerns. Appearing to be uniquely modern, however, are the nearly automatic association of love with marriage and subsequent challenges to that equation in the past few decades.

Love and Marriage in the Past

Most people assume that love and marriage have always gone together—as the song says, "like a horse and a carriage." But putting the two together is probably a relatively recent invention (Murstein, 1974). In most societies throughout history, and in many societies throughout the world today, people marry out of obligation to parents and family. In the typical case, a strong sense of family duty and obligation to parents is symbolically transferred on marriage to a spouse who is chosen by one's parents or grandparents.

In various societies around the world, older family members have followed elaborate cultural customs in selecting mates for younger people, whose choice in the matter has often been severely constrained. In tribal societies, for example, kinship rules specified who should or should not marry whom (e.g., a cousin on the father's side might be preferred, but a cousin on the mother's side might be taboo, according to custom). In many societies reliant on fishing, herding, or primitive horticulture, the family or clan of the wife received valuables such as furs, shells, or livestock as part of the marriage exchange (Lévi-Strauss, 1969; Rubin, 1975). In more technologically advanced societies, arranged marriages were especially common in the higher social classes, where they were used to form alliances and maintain family control of wealth and property (Boulding, 1976; Searle, 1988). But even among common people, older family members have usually identified potential marriage partners and effectively encouraged or discouraged young people from seeing one another or getting married. This does not mean that young people did not develop affectionate bonds or have some influence over the selection of a mate, but the idea of marrying solely on the basis of love was practically unheard of (Goode, 1963; Goody, 1983). In most traditional societies, such as ancient China, the Middle East, and medieval Europe, love matches such as the famous one between Romeo and Juliet were considered dangerous precisely because they had the potential to disrupt the existing social order (Laslett, 1977).

Although most marriages were arranged, the idea of love was present in many past societies, as evidenced by ancient myths and stories from around the world. For example, in India, one of the most popular gods of Hinduism, Krishna, was sometimes depicted as a flute-playing beloved of the cow maidens (*gopis*) or as a prince consorting with his lover, Radha. Krishna combined the sensitive sentiments of erotic love with a more religious yearning for salvation. The *Kama Sutra*, a Hindu treatise on the art of love attributed to Vatsyayana (1963), was composed sometime between the first and fourth centuries A.D. *Kama* is the Hindu word for love (or pleasure and sensual gratification); *sutra* are aphorisms (truthful sayings). The *Kama Sutra* provides love advice, including explicit sexual instructions, as well as advice on courtship and marriage. For example, a girl is told to use indirect tactics in showing her love:

> She never looks the man in the face, and becomes abashed when she is looked at by him; under some pretext or other she shows her limbs to him: she looks secretly at him, though he has gone away from her side; hangs down her head when she is asked some question by him, and answers in indistinct words and unfinished sentences, delights to be in his company. (pp. 183-184)

Like other ancient records of love advice from around the world, the *Kama Sutra* describes the erotic pleasures of wealthy nobles who led a life of relative leisure (Archer, 1957).

Romantic love with a spiritual quality was also present in the wealthy courts of 11th-century Japan. The most famous of all Japanese novels, *The Tale of Genji*, was written by a noble lady of the high court for the amusement of the emperor and his nobles (Shikibu, 1976). The book tells of Genji, the indulged son of an ancient emperor, his travels, and his many loves. Not only does the novel depict the intricacies of court life in Kyoto, but it describes the prince's erotic impulses, feelings of romantic longing, and elaborate plans for wooing the beautiful young Murasaki (Seidensticker, 1977).

The ancient love myths familiar to most Westerners come from southern Europe and the area surrounding the Mediterranean Ocean. For example, Venus was the goddess of love in ancient Rome, and her son, Cupid, was the pudgy little archer whose arrows turned men and women into helpless lovers. Before then, the Greek goddess Aphrodite and her son Eros symbolized passionate love. But in these myths, like most others, passionate love is not usually depicted as something attainable by common people, and rarely is it shown as a normal part of marriage (Hadas, 1950; Reiss, 1971).

Greek philosophers and poets celebrated sexual love, but it was not the mutual form of love we think of today. In Greek mythology, Hera, the goddess of marriage, was embarrassed by the sexual affairs of her husband, Zeus, and plotted against the love goddess, Aphrodite. The erotic love that Plato and other Greek philosophers idealized was a combination of the purely physical and the extremely spiritual. Sex and beauty were its goals, but it was not focused on one's marriage partner. Greek men kept their wives locked up inside their houses while entertaining themselves with cultivated prostitutes called *hetairai* (Pomeroy, 1975). The highest form of love in ancient Greece was not even heterosexual; it usually involved an older man's one-sided infatuation with a beautiful adolescent boy (Dover, 1978).

A similar gap between love and marriage can be seen in medieval Europe. The arrival of Christianity promoted the idea of the love of God, but this was a spiritual love different from Plato's ideal forms or the sensuality of pagan rituals. The Christian church considered the overt sexuality and eroticism of the Greeks, Romans, and pagans as an immoral abomination. Early Christianity placed a strong emphasis on asceticism, and the ideal person was expected to deny all desires of the flesh to attain holiness (Queen & Habenstein, 1967). If people could not remain celibate, they could marry, but even sex in marriage was suspect. The Penitentials of Theodore, seventh-century archbishop of Canterbury, contained a list of punishments for those who could not abstain: "A man who had intercourse with his wife must take a bath before entering the church. Newly married persons or women who had given birth were likewise barred from church for a period, followed by a set penance" (Williams, 1993, p. 96). Marriage ceremonies were not holy enough to take place inside the church, so they were held just outside the church doors. Even today, wedding guests continue this ritual when they gather outside church doors to throw rice at the newlyweds.

In medieval society, most people married not because of love but because of practical concerns. This was especially the case among the upper classes, but it was also true for ordinary people (Power, 1975). Among kings, queens, and other nobility, marriages were a form of diplomacy. Some of the most important treaties of the time were the result of complicated political marriages and agreements about royal inheritance and ascension to the throne (Boulding, 1976; Searle, 1988). Among the lower ranks of the aristocracy, marriages were also arranged to ensure the prestige of the family line and the growth of property holdings. Among middle-class shop owners and small farmers, spouses were often chosen on the basis of their ability to help out with the business. Even among the peasant and working classes, economic considerations often shaped marriage decisions (Shorter, 1975). For example, peasant children were likely to be hired out as servants during their young adulthood and married only when they could afford a cottage or a little plot of land. In England, individual men and women would coordinate their economic activities by deciding if and when to marry, whereas in eastern and southern Europe, most marriage choices were made by families, rather than by individuals. In both places, however, marriages were based primarily on economic considerations. If people were too poor, they often had to remain single for their entire lives (Goody, 1983; Laslett, 1971).

Although people did not marry just for love, the marriage bargain almost always included sex. But this was not the mutual and flirtatious sexuality that we normally associate with dating and courtship. People sometimes had sex before marriage, but sexual activity, especially for women, was severely restricted by the family. Chastity, or sexual abstinence, was promoted by keeping young women apart from young men or (rarely) through protective devices such as chastity belts. The unchaste maid was no longer marriageable and thus worthless to her father (Williams, 1993). Once married, however, women were expected to have sex with their husbands: "Wives, submit yourselves unto your husbands, as unto the Lord. For the husband is the head of the wife, even as Christ is the head of the church" (Ephesians 5:22-23, King James Version).

According to custom and religious teachings, sex was an obligation married women bore to produce heirs or able-bodied children who could help with the work of the household. This does not mean that men and women in the past weren't sexually attracted to each other or that they didn't enjoy having sex. For example, even though the church promoted a sexual double standard and devalued women's sexuality, the Old Testament also reveals a sensual and earthy consciousness of sex (Williams, 1993, p. 97). Documents from the Middle Ages, such as the love letters of Héloise to Abelard, or the open sensuality of Chaucer's Wife of Bath, suggest that some women appreciated the pleasures of sex (Edwards & Spector, 1991; Murstein, 1974). It's just that sex, love, and marriage didn't necessarily come together in a common package as we think they should today.

The Birth of Courtly Love

The ideal of courtly love that emerged in Europe during the Middle Ages provides some of the precursors to our modern version of love and marriage. During those days, countries and governments did not exist as they do today, and feudal lords with their own armies exercised control over the land and the peasants who lived on the land. People from all walks of life had to pay homage to these powerful lords. Men of higher social rank expressed their allegiance to their lords through the giving of gifts and symbolic gestures such as kneeling and kissing (Collins, 1975; Dickens, 1977).

Through the centuries, families with successful warriors solidified their social ranking by cultivating these aristocratic manners. Gradually, they established a system of hereditary knighthood that benefited their own children. As the knights' expressions of symbolic allegiance began to focus on the lady of the feudal estate as well as on the lord, these courtly courtesies took on flirtatious and romantic overtones. This marked the beginning of chivalry and a style of courtly love that set the stage for our own modern version of romance—aptly called *court*ship (Collins, 1986; Macfarlane, 1986).

Among the upper classes of medieval Europe, and especially in France, a unique class of minstrel knights called *troubadours* traveled among the courts of lords and nobles. The troubadours were minor nobles themselves, rather than commoners, and as they traveled around, they sang the praises of idealized aristocratic noblewomen. In elaborate lyrical poems and songs, they spun tales of beautiful and superior ladies who remained inaccessible to their suitors. Fine young noblemen diligently pursued the lovely ladies, but no matter how much they pleaded and suffered, the gentle and noble ladies always said "no" (de Rougemont, 1956).

Just as they had done to the lords of patrimonial castles, troubadours and knights would swear loyalty to high-ranking ladies of the court, using symbolic gestures. But these gestures soon began to take on sexual overtones as well. During this time, knights began the chivalrous custom of wearing a lady's scarf or other token in a tournament or a battle. Troubadours and knights often attended ladies who were left in charge of their castles while their husbands were away traveling or fighting. Because the lord and lady of the castle had not usually married out of love or developed a close personal attachment, erotic courtly romances frequently developed between ladies and visiting knights. Adultery was common. Aristocratic love affairs began to take up much of the nobles' time and were celebrated in song and poem. The elaborate and mischievous seduction games of the wealthy classes continued into the 18th century, as depicted in the film *Dangerous Liaisons*.

The courtly love affairs celebrated by troubadours were not just spontaneous expressions of sexuality or intimacy. Because an elaborate set of allegiances governed wealth, property, and virtually all social relations within the aristocracy, flirtation and adultery had to be tightly regulated. The courtly love affairs thus followed a complicated set of rules and customs that fitted nicely into the status hierarchy of medieval military households among the upper class (Collins, 1986). The love rituals of the nobility, however, laid the groundwork for more popular ideas about romance among the general population (Macfarlane, 1979).

The cult of courtly love was a break from earlier idealizations of love because the lady was exalted in a spiritual sense. Her beauty and remoteness were worshiped as never before. As it is commonly referred to today, she was "placed on a pedestal." One might flirt with her and perhaps even have sex with her if all the right moves were made, but she remained unattainable as a permanent love object. This form of chivalrous love was confined to a small segment of the population and was not associated with marriage, but important elements of it have survived to this day.

As the political and economic structure of society underwent massive changes after the medieval period, marriages became more private affairs for the couples involved. At the highest levels, diplomatic alliances were still formed through marriage, but the growth of large standing armies and bureaucratic government made courtly marriage politics less important. Among the middle and lower classes, marriage also became less a matter of practical economic necessity and more a private matter of acquiring a sexual and domestic partner. We will see in the next chapter that, as the market economy developed and capitalism spread, the ideal of a separate domestic sphere began to develop. Because marriages were no longer held together as tightly by the larger political and economic structures, a newer, more internal motivation for marriage emerged: the sentimental ideal of modern love (Flandrin, 1979; Shorter, 1975; Stone, 1977).

Sentimental Love and Modern Marriage

Today, we think of love as a mutual emotional bond between a man and a woman that occurs within marriage. We tend to think that there is something wrong with people if they are not in love when they get married. But as the Greek and medieval examples show, what seems natural and inevitable to us now is actually a relatively new idea. Unlike the erotic passions of ancient times or the adulterous games of courtly love, the new ideal says that love should include mutual caring that lasts a lifetime. Most important, the new ideal says that love should be a part of marriage and that it should stay confined within it.

Why did the new ideal emerge? For the most part, changing patterns of production and consumption transformed almost all aspects of society in profound ways. Because of changes in the marketplace and the political arena, men gained less from marriage than before, although they still received domestic services and sex from wives. Because women's labor became less necessary under newer forms of production, they were forced to ensure their own economic well-being through other means. Wives now found it increasingly important to attach men to themselves personally, and with a strong and lifetime tie. This is what the new love ideal did (Collins, 1971). In a way, love became a sort of emotional insurance that kept a woman and her loyal breadwinner husband tied together "until death do us part." For this to work effectively, however, it was also necessary to develop a new cultural attitude toward sex, one that connected it to love and kept it confined to marriage.

Sex as Marital Property

People resist thinking about sex as something that can be owned or exchanged, especially today, when most young people experience sex outside marriage. But when we compare different societies throughout history, we can see that sex has often been treated as a form of property (Collins, 1971; Rubin, 1975). The dispensing of sex through prostitution or the use of concubines shows that sex can be bought and sold like property, but more "normal" sex can also be seen as a type of property. Getting married has meant that a husband can have sex with his wife and other people cannot; the man is like an owner of the woman's sexuality, insofar as he is granted rights of access and control. In our society, the corollary pattern is also supposed to hold for women controlling men's sexuality (although in practice, men have had more license to have affairs or visit prostitutes). When men control women's sexuality, but not the reverse, it is called unilateral sexual possession. When women can also "own" a man's sexuality, as in our own modern form of marriage, we call it bilateral sexual possession. In the same way that spouses have rights over each other's sexuality, in many societies, fathers (or mothers, uncles, grandparents, etc.) have regulated their daughters' sexuality, prohibiting them from having sex until a marriage to the right man has been arranged.

When we look back across all the different types of societies that have existed throughout history, we can see an interesting pattern in the treatment of sex as property. If family alliances and marriage politics are more important to the organization of the society, men are more likely to treat women's sexuality as a form of property. In simple tribal societies that rely on hunting and gathering, there is usually little control over sexuality. Premarital intercourse is frequently allowed with any choice of partners, and sometimes marriage is a trial arrangement that can be easily broken up if unsatisfactory. Not all less-developed societies have been this sexually permissive, but few require a woman to be a virgin at marriage.

Societies that are more developed tend to have more status differences throughout the society and are much more likely to require that brides be virgins. The great historic civilizations of Egypt, the Middle East, China, Japan, India, ancient Rome, and medieval Europe fall into this category and had fairly tight controls over women's sexuality and strict controls over marriage. Not only was virginity usually required, but also there were practices of early marriage, wherein a girl would be betrothed well before the age of puberty to ensure her sexual purity. In these societies, if a girl had any sexual experience, it was considered a serious insult to her future husband and a violation of the alliance and exchange between the families contracting the marriage. To promote chastity, women were often secluded, veiled, and tightly chaperoned. Premarital sex, like adultery, was often punishable by death or by the sale of the woman into slavery or prostitution. This extreme treatment of sex as property was one-sided because only women were supposed to be virgins at marriage. Men, in contrast, were expected to use prostitutes and could often get away with raping more vulnerable women in the lower social classes or the women of a defeated enemy in war. The sexual double standard in these male-dominated agrarian societies encouraged men to have sex at the same time that they controlled the sexuality of their own wives and daughters. Protecting women as a valuable form of sexual property was also most common among the upper social classes because peasant women had to work and could not be locked up in exclusive women's quarters (Goode, 1967).

With the growth of a market economy and the rise of smaller private households in England and Europe following the medieval period, the marriage system was slowly transformed. Love became more associated with marriage, and the old male-dominated double standard of agrarian societies gave way to a new, more equal, but puritanical, sexual standard. This was not a swift or even transition, but gradually the new marriage ideal called for fidelity for both husbands and wives, rather than just for wives. The new ideal was often violated, especially by the men, but the idea of marriage implying a mutual sexual bond gradually gained in symbolic importance (Flandrin, 1979; Laslett, 1971; Shorter, 1975; Stone, 1977; Williams, 1993).

From the 1700s on, but especially during the so-called Victorian era of the 1800s, named after the reign of Queen Victoria of England (1837-1901), sexual prudishness reached its height. In the public dealings of the middle and upper classes, women came to be seen as the "delicate sex," and men attempted to keep "improper" subjects from their ears (Cott, 1978). Respectable people were admonished to refrain from talking openly about sex, references to pregnancy and childbirth were considered obscene, and it was considered improper for a woman to expose even her ankle to a man (Haller, 1972).

The extreme prudery of the Victorian era accompanied the separation of male and female spheres. Although the public ideal was for mutual fidelity, a masculine backstage of private clubs, saloons, hunting trips, the theater, and prostitutes flourished during this period of history. Prostitution had existed since ancient times and was openly accepted in most ports and military towns, but during the Victorian era, it was pushed further underground. The masculine backstage of "bad girls" and "fallen women" became a contrast to the cult of true womanhood and an ideal of domestic purity (Welter, 1966). A public battleground developed, especially among the middle class, in which women worked hard to make the men behave "decently." The ideal path for women was to be pious and submissive, but they had to cultivate an image of passionlessness to escape being an object of men's sexual desire. Consequently, women were encouraged to embrace the home and motherhood but to distance themselves from any form of sexuality (Cott, 1978; Haller, 1972; Walter, 1974).

As the new individual marriage market began to supplant the older arranged marriage market, sex became an important part of marital bargaining. Women could no longer count on being married off by their parents, and their worth as workers in the emergent wage labor economy made them less desirable as marriage partners. Instead, they began to rely on getting potential marriage partners to fall in love with them on the basis of their personal attractiveness. By the latter part of the 19th century, a formal pattern of courtship called *calling* had developed among the middle and upper classes. Men would be invited to call on young women at home, and visits were supervised by the woman's mother. Often, a woman would designate certain days on which she would receive callers, and she might have several suitors at one time. A man might be told that the woman was not at home to receive him, and he would then be expected to leave his calling card. If this happened frequently, he was supposed to get the message that his visits were no longer welcome (Whyte, 1992). In this way, calling was an early form of dating, and its purpose included providing both men and women the opportunity to examine potential marriage partners (Bailey, 1988).

The moral code at the turn of the century confined sex to marriage, and the prudishness of the time encouraged women to withhold sex from potential suitors to get them to propose. Among the elite upper classes, a few still played a version of the courtly love game, and among the lower classes, sexuality was more overt and less regulated. As the middle class grew in size, however, popular cultural ideas about love, sex, and marriage became more widely accepted. Separate spheres for men and women, sentimental love as the basis for marriage, and sexual fidelity for both husbands and wives gained acceptance among a larger segment of the population than ever before.

The development of a morally pure sphere for women gave them some leverage with men and provided them with some distinct advantages. They were idealized (at least in public), and most middle-class women were guaranteed the economic support of marriage at a time when they were excluded from independent careers of their own. The price they paid, however, was that they were confined to the home. The "female" home came to be seen as the opposite of the "male" world of business, politics, and pleasure. Women were supposed to be asexual, have a decorous courtship with a prospective husband, and save themselves for marriage. This ideal of separate spheres had profound implications for the organization of paid and unpaid work, as I discuss in Chapter 3, and was influential in shaping modern ideas about parenting and family, as discussed in Chapter 4.

The Continuing Significance of Romantic Love

Vestiges of courtly love and Victorian ideals remain in 20th-century advice columns and popular culture portrayals of romance, although many of the social and economic circumstances that produced these ideals have faded from the scene. We are still exposed to countless images of pure, beautiful damsels in distress who are saved by strong, chivalrous knights in shining armor (except these days, the "fair lady" usually shows most of her body and the "troubadour" usually can't sing). Like their fairy tale forebears, most women in movies, television, and novels still lure their men through personal beauty, act coy and withhold sex during courtship, and appear blissfully happy on their wedding days. The happily-ever-after of marriage and children is rarely spelled out in any detail, but the theme of women winning a husband through courtship is still very much with us today.

The romantic love ideal that we have inherited from earlier times encourages men to focus on women's beauty and to idealize their potential mates. Women focus on their physical appearance, get men's attention through flirting, and win them over by being coy. This is what we see in most of the love advice manuals. In this pattern, the woman becomes an idol who is placed on a pedestal and worshiped by the man. Like the troubadours of old, he tries to impress her and win her favor. After he courts her and perhaps seduces her, however, he must protect her and ends up having to hide her away from other potential suitors. This romantic script still influences modern dating rituals and continues to define what it means to be a man or woman today.

The romantic love ideal encourages men to glorify women but, at the same time, tends to imprison them. The woman is a trophy to be admired, but she is also kept dependent on the man and locked away as his treasure. Ironically, after he is finally sure of possessing her, he may begin to lose interest. No longer a mysterious beauty to be conquered, the woman turns into an ordinary person, and the man begins to find fault with her and withdraw (Collins, 1971). According to most 20th-century love guides, women can avoid this potential problem by turning the marriage into a perpetual courtship game, preening herself and coyly seducing her mate in a continuing way. According to many theorists, the tendency of women to use their sex appeal to attract men is a trap for them because men's idealization of women's beauty often includes a subtle contempt for women. Romantic love ideals are thus linked to a system of gender relations that keeps women in a subordinate position (Collins, 1971; Rapp, 1992).

Love Matches and Marriage Markets

This chapter has shown that the linking of love, sex, and marriage developed as changes in the economy and the society encouraged people to put more emphasis on their emotions. As people paid more attention to love, they took more active roles in choosing their own sex and marriage partners. These relationships, however, are still "arranged" by larger social forces. Most people who become lovers or marry are surprisingly similar in important social characteristics. Even today, how people fall in love, when they do it, and with whom are still remarkably predictable.

Because we are so preoccupied with being in love, we tend to ignore that selecting sexual and marriage partners is still strongly influenced by our social circumstances. To begin with, we must have contact with others before we can fall in love with them (or even "in lust" with them). People who end up having sex or marrying usually meet where they spend most of their time: in the neighborhood, at school, on the job, at a friend's house, and so forth. So the first thing shaping love matches is propinquity or nearness. The places in which people spend time, and the people we come into contact with, tend to be divided according to social class and ethnicity.

Sexual Exchanges

One of the most consistent findings from research on social relationships is the tendency toward *homophily,* or association with similar and equal-status others. People tend to initiate and maintain relationships with people who possess comparable social characteristics, such as social class, age, race, education, and religion (Laumann, 1973; Marsden, 1988). In sexual relationships, this is especially the case. Recent research shows that most sexual partners were introduced by friends or family, and most partners met through school or work (Laumann, Gagnon, Michael, & Michaels, 1994). Because of residential and occupational segregation, this means that people get together with people like them.

Contrary to popular stereotypes, homophily is common for those who have short-term sexual relationships (under one month), as well as for those who have longer-term sexual relationships. A national random sample found that 91% of short-term sexual partners were of the same race/ethnicity, 87% were similar in educational achievement, 83% were within five years in age, and 60% had a similar religion (Laumann et al., 1994). The same tendency is found among cohabiting partners, whether they are heterosexual or same-sex partners (Laumann et al., 1994; Schoen & Weinick, 1993). Among married couples, the tendency to be paired with a similar other is even stronger (see Table 2.1).

TABLE 2.1

Who Has Sex With Whom? Most Sexual Relationships Include People Who Are
Similar to Each Other

	Percentage in Relationship With Similar Other			
	Type of Relationship			
Similar Characteristic	*Marriages*	*Cohabitations*	*Long-Term Partnerships*	*Short-Term Partnerships*
Race/Ethnicity	93	88	89	91
Age	78	75	76	83
Education	82	87	83	87
Religion	72	53	56	60

SOURCE: Adapted from Laumann et al., 1994, Table 6.4, p. 255, © University of Chicago Press;
used with permission.
NOTES: Sample is based on a national sample of U.S. residents ($n = 3,432$).
Sexual relationships include both heterosexual and same-sex couples.
Marriages and cohabitations include only those who had relationships that began within the
past 10 years.
Short-term partnerships are sexual relationships lasting less than one month.
Long-term partnerships are sexual relationships lasting a month or more.
Missing data and "other" are excluded from race/ethnicity and religion.
Age similarity is defined as a difference of no more than five years.
Educational similarity is defined as a difference of no more than one educational category (less
than high school, high school graduate, vocational training, four-year college, and graduate
degree).

Exposure to potential mates provides the opportunity for love to develop
among similar others. But what is love, and when does it occur? According to
various theories and literary traditions, love can involve sexual passion, romantic
idealization, affection, companionship, altruism, dependence, attachment, and
shared experiences (Cancian, 1994; Hendrick & Hendrick, 1996). Social science
theories about love focus on how similar (or different) potential mates are, what
they get from the relationship, whether the relationship seems fair or equitable to
them, and how ritual interaction promotes intense feelings of love and attachment
(e.g., Berscheid, 1985; Collins, 1975; Walster & Walster, 1978). But regardless of the
type of love predicted or the stages that the love relationship is supposed to go
through, most theories assume that love involves a market exchange.

When we think about sex, it is not too far-fetched to think of a market. In most
cases, the market does not involve a product being exchanged for money but
instead entails bartering between two people. Each prospective partner offers a
set of physical attributes, personality, skills, and so on that are exchanged for those
of a partner who seems interesting (Laumann et al., 1994, pp. 11-13). The exchange
is made explicit in personal newspaper advertisements, such as the ones below
from a major newspaper in 1996.

DATELINE PERSONAL ADVERTISEMENTS

SAF, 24, 5', 100 lbs, n/s, drug-free, no kids, enjoys fine wine and beach. ISO SA/WM 25-36, Thai-spkg, w/similar interests.

SAF, passionate, athletic, educated, high integrity, delicate, feminine, luvs rose gardens, 30s, slim, wants 1 special Gent!

SAF, attractive, honest, simple, seeks feminine, intelligent B/H/AF, with good heart for good times.

SBF, attractive, funloving, warm, 43, good sense of humor, looking for my hero. ISO SBM, 40-50.

SBF, cosmopolitan, 28, ISO well-edu SB/H/WM, 25-40, 6'+, mature, open-mind, n/s, n/d; friends, dance, books, movies. No airheads please!

SBF, attractive, feminine, articulate, intel. ISO SBF, 26-36 5'5"+ 4 friendship, movies, dining and possibly more.

SJF, slim, strawberry blonde/blue, 53, loves opera, theater, trvl. ISO DJM, affluent, 50-60. Let's explore life's pleasures.

SJF, beautiful, dimpled, vivacious, blonde with knock-out figure ISO tall, fit, witty, adventurous SJM with champion personality, 48-58, n/s.

SHCF, 41, 5'3", 123#, meticulous, stable, no vices. ISO phys fit M, 39-49, avg build, 5'9"-6'2", 170-200#, finan. secure, similar quals, no kids.

SHF, beautiful, full figured, college student, likes dancing, roller skating ISO SM 21-40, financially secure.

DWF, very attractive, prof, brown/green, 5'8", slender, young-looking 45, ISO SWM 40s, attractive, honest, sense of humor, outgoing.

SWF, stunning figure, tall, leggy, blonde, sense of humor, n/s, n/d, ISO fin sec entrepreneur, humor, knight in armor. Friendship 1st.

SWF, attractive, fem, fun, erly 40s, gnuine, sxy, crtive, enjys thtr, mvies, rstrnts, ISO fem attr SWF, prefer blnd, hnst, 30s-40s.

GWF, caring, 34, prof, slim, fem, with young son. ISO soft butch, to share fun and love. n/d. No games.

SHM, financially sec, 40, 5'10" 175# jewelry desgnr ISO slim, pretty, well-balncd W/HF, 24-38, n/s, 4mus, dining, romance.

SHM, 27 ISO 50-60, < 5'7" AM for gd times, frnshp.

SHM, 27, 5'8" 160# clean, honest, fun, fit. ISO SAF, 22-30, 4 LTR, enjoy life, n/d, n/kids, let's talk.

SHM, 33, attr, prof, ISO SW/HF 4 fun, adventure, and romance.

SAM, 39, 5'6" 160#, computer prof, ISO SWF, < 35, tall, full-figured, single mom OK. prefer policewoman.

SWCM, 6'5" handsome, athletic, fun-loving, intelligent, well-educated, strong, tender, sensitive, ISO sim S/DW/A/HCF.

SWM, tall, attr, 35, fun, intel, stable, knight in dull armor. ISO bright creative, very curvaceous, sweet princess w/ polish.

SWM, affluent, trim, athletic, 5'8", generous nature, ISO attr. petite curvaceous, n/s lady for mutually rewarding rel.

GWM, 50, 5'10", 180#, vry masc, good-lookng, HIV-, ISO masc, pot-bellied WM, 25-45.

GWM, prof, 33, 5'7", 145#, masc, rmtc, down-2-earth ISO HIV-, str8-act, fit Guy, 18-38, safe desrt, 4 fun.

GAM, 28, 5'6", 125#, fit, enjoy conversation, movies, and wlks on the beach, ISO WM, 30-40, for long-term relationship.

BiBM, smart handsome, 39, safe, tall slim, fit, ISO manly HM, 25-45.

SWM, romantic, tall, good-looking, affluent, ISO bright, vry attractive, warm SWF, 40s.

SJM, attorney/fin. prof, cute, ISO exotic lady w/dk hair, 28-39, smart, funny, pretty for romance, travel, and more.

SWM, 50, 5'10", 170 lbs, n/s, creative, rom, hndsm, ISO queen-sized Dolly Parton/Anna Nicole Smith-type, vibrnt, affec.

Abbreviations:	
A	Asian
B	Black
C	Christian
D	Divorced
F	Female
G	Gay
H	Hispanic/Latino
J	Jewish
L	Lesbian
M	Male
S	Single
W	White
ISO	In Search Of

SOURCE: Excerpted from "Dateline," *Los Angeles Times,* 1996, pp. E5-E6.

Researchers and other observers have noticed how personal advertisements such as these tend to differ according to gender. Ads written by men seeking women tend to emphasize the importance of conventional physical attractiveness, using terms such as *attractive, slender, petite,* and *sexy.* Women's ads may ask for attractive male partners but are more likely to emphasize status and success with words such as *secure, affluent, professional,* and *successful* (Davis, 1990; Smith, Waldorf, & Trembath, 1990; Wood, 1994a). In addition, heterosexuals seeking partners tend to emphasize the same things about themselves, that is, women tend to say they are pretty and men tend to say they are successful. The ads thus reflect conventional expectations for men to be providers and for women to be objects of beauty.

The ads also show how people are figuratively trading valued sexual and emotional commodities in a type of intimate relationship marketplace. Some of the ads are more about sex, and some are more about companionship, but they all attempt to match people according to valued characteristics. Note, too, how many of the ads advertise for people similar to themselves in physical characteristics, age, education, race, ethnicity, social class, and so on. There is some variation, especially in ads for same-sex or bisexual relationships, but even in these cases, gender stereotypes are at play when lesbians describe themselves as "feminine" and when gay men describe themselves as "masculine"—the more valued gender characteristics in our society.

Marriage Exchanges

The relationship want ads show how people are exchanging sexual or emotional goods. Similarly, theories about marriage tend to focus on exchanges, either between families (as in the past) or between individuals (as in today's environment). Marriage can thus be seen as an exchange system in which the personal attributes of men and women are matched up or traded off. The whole process of dating, courtship, and marrying is viewed as a giant sorting and matching marketplace—the marriage market. Although it sounds cynical, romantic love is a feeling that appears at predictable times in this bargaining and matching process. Everyone has a "market value," and whom a person will be able to "trade" with depends on what resources each can bring to the exchange.

This type of rating and ranking is not always acknowledged and usually does not seem as cold and calculating as the market metaphor makes it sound (except on those television dating shows that emphasize the "meat-market" aspects of the process). But virtually every romantic encounter involves an implicit comparison: How attractive is the other person, and how confident are you that you can "strike a deal"? Many things go into such calculations, but the filtering and sorting process that occurs is part of the overall marriage market. Most of us can understand that those possessing the more desirable personal traits can do better on the market or, at least, are able to "catch" someone who is their equal. We can get a better idea of how this market operates today by looking at the demographics of marriage—who marries whom and when.

Contrary to popular rhetoric about the disappearance of marriage, the number of married people in the United States continues to grow. Although people are more likely than they were in the 1950s to have sex with someone to whom they are not married, most sex still occurs between marital partners, and the vast majority of Americans still marry (Laumann et al., 1994). Between 1970 and 1995, the number of married people actually increased by more than 20%. Primarily because people marry later and divorce more, and because most people now live together for a while before getting married, the proportion of all adults who are married has declined somewhat. Nevertheless, more than 90% of Americans still get married (Ahlburg & DeVita, 1992).

Marriage rates vary according to many factors, including trends in fertility and population size, average age at marriage, school attendance, labor force participation, economic prospects, social conditions, and cultural traditions. For example, the stagnation of men's wages during the 1970s and 1980s made marriage less affordable for many men, and marriage rates dipped, just as they had during the Depression in the early 1930s (Cherlin, 1992). Most people are pragmatically taking employment and earnings into account when deciding whom and when to marry (DeVita, 1996). Because African American men are less likely to find good-paying jobs than are white men, it is not surprising that rates of marriage for African Americans, especially women, are among the lowest in the nation. When African American men have access to good-paying jobs, however, the chances of getting married and staying married increase dramatically (Mason, 1996).

It is projected that more than 90% of Americans will continue to marry in the future (DeVita, 1996). The overall marriage rate in the United States, although lower than it was in the 1970s and 1980s, is still much higher than those of most other industrialized countries (DeVita, 1996; Sorrentino, 1990; see Figure 2.1). At the same time, U.S. divorce rates are almost twice as high as other countries'. Americans are thus more likely to marry but also more likely to divorce than people in other industrialized countries. This general pattern has existed ever since reliable cross-national statistics have been recorded.

Most people who divorce also remarry, with about a third of all Americans expected to marry, divorce, and remarry (Cherlin & Furstenberg, 1994). Remarriage rates have exceeded marriage rates for more than 50 years, with about half of all U.S. marriages now remarriages (DeVita, 1996; U.S. Bureau of the Census, 1992b). Although remarriage rates are still high, they have been decreasing since the 1960s: Today, about two thirds of separated and divorced women will remarry, compared with three quarters in the 1960s; three quarters of men will remarry, compared with more than four fifths in the 1960s (Cherlin & Furstenberg, 1994). Remarriage rates also differ between ethnic subgroups: About half of white women are expected to marry within five years of their separation, compared with one third of Mexican American women and one fifth of African American women (Sweet & Bumpass, 1987).

On the overall marriage market, who marries whom? As in sexual encounters and cohabitation, people tend to marry those who resemble them in age, social class background, race, religion, education, and even personal traits such as body type or personality (Kalmijn, 1991; Laumann et al., 1994; Mare, 1991; Schoen & Weinick, 1993; see Table 2.1). This certainly does not mean that everyone follows the pattern, because most of us can think of counterexamples: a tall person married

FIGURE 2.1

Marriage Rates for Selected Countries, 1960 to 1992
SOURCE: DeVita, 1996, Table 7; U.S. Bureau of the Census, U.S. Statistical Abstract, 1991, Table 1439, and 1995b, Table 1366.

Marriages per 1,000 population ages 15-64

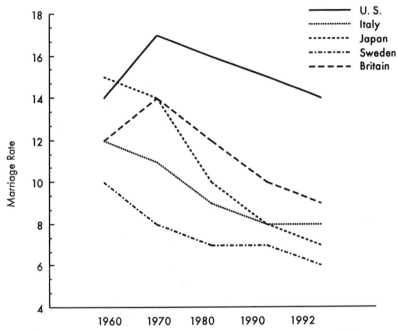

to someone short, an African American with a European American, a Catholic, with a Protestant, or an older man with a younger woman. Some of these contrasts are even romanticized in contemporary films, such as *Pretty Woman*, in which a street prostitute (Julia Roberts) marries a rich businessman (Richard Gere). In real life, such extreme cross-class marriages are rare, although there is a gradual increase in the numbers of people marrying across various social categories.

Homogamy

Social scientists call the tendency to marry those with similar social characteristics *homogamy* (literally "same-marriage"). Religious homogamy has been decreasing faster than other forms of homogamy, but most people still marry someone from the same religion (Johnson, 1980; Surra, 1991; see Table 2.1). In recent national surveys, two thirds of Catholics are in intimate relationships with other Catholics, as are two thirds of fundamentalist Protestants. Protestants of other denominations and people citing no religious preference, on the other hand, are coupled with similar others only about one third of the time (Laumann et al., 1994). Individual beliefs and preferences play an important part in the mating and matching process.

FIGURE 2.2

The Number of Interracial and Interethnic Marriages Is Increasing
SOURCE: U.S. Bureau of the Census (1992a, 1993a, 1994b).
NOTE: 1960 Hispanic/Other estimated.

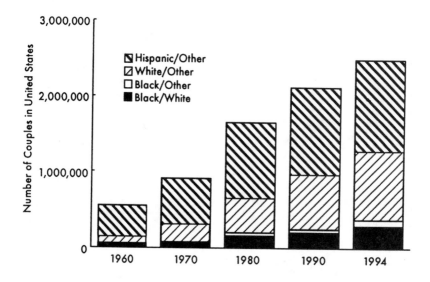

Homogamy rates are even higher for race, age, and social class than they are for religion. For example, more than 9 of 10 married people in the 1990s had spouses who were the same race/ethnicity (see Table 2.1). For some ethnic/gender categories, such as Asian American women, rates of out-marriage are high, whereas for others, such as Asian American men or African American women, rates of out-marriage are low (Kitano & Daniels, 1988; O'Hare, 1992). The reasons for these patterns are too complex to cover in detail here, but most revolve around patterns of discrimination and institutional racism. When the U.S. Supreme Court declared laws against interracial marriages to be unconstitutional in 1967, 17 states still had antimiscegenation statutes. Other factors influencing in- and out-marriage rates for specific subpopulations include the number of available potential partners, historical immigration policies, spatial segregation, job discrimination, stereotyping of Asian women as exotic and desirable by white men, and long-standing patterns of self-reliance among African American women (Chow, 1994, 1996; Dill, 1988; Espiritu, 1997; Hamamoto, 1992; hooks, 1984; Jaynes & Williams, 1989; Massey & Denton, 1993).

Although studies show that rates of race/ethnic homogamy remain more than 90%, both the number and percentage of interracial and interethnic marriages have increased rapidly in the past two decades (O'Hare, 1992; see Figure 2.2). Although interracial marriages are still stigmatized by some people, they are becoming more accepted. With the combined ethnic minority population (African Americans, Asian Americans, Pacific Islanders, Native Americans, and Latinos) projected to increase from about one quarter of the U.S. population to more than one third in the next 25 years, higher rates of intermarriage can be expected in the future, with concomitant shifts in the social norms surrounding interethnic marriage (DeVita, 1996).

When there is a difference in the social class or education level of spouses, the difference tends to be in a predictable direction with regard to gender. Women have tended to use marriage to improve their overall social standing, a practice referred to as *hypergamy* or "marrying up." Although the practice is weakening, women still tend to court and marry men with higher social standing and resources than themselves. In other words, some women still use marriage as a path to financial security and upward mobility.

As discussed above, women's dependence on marriage has made it less likely they will impulsively fall in love and more likely that they will work on their own feelings to make them fit the practical aspects of relationship possibilities. In contrast, men have been able to follow their impulsive feelings and trade their wealth or earning power to get a desirable wife, often marrying more attractive women slightly below them in social class. Such marital bargains tend to reinforce power differences between men and women in the larger society (Cancian, 1987; Sattel, 1992). Women are still more practical about marriage than are men, but as women have gained more education and more earnings, they are less likely to rely on marriage to improve their social standing (Surra, 1991). It is likely that the ways women and men approach marriage will become more similar in the future, provided that women's resources and opportunities on the job market continue to improve.

These days, most Americans wait until their mid-20s to marry, a pattern that was also true about a hundred years ago. In the United States at the turn of the century, men were likely to marry around age 26 and women around age 22. The average (median) age at first marriage gradually fell, until it was about 23 for men and about 20 for women during the 1950s and 1960s. The average age for men is now back up to nearly 27, and for women, nearly 25 (U.S. Bureau of the Census, 1995b). This means that Americans have more time to date, experiment sexually, and cohabit before marrying than they did during the middle part of the century. But these figures also reveal another persistent gender difference: Men tend to be older than the women they marry (the technical term is *age hypergamy*). This male-female age difference made more sense in the days when women needed to look for occupationally secure mates who could provide for them and take care of them financially. As with many gender differences, the age gap in marriage is smaller now than it was in the past, but it is still in evidence today.

What difference does it make that husbands tend to be older than wives? The older person in a relationship tends to have more experience and higher earnings than the younger, so age differentials can also reflect the relative distribution of status or economic leverage in marriages. The younger person is not necessarily the one with fewer resources, but as a rough rule, the younger partner tends to be in a weaker bargaining position. The slow reduction in the age difference between husbands and wives through the years (from four years to two years) may thus indicate a shift toward more equitable marital relations as well (West & Iritani, 1986).

Concluding Thoughts on Love, Sex, and Marriage

The main point to remember from this chapter is that we cannot understand love, sex, or marriage without looking at how they are shaped by cultural notions of gender. Similarly, we cannot understand gender without seeing how it is shaped by social practices of courtship and romance. Men and women learn to feel differently about love and marriage because they are exposed to different romantic messages from the culture and play different roles in scripted courtship rituals. In later chapters, we will see how gender differences are also promoted by divisions of labor in marriage and families, by child socialization practices, and by legal and institutional definition of family roles. The historical and contemporary examples in this chapter remind us that men's and women's romantic lives cannot be understood without reference to larger social processes. As the society around us changes, we can expect that both gender relations and the love ideals associated with them will continue to change.

CHAPTER 3

Paid Work and Family Life

Chris and Pat had been living together for three years before they decided to have kids. Now that they had a one-year-old, both agreed that having Emily was more work than they anticipated. Before children, both worked full-time and still had time for romantic evenings and plenty of opportunities to go out with friends. Since becoming parents, however, it seemed as if they never had enough time, even with Pat working part-time. To get an idea of their normal daily routine, take a look at an average daily log of their activities:

Chris and Pat's Activity Log

	Pat's Activities	Chris's Activities
4:30 a.m.	Wake up to Emily's cry, get out of bed. Change Emily's diaper, give her a bottle.	Sleep.
4:45 a.m.	Back to bed for some rest (half-sleep).	Sleep.
5:45 a.m.	Wake up to alarm, get out of bed.	Wake up to alarm, get up.
5:50 a.m.	Start coffee and toast, heat oatmeal, peel banana, make sandwiches.	Take shower, get dressed.
6:05 a.m.	Wake Emily and change her diaper. Begin feeding Emily her breakfast.	Eat breakfast.
6:15 a.m.	Take shower, get dressed.	Take over feeding Emily.
6:30 a.m.	Entertain Emily while finish dressing.	Say good-bye, leave for work.

	Pat's Activities	Chris's Activities
6:40 a.m.	Dress Emily. Collect dirty clothes. Put wet clothes from washer in dryer.	Drive south to highway.
6:50 a.m.	Clean up kitchen, wash breakfast dishes.	Turn off highway to Main St.
7:00 a.m.	Load dirty clothes in washer, fold clean clothes from dryer. Emily "helps."	Arrive at Cityville Post Office, clock in with time card.
7:10 a.m.	Find Emily's shoes (who put them under the bed?) and get them on.	Pick up letter sacks, take to racks for Route #17.
7:20 a.m.	Take Emily to car, buckle into car seat.	Begin sorting letters.
7:30 a.m.	Drive to baby-sitter's house.	Continue sorting letters.
7:40 a.m.	Take Emily into sitter's, kiss good-bye, pry clutching fingers from leg.	Continue sorting letters, joke with carrier for Route #18.
7:45 a.m.	Drive south.	Continue sorting letters.
8:00 a.m.	Arrive at Indemnity Insurance Company. Prepare coffee, begin taking calls.	Continue sorting letters.
8:30 a.m.	Continue taking calls, file billing notices.	Pick up parcels.
8:45 a.m.	Continue filing billing notices.	Sort parcels.
9:00 a.m.	Brief boss on appointments for the day.	Take break with other carriers.
9:30 a.m.	Take calls, greet clients, continue filing.	Pick up certified/registered mail.
9:45 a.m.	Continue filing, taking calls, etc.	Pull mail and load into trays.
10:00 a.m.	Take break, call pharmacy about Emily's ear medicine.	Load jeep, leave for route.
10:15 a.m.	Take calls, greet clients, transcribe letter.	Begin delivering mail.
11:00 a.m.	Continue with calls, clients, letters.	Continue mail delivery.
11:30 a.m.	Continue with calls, clients, letters.	Eat lunch at park on route.
Noon	Eat lunch with secretary from office.	Continue mail delivery.

	Pat's Activities	Chris's Activities
1:00 p.m.	Open office mail, sort, file.	Continue mail delivery.
2:00 p.m.	Leave work, stop at pharmacy.	Continue mail delivery.
2:20 p.m.	Arrive at sitter's to pick up Emily.	Finish mail delivery.
2:30 p.m.	Take Emily to market, buy milk, juice.	Drive back to post office.
3:00 p.m.	Arrive home, put Emily down for nap.	Return slips, undeliverable mail.
3:15 p.m.	Put groceries away, change clothes, load damp laundry into dryer.	Check to see if supervisor needs overtime workers (yes).
3:30 p.m.	Write note to sitter about Emily's new ear medicine. Tidy up living room.	Begin sorting parcels.
4:00 p.m.	Fold clothes. Wash vegetables for salad.	Continue sorting parcels.
4:20 p.m.	Emily awakes. Change diaper, cuddle.	Chat with coworkers.
4:30 p.m.	Bring Emily to kitchen, continue dinner.	Clock out. Begin drive home.
5:00 p.m.	Continue with dinner. Watch Emily.	Arrive home, wash up.
5:15 p.m.	Set table, finish dinner.	Take Emily, watch television.
5:30 p.m.	Serve and eat dinner.	Eat dinner.
6:00 p.m.	Clear table, put leftovers in refrigerator, wipe counters, rinse dishes.	Back to television with Emily, play tickle games.
6:30 p.m.	Sit down with Emily, feel wetness, change diaper, return to television, sit (finally!).	Finish washing dishes. Take trash out.
7:00 p.m.	Watch television together.	Watch television together.
7:30 p.m.	Read good night story to Emily.	Kiss Emily good night.
8:00 p.m.	Read novel.	Read newspaper.
8:30 p.m.	Fall asleep in chair.	Watch television.
9:30 p.m.	Go to bed.	Watch television.
10:00 p.m.	Sleep.	Go to bed.

What do you notice about this activity log? To begin with, Pat and Chris are doing quite a bit of work in a typical day. Some of the work is employed labor, such as Chris's job with the post office and Pat's job with the insurance company. You might also notice that much of the work that routinely happens is unpaid family work such as cooking, cleaning, shopping, and tending to children. But who does which type of labor? In this household, Pat does more of the housework, and Chris spends longer hours on the job. Chris probably gets paid more on the job, and Pat does more of the mundane everyday tasks.

You probably assumed that Pat is a woman and Chris is a man, although no pronouns indicating sex were used in the introduction or the time log. Hypothetically, Pat could be a man, because the name "Pat" is used to stand for Patrick almost as often as it is used to stand for Patricia. Similarly, Chris could be short for Christine or Christina, rather than for Christopher or Christian. Pat and Chris could both be men, or both could be women. Nothing in the story indicates the sexual orientation of either person, and nowhere does it say that Chris and Pat are married. Nevertheless, most people reading this story assume that Pat and Chris are a married heterosexual couple, and virtually everyone thinks Pat is a woman. Why?

People make assumptions about sexual orientation and marital status because of widely held social norms. This is so although gay and lesbian couples can be and often are parents, and even though heterosexual couples can and often do have children without being married. Social norms and expectations about work also encourage us to view Pat as the woman and Chris as the man. Because housework and child care have been considered "women's work," we think Pat must be a woman. We expect Pat, as a woman, to be responsible for family and home, even though she has a job. Because Chris does little housework and spends more time on the job, we think Chris must be a man. Although both have paid jobs, we assume that the man is the "real" breadwinner.

The expectation that a man's duty is to be a provider and a woman's duty is to be a homemaker is part of a larger ideal of separate spheres. Most people assume that having separate spheres for men and women is desirable, if not natural and inevitable. Like courtly love, however, the separate spheres ideal developed relatively recently (Bernard, 1981; Hood, 1986). In this chapter, I look at how the ideal developed and how it continues to influence the division of housework and paid work. In the next chapter, I look more closely at how the ideal contributes to different images of mothers and fathers and how separate family roles have promoted different styles of caring in men and women. Although the ideal of separate spheres influences virtually all Americans, it has been more of a myth than a reality, especially for working-class families and people of color. The separate spheres ideal is becoming even more unrealistic as the roles of men and women converge (Bose, 1987; Ferree, 1990).

Work and Family Life

As the opening story about Pat and Chris illustrates, both paid and unpaid work are central to family life. People tend to think of paid employment as the real work, but unpaid work is also important because it takes considerable time and effort to make households and families run smoothly. There are vast differences in the living conditions of different families and differences in the ways that basic needs of food, shelter, clothing, and rest are provided. But in virtually all families, domestic tasks such as cooking and cleaning have to be done by someone. In many households, domestic work seems invisible to the men and children who are its primary recipients but salient to the women and children who perform the daily tasks. For many women of color, domestic work is both paid (because they clean wealthier families' houses, cook for them, and care for their children) and unpaid (because they still perform these tasks for their own families; Dill, 1994; Rollins, 1985; Romero, 1992).

Family work is usually unseen because it is done in private homes. It is often unacknowledged because of cultural assumptions that a wife or mother should do the housework, even if she also holds a job outside the home. Paid work, on the other hand, is much more public and continues to be associated with men. Holding a job and earning a regular paycheck is considered to be a husband's primary family obligation. Why do we make these assumptions about the types of work men and women should do? To answer this question, we need to look at how different societies have divided work in the past.

Separate Spheres: Myth or Reality?

Studies by anthropologists and sociologists show that in all societies, some tasks are the province of men, whereas others are the province of women. But we need to be careful about what the historical and cross-cultural record reveals. Modern-day caricatures of ancient and so-called primitive societies suggest that men were aggressive macho types who hunted big game, were always engaged in war, and were forced to defend vulnerable children and wives. Women, it is assumed, were passive stay-at-home types who were content to mind the children and serve their he-man husbands. Most of these popular media portrayals suggest that men and women have always performed separate tasks for family survival. These caricatures and myths are misleading.

Divisions of labor in most nonindustrial societies were much more flexible and cooperative than popular myths imply. Except for breast-feeding and the earliest care of infants, there appear to be no cross-cultural universals in the tasks that women did and men did (Johnson, 1988; Rosaldo, 1980; Tiffany, 1982). In some societies, the worlds of men and women were so separated that they had little contact with one another and rarely performed the same tasks (Gelber, 1986; Herdt, 1981; Spain, 1992). In other societies, however, women routinely shared tasks such as hunting, and men routinely shared tasks such as caring for babies (Coltrane, 1988, 1992; Johnson, 1988). In most societies, the majority of tasks could be performed by either men or women, and a great many tasks were performed jointly or cooperatively between them (Sanday, 1981; Whyte, 1978). This does not mean that these societies thought men and women were interchangeable in all matters; most considered the sexes to be different from one another in at least a few important ways. But the cross-cultural record clearly reveals that the tasks men and women are supposedly suited for vary enormously from society to society (Mead, 1949). In some Native American societies, only women were supposed to erect dwellings, whereas in others, only the men could do it. In some European peasant villages, the men were supposed to harvest the wheat, and the women were supposed to thresh it (separate the wheat from the chaff). But in other villages, this was reversed, with women called on to do the harvesting and men to do the threshing. This suggests that biology does not require women to perform a fixed set of domestic tasks or dictate that men should be good providers. In other words, gender activities are culture based. To understand how our own modern version of separate spheres for men and women developed, we must therefore turn our attention toward our own social and economic circumstances.

From Home Production to a Market Economy

In older nonindustrial societies, production was organized in and through the family household. This was true in small clans of hunter-gatherers as well as in large and complex feudal societies with lords and peasants. In modern industrial societies, in contrast, production has generally been separated from the family household. More than anything else, this change from home production to a market economy brought about the possibility for a belief in separate spheres for men and women (Skolnick, 1991).

The colonial economy of 17th- and 18th-century America was based on agriculture and the family household. For the many families who owned farms or small artisan shops, one's place of work was also one's home. Slaves, indentured servants, and other poor people were expected to work on family estates in return for food, a place to live, and sometimes other rewards. In this model of family-based production, men, women, and children worked side by side, along with hired hands, servants, slaves, and apprentices. Fathers and mothers often did different work, but much of the labor was interchangeable.

In the 19th century, the United States shifted from a largely rural agricultural society to an urban industrial one. Figure 3.1 shows how the percentage of U.S. workers in farm and nonfarm occupations switched places in 100 years.

As a result of the growth of commercial markets and industrialization, men were drawn out of the home into work for wages. The pace of this change accelerated dramatically between 1870 and 1900, when centralized industrial production increased fivefold. As late as 1871, two thirds of the American population was still self-employed, but by the early 20th century, a majority of Americans depended on wage labor to support their families. An increasing percentage of men became breadwinners who sought work outside the home, leaving their wives to run the household and look after the children (Bose, 1987; Griswold, 1993). In the older agricultural model, people worked together at home, but in the newer model of industrial production, family members left home to sell their labor for wages. This contrast is much too simple, of course, because the economic changes did not happen all at once and were not the same for all families.

FIGURE 3.1

Percentage of U.S. Workers in Farm and Nonfarm Occupations, 1820 to 1930
SOURCE: U.S. Bureau of the Census, 1975, Part 2, Series D-75-84, p. 134.

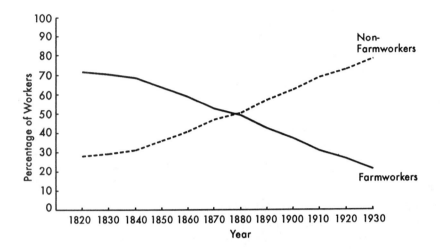

We tend to think that it was only men who joined the wage labor force under industrial production, while the women stayed home. But in the early stages of this transition, from about 1820 to 1850, it was actually young farm women who were the most likely to work in factories, and it was only later that this work was performed predominantly by men (Kessler-Harris, 1982). Work for wives and daughters of the poor in England and America was already commonly accepted, so no shift in values was needed for lower-class women to work outside the home in the 19th century (Scott & Tilly, 1975). Most of the jobs into which poor women moved were related to some of their earlier duties in home production. For example, large numbers of poor single white women were employed in garment making in textile factories, and some were employed as domestic servants in more affluent households. Black women and immigrant women were most likely to be hired as domestic servants or agricultural workers, working long hours for low pay (Romero, 1992).

The experience of middle-class families was somewhat different because most did not need to send the wives and daughters out to work. Working-class households were forced to depend on the earnings of several family members, but in middle-class households, men's earnings were often enough to support a wife, children, and several servants at a comfortable level (Baxter, 1993; Bose, 1987). In these households, women relied on servants to perform many of the daily chores. In some households, women continued to combine family responsibilities with income-generating work by taking in boarders, tending gardens, sewing, or doing other productive work at home (Boydston, 1990; E. Pleck, 1983).

For the entire economy, however, home production steadily declined, and the majority of married women were excluded from the emerging wage economy. Although the total number of U.S. women workers increased between 1870 and 1900, these were predominantly unmarried women. In 1890, when the census began to distinguish between white and "coloured" women (Native Americans, blacks, and some Chinese or Japanese), 16% of white but 38% of nonwhite women were in the labor force, with nonwhites concentrated in agricultural and domestic work (Bose, 1987). By 1920, only 7% of married European American women worked for pay, compared with one third of married African American women and 18% of Asian American women (Reskin & Padavic, 1994). The labor force participation rates for unmarried women were much higher: 45% of European Americans, 59% of African Americans, and 39% of Asian Americans (Amott & Matthaei, 1991).

The overall economic shift toward wage labor for married men, but not for married white women, had a profound effect on assumptions about men's and women's inherent "natures." The ideal white middle-class woman gradually came to be seen as pure but frail. Her weak constitution rendered her unsuitable for the harsh and competitive world of paid labor, and as discussed in the next chapter, her virtuous nature linked her to home and family. The doctrine of separate spheres associating women with family and men with jobs originated among the English upper-middle classes, but it quickly spread to the United States (Baxter, 1993; Reskin & Padavic, 1994; Skolnick, 1991).

The ideal of separate spheres drew sharp contrasts between women and men, home and work. Middle- and upper-class women wore tight corsets that symbolized women's incapacity and made it virtually impossible to perform hard labor. Well-to-do families kept the parts of the house devoted to productive work—such as cooking and washing—isolated and out of sight. The areas of relaxation—such as the parlor and dining room—were more public and visible, creating the illusion that the home was not a place of work (Davidoff & Hall, 1987; Reskin & Padavic, 1994).

As images of the ideal middle-class woman became more fragile, images of the ideal middle-class man shifted toward rugged individualism. Because men's and women's underlying physical and emotional capacities changed only slightly during this period, we must look elsewhere to understand why the contrast between men and women was drawn so sharply. Some scholars suggest that men's and women's ideal natures diverged because of changes in the labor market and increased competition between them for jobs. The 19th century was marked by a huge influx of men into wage labor of all types, but because of the expansion of the economy near the turn of the century, unprecedented numbers of unmarried women also entered the wage labor force. Many joined the ranks of formerly all-male occupations such as clerks, typists, bookkeepers, cashiers, and sales personnel. This influx of women into what were previously men's jobs contributed to a masculinist backlash and promoted a rigid Victorian-era belief in separate spheres for men and women (Degler, 1980; Kimmel, 1987).

During this time, all-male fraternal orders such as the Odd Fellows and Freemasons gained thousands of members in the United States by putting men through an elaborate sequence of masculine initiation rituals. Although gentlemen in an earlier era tended to avoid physical exertion, the late 19th and early 20th century saw an enormous growth in outdoor sports and camping, which were idealized for their contributions to masculine character. Popular magazine depictions of male heroes at the turn of the century shifted from earlier praise of piety, thrift, and industry to appreciation of vigor, forcefulness, and mastery. This was also the era in which the Boy Scouts, with their emphasis on turning boys into "red-blooded, moral, manly men" grew to unprecedented size (Carnes & Griffen, 1990; Hantover, 1995). Fears of emasculation rose to new heights as men were spending less time at home and as the father's authority inside the family was being eroded by larger social and economic forces. In response to competition from working-class women, children, and immigrants, men defended their privileged position by asserting their "inherent" ruggedness and suitability for "men's work."

History shows that beliefs about gender and family tend to follow changes in the economy. In the 17th and 18th centuries, agricultural production and the household economy maintained men's authority in the home and in the society. As market economies grew, men came to be viewed as breadwinners, and individualism flourished. As traditional forms of authority weakened and men's direct participation in daily family life decreased, women's nature came to be seen as pure and virtuous, and domestic activities were elevated to a revered status. When unmarried women later challenged men's monopoly on wage work, men's nature came to be seen as even more tough and rugged.

Cultural ideals about the inherent natures of men and women shift when family members play different roles in the overall economy. In the same way, the types of jobs open to different ethnic groups lead to cultural labels and prejudices that serve to justify continued occupational tracking and job discrimination. Some people assume that deep-down natural predispositions are the cause of gender or ethnic group differences and job capabilities, but it is usually differential economic and social opportunities that shape our ideas about the type of work men or women, whites or blacks, or Anglos or Latinos are supposed to do. As many scholars suggest, we also need to pay attention to the ways that gender and race/ethnicity intersect, because although both are influenced by economic opportunities, neither is experienced in isolation, and neither can be understood without reference to the other (Chow, 1987; Collins, 1990; Espiritu, 1997; Romero, 1992; Stacey & Thorne, 1985). For example, in a 1990s update of her study of American working-class families, Lillian Rubin (1994) found that when faced with shrinking economic opportunities, men often blamed other ethnic groups and women for their lack of money or job prospects.

History teaches that in response to economic and social forces, cultural ideals about appropriate work activities for men or women change, but the underlying biological facts change little. Thus, gender and work ideals are socially constructed. The ideal of separate spheres is therefore a work in progress, insofar as it has always been, and will continue to be, molded and shaped as individuals within families respond to shifting economic circumstances. Because the specific conditions faced by men and women of different social classes and ethnic groups in various geographic regions differ, there is always variation in the actual separation between the spheres of home and work. Even during the heyday of separate spheres in the early part of the 20th century, minority women, young single women, widows, and married women whose husbands could not support them worked for wages. Married immigrant women and former slaves were the most likely to be employed because staying out of the labor force would have meant starvation (Reskin & Padavic, 1994). The spheres were not as separate as the middle-class ideal suggested.

The Persistence of the Ideal of Separate Spheres

The separate spheres ideal persisted in the United States during the 1920s and 1930s, as indicated by the love advice reviewed in the last chapter. During the 1940s, wartime increases in women's labor force participation and "Rosie the Riveter" imagery briefly challenged the ideal of separate work spheres for men and women. During the 1950s and 1960s, however, the ideal enjoyed renewed and unprecedented acceptance, although most poor women continued to be employed.

With Ozzie-and-Harriet families as the 1950s model, women surprised demographers by marrying earlier and having more children than any group of U.S. women before them. Rapid expansion of the American economy fueled a phenomenal growth of suburbs throughout the country. The consumer culture that developed from that era idolized domestic life on radio and television. Isolation in suburban homes was certainly not trouble-free for many women, as reflected in higher than average depression levels among stay-at-home housewives in the 1950s and 1960s (Collins & Coltrane, 1995). Nevertheless, many working-class women aspired to full-time homemaker status, and if middle-class mothers actively pursued careers, their womanhood was sometimes called into question (Rubin, 1976).

Idealized visions of domestic life lost some of their luster in the face of the women's movement of the 1970s and shrinking family resources during the 1980s and 1990s. But the idea that women's real place was in the home did not disappear. A resurgence of glorified domestic imagery began to appear in the 1980s, with women's magazines celebrating the "new traditionalists"—stay-at-home moms who gave up jobs to be with their children on a full-time basis (Coontz, 1992; Pogrebin, 1983; Sidel, 1990; Skolnick, 1991). The popular media sometimes ridiculed independent women who put career ahead of family; a *Newsweek* cover story reported that a 40-year-old woman's chances of getting married were so low that she was "more likely to be killed by a terrorist" ("Too Late for Prince Charming," 1986, p. 54; see also Faludi, 1991). In the 1990s, then Vice President Dan Quayle attacked the television character Murphy Brown for having the audacity to have a baby out of wedlock, and the next year, an *Atlantic* magazine cover article proclaimed, "Dan Quayle Was Right" (cited in "Riding Murphy Brown's Coattails," 1992, p. C1; Whitehead, 1993). Although the language changed through the years, the separate spheres message remained essentially the same: A woman's place is the home, and her true calling is to serve a husband and raise children. We will explore the domestic side of this imagery more fully in the next chapter.

Separate Spheres and Gender Inequality

Many feminist scholars argue that the cultural ideal of separate spheres has been so persistent because it helps privileged men maintain power over women (Bose, 1987; Coontz, 1992; Delphy, 1984; Ferree, 1990). Like most modern systems of social control, the separate spheres ideal perpetuates an image of the subordinate group (women) as fundamentally different from the dominant group (men). An assumption of difference typically makes it easier to exploit the labor and resources of the subordinate group, particularly when the assumption is incorporated into laws and government policies (see Chapter 6). In the case of the separate spheres work ideal, women are assumed to be inherently suited to serve men, which renders them naturally prepared to perform unpaid labor for them. In conjunction with being economically dependent on men and fearing violence from them, the separate spheres ideal perpetuates the idea that women are naturally in need of protection and provision. Seen in this light, the assumption of separate work spheres for men and women is far from benign.

In addition, the separate spheres ideal helped structure modern labor markets. According to Barbara Reskin and Irene Padavic (1994),

> The doctrine of separate spheres contributed to the gendering of work in the 20th century in several ways. First, men gained social approval as workers, but women's work became invisible because it was done at home. Second, social values that encouraged employers to ban women from many jobs made sex discrimination commonplace. Third, employers could justify low pay for women because men presumably supported them. Indeed, people came to define pay as what one earned for going to work; women's relegation to the home put them outside the system of pay for labor. Finally, the sexual division of labor that assigned men to the labor force and women to the home encouraged employers to structure jobs on the assumptions that all permanent workers were men and that all men had stay-at-home wives. (p. 23)

Feminists who challenge the cultural ideal of separate spheres do not claim that men and women should be exactly the same, nor do they disparage cooperation or complementarity between them. Rather, they find that the problem lies in the ways that the separate spheres ideal has been used to further men's interests at the expense of women's. As economists and sociologists have shown, the belief in fixed and natural distinctions between men's and women's aptitudes, obligations, and social roles has helped exclude women from jobs, kept their pay low, and blocked their access to better positions (Epstein, 1988; Reskin & Hartmann, 1986; Reskin & Padavic, 1994; Reskin & Roos, 1990).

As noted above, a rigid split between domestic work and productive work has always been something of a myth, because most women had to bring in resources with their labor. Working-class women and most women of color have always had to engage in some form of productive labor just to get by (Zavella, 1987). Middle-class women have always performed work that feeds into the larger economy because they feed, clothe, and care for men who are paid workers, managers, and proprietors, and for their children (Bose, 1987; Ferree, 1990; Kessler-Harris, 1982).

Even upper-class women have contributed to the economic system, insofar as their charities have ameliorated some of the harsher inequities of capitalism, and their art patronage and social activities have solidified allegiances and perpetuated class boundaries (Daniels, 1988). Just as in earlier models of household production, after the transition to a market economy and eventual industrialization, women's activities and labor continued to contribute to the total economy. A more complete discussion of the ways that family work and paid work depend on each other is beyond the scope of this book; remember, however, that they are mutually interdependent, not fundamentally separate as the Victorian cultural ideal implies.

The ideal of separate work and family spheres developed in response to specific historical circumstances. Like the romantic love ideals discussed in Chapter 2, the ideal of work-family separation was always more important as a cultural symbol than as an actual code of conduct (Coontz, 1992; Skolnick, 1991). Nevertheless, it has provided a belief system and set of ritual practices that continue to disadvantage women in the marketplace and discourage men from doing family work. The social and economic conditions initially promoting the separate spheres ideal have changed dramatically, but our ideas about the natural predispositions of men and women have changed more slowly.

Modern Labor Market Trends

Some of the biggest changes in family life in the latter part of the 20th century have been precipitated by women's increased participation in wage labor. Although it used to be optional for most women to work, it is now much more of a necessity. Figure 3.2 shows how the labor market has changed in the 20th century.

The gap between men's and women's labor force participation rates has narrowed dramatically. In 1890, 84% of men over the age of 14 were in the paid labor force, compared with only 18% of similar women (although the census did not count farmwives or women who ran boardinghouses). Men's labor force participation has inched down to 77% in 1994, whereas women's has steadily increased to 59%. More than three quarters of women between the ages of 35 and 44 are now in the labor force, and experts predict a continued narrowing of the gender gap in levels of employment (Reskin & Padavic, 1994).

As noted in the historical review presented above, single women and poor married women have always worked for pay. The most significant new development is that married women and mothers have entered the workforce in record numbers. In 1960, fewer than 20% of women with preschool children were in the paid labor force, but by 1990, about 60% were (see Figure 3.3). Similarly, in 1960, only about 40% of women with school-age children were in the paid labor force, but by 1990, more than 70% were employed. The employment rates for women without children under the age of 18 started higher but increased more slowly, from about 35% in 1960 to about 50% in 1990. The increase for mothers of babies was the most pronounced, with more than half of all mothers with children under one year old in the 1990s holding jobs in the paid labor force (U.S. Bureau of the Census, 1992a). In a dramatic break from midcentury, by the early 1990s, more

FIGURE 3.2

Trends in U.S. Labor Force Participation Rates by Sex, 1890 to 1994
SOURCE: U.S. Bureau of the Census, 1975, Series D-29-41; U.S. Bureau of the Census, 1995b, Tables 636, 637.

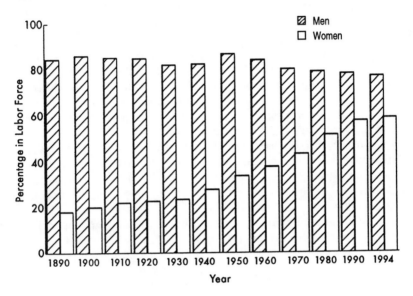

FIGURE 3.3

Rates of Employment for U.S. Mothers Have Increased Rapidly
SOURCE: Current Population Surveys; U.S. Bureau of the Census, 1975, Part 2, Series 63-74; U.S. Bureau of the Census, 1995b, Table 639.

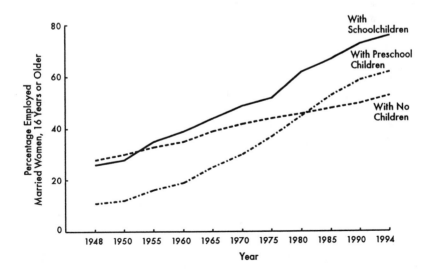

than two thirds of all children under 18 years of age were living with mothers who were employed.

Not only are mothers increasingly likely to be employed, but most work full-time. Although many mothers arrange their work schedules around the care of children, and even though women constitute the bulk of part-time workers in the United States, two of three employed mothers work full-time (Phillips, 1989). Not surprisingly, women without children are more likely to work full-time than those with school-age children, and those with preschool children are the least likely to work full-time. Nevertheless, between 62% and 70% of women with children under the age of five are in the labor force on a full-time basis (Hernandez, 1993, pp. 148-149). Since the 1980s, the proportion of male workers employed part-time (and the proportion of male and female teenage workers employed part-time) has increased, whereas the percentage of adult women workers employed part-time has declined (Lester, 1996). In the next two chapters, I will review some impacts of these employment patterns on child-rearing practices in American households.

When the economic recession hit in the early 1990s, some political pundits misinterpreted labor statistics and assumed that women were quitting their jobs to return to full-time motherhood. As it turns out, young women (mostly childless) were not able to obtain jobs at the bottom end of a constricted job market. After analyzing national employment data in 1994, the U.S. Department of Labor, Bureau of Labor Statistics (1994) reported that American women were continuing to enter the labor market in record numbers and that they were not forsaking jobs to return to the home: "Looking closely at trends in women's labor force activity, it is difficult to find any evidence that women might be leaving the labor force in large numbers to take up homemaker roles" (p. 2).

Why have women been entering the labor market in record numbers? Some women take jobs for personal fulfillment, for career motivation, or to be able to afford luxury items. But most women go to work to make wages from necessity. Census demographers note that the need for women to work for basic living expenses has increased dramatically in the past two decades, and national surveys find that more than 80% of Americans now agree it takes two paychecks to support a family (Hernandez, 1993; Wilkie, 1993). Single-mother families must rely on one income that is, on average, only about two thirds an average male worker's (Reskin & Padavic, 1994). Between a quarter and a third of all children needed a mother's income to lift the family out of poverty during the 1980s (Hernandez, 1993, p. 396). Despite so many mothers entering the workforce, nearly one in four children is now forced to live below the official federal poverty level (Hernandez, p. 431; O'Hare, 1996).[1]

Whether people see the increased need for women to work as good or bad is somewhat beside the point: Most people still harbor a belief in separate work spheres for men and women at a time when it is virtually impossible to enact. Because cultural symbols are constantly undergoing change, gradual changes are occurring in the ideal notion of what type of work men and women should do. To the extent that the actual work patterns of men and women change, we can expect even more change in the future. As the next chapters show, however, the problem today is that economic conditions and gender ideals do not seem to be changing at the same rate. This cultural lag causes difficulties because the old gender ideals tend to govern people's thoughts and feelings, but the new economic and social realities tend to govern people's actions. This makes it an exciting time to be alive, but it also means that many families and individuals are having a hard time adjusting.

Work-Family Linkages

Sociologist Rosabeth Kanter (1977) was one of the first scholars to point out that it has always been misleading to treat work and family as separate spheres. Rejecting popular beliefs about the separation of workplaces and families, she called for examining the interconnections between the two and studying how and why people make and sustain attachments to each. Today, most social scientists recognize and appreciate the numerous mutual influences between the two (for reviews, see Aldous, 1982; Bielby, 1992; Ferree, 1990; Menaghan & Parcel, 1990; Piotrkowski, 1978; Spitze, 1988; Thompson & Walker, 1989; Voydanoff, 1987).

Although linkages between work and family are many and varied, most researchers have focused on the one-way effects of jobs on family life. For example, some studies look at how economic resources affect marital functioning (e.g., Booth, Johnson, & White, 1984), health and well-being (e.g., Mirowsky & Ross, 1989), or parenting practices (e.g., Kohn, 1977). In general, longer hours, harsher working conditions, and lower wages are associated with more family and health problems, and closely regulated work environments are associated with more restrictive parenting practices. Other work-family studies focus on how people use different strategies to coordinate market labor and household labor (Pleck, 1985), who does the housework (Robinson, 1988; Shelton, 1992), or how people balance commitments between the two (Bielby, 1992; Coltrane, 1996; Gerson, 1985, 1993). Results are too varied to detail here, but most studies find that job demands have important impacts on family life and individual well-being and that the ideal of separate spheres continues to influence the allocation of paid and unpaid work.

Although women are more likely to be employed than ever before, it is still men who tend to be identified most strongly with paid work. Masculinity and men's authority are still associated with success on the job. Although male-breadwinner families with stay-at-home wives are now relatively rare, the men's work still tends to count for more than the women's. The provider role is undergoing some changes, and most families now give some recognition to women whose incomes are essential, but men tend to retain symbolic responsibility for earning money and get more credit for doing it. Many men are still reluctant to accept wives as equal providers, even when both spouses are working full-time (Bernard, 1981; Coltrane & Valdez, 1993; Gerson, 1993; Haas, 1986; Hochschild, 1989; Hood, 1983; Lamphere, Zavella, & Gonzales, 1993; Pyke & Coltrane, 1996).

In working-class couples in which wives take jobs because of financial necessity, they are more likely to see themselves, and are likely to be seen by their husbands, as sharing the provider responsibility. This is particularly so when wives' earnings approach those of husbands, a still rare, but increasingly common, situation.

Within couples, the wage gap is smallest, on average, between working-class spouses. Nevertheless, most studies of work-family issues in two-earner families have been conducted with middle-class samples. Considerable research attention has been paid to upwardly mobile professional couples who focus on their careers and espouse egalitarian beliefs. Some researchers conclude that such marriages are "more equal than others" (Hertz, 1986). Nevertheless, professional men's salaries are usually considerably higher than those of their wives, so the women may have a harder time receiving recognition as providers than do their working-class counterparts (Ferree, 1987). It may be that well-educated professional couples talk more about the importance of sharing, which leads researchers to report more equality than actually exists (Coltrane, 1996; Hartmann, 1981).

Job and Family Commitments

Today, most people say they hold jobs to make money, but the majority also report that they get personal satisfaction from their paid work. This is now as true for women as it is for men. Satisfying well-paid work is related to enhanced well-being for both men and women (Baruch & Barnett, 1986a, 1986b; Thompson & Walker, 1989). The only exception seems to be when people believe that they should *not* be working, but circumstances force them to take jobs or work longer hours than they want. Things are especially bad for women who want to spend more time with their children but whose families cannot survive without their income. The problem is particularly acute for single mothers, who are usually both sole caregivers and major financial providers for their children. Many must work long hours to earn a living wage and then feel guilty that they cannot give more time to their children (Kurz, 1995). In general, however, as men's and women's jobs and work histories begin to look more alike, men and women are also likely to share similar family concerns. Recent polls find that more than 70% of American men and more than 80% of American women feel torn between the demands of their jobs and wanting to spend more time with their families (Gerson, 1993).

Because of the old ideal of separate spheres, it has been easier for men to feel that they are fulfilling their family commitments by working and being financial providers. Women, on the other hand, have had to justify why having jobs does not make them bad mothers. Pleck (1977/1984) suggests that the boundaries between work roles and family roles are "asymmetrically permeable" (p. 16) for men and women. Men have typically been able to keep family commitments from intruding on their work time and have been able to use job demands to limit family time. In the example at the beginning of the chapter, Chris did not feel obliged to make the breakfast or start the laundry in the morning because of work demands. Similarly, Chris could ask for and receive overtime work without checking in with Pat because it was assumed that Chris's paid work took precedence. Such behavior makes us assume that Chris is a man. Men have traditionally been more able than women to keep their paid work and family life as separate spheres, although these patterns are converging as men's and women's jobs become more similar (Coltrane, 1996; Gerson, 1993; Thompson & Walker, 1989).

In contrast to men's family obligations, women's family obligations have traditionally been allowed to penetrate into the workplace. For example, while she was on the job, Pat called the pharmacy about Emily's medicine. In addition, it is usually mothers who take time off from work when a child becomes ill, although there is a small increase in the number of fathers doing this (Coltrane, 1996). As another example of permeable work-family boundaries, Pat was the one to cut back from full-time to part-time work. This is a more typical pattern for women than men, as women often move in and out of the labor force, regulating the number of hours they are employed in response to child care demands and other family needs (Moen, 1985; Presser, 1989).

Researchers have attempted to measure people's work and family attachments by asking questions about how committed they are to each. Although somewhat superficial, answers to these survey questions indicate whether respondents gain special meaning from family and work activities and how willing they might be to cut back on one or the other. As noted above, both men and women say they are strongly committed to both work and family. Nevertheless, on average, men tend to be slightly more identified with work than with family, and women to be slightly more identified with family than with work (Bielby, 1992). This fits common notions of gender-linked priorities and resonates with the cultural ideal of separate spheres.

Men's commitments to work have remained relatively stable during the last three decades, but women's have been increasing. Overall gender differences in commitment to work are thus diminishing. As women receive more education and as job opportunities and rewards open up to them, they become more attached to their careers. If women have work statuses and experiences similar to men's and have the opportunity to identify as strongly with the work as do men, gender differences in commitment to work and family disappear (Bielby & Bielby, 1988; Rosen, 1987). In recent studies, job conditions and opportunities are the strongest determinants of work commitment, with marital and family status having little if any impact (Bielby, 1992, p. 290). Despite much less research on the family side, there is also evidence that when men have household responsibilities similar to those of women, they are as strongly committed to the family as are women. As we will see in the next chapter, when men perform the routine family work that mothers have traditionally done, they also tend to develop the attentive and caring dispositions that have been assumed to belong only to women.

Who Does the Housework?

Because of the assumption that men should be breadwinners and women should be homemakers, family studies before the 1970s tended to ignore men's participation in everyday family work. This makes it hard to estimate how much has really changed since women began entering the paid labor force in record numbers. In the past few decades, however, researchers have begun to pay more attention to what men do (and do not do) around the house and for other family members (Coltrane, 1996; J. Pleck, 1983). Some observers predicted that men would immediately begin doing more housework as their wives entered the labor force. Although most men did increase their contributions to child care, increases in housework were much smaller, and few men assumed significant responsibility for the routine cooking, cleaning, and washing that are needed to keep families functioning (Miller & Garrison, 1982).

For most routine housework tasks, not only have men been reluctant to pitch in, but many have failed to notice that the chores need doing, and some feign incompetence to get out of the work. They usually get away with it. In general, women do more of the actual work around the house and perform a wider range of chores, at different times and under different circumstances, than do men. Women also do most of the least pleasant tasks, such as cleaning toilets and scrubbing floors, even though they require hard physical labor. For these reasons, but also because family work can represent love, women tend to experience housework differently than do men (Hochschild, 1989; Luxton, 1980; Thompson & Walker, 1989). We will explore how and why, but first let's review what surveys tell us about who does what in modern American households.

In the 1960s and 1970s, studies showed that women did about three quarters of the total family work, but four fifths or more of the indoor housework. For instance, a rare national study that included men, conducted in 1965, found that women spent an average of more than 24 hours per week on the indoor tasks of cooking, meal cleanup, housecleaning, and laundry, whereas men spent an average of just 2 hours on these tasks (Robinson, 1988). Throughout the 1960s and 1970s, men tended to focus their at-home family work on outside chores such as mowing the lawn or taking out the trash, tasks that took substantially less time than the chores their wives were doing inside the home. On average, husbands increased their hourly contributions to the inside domestic chores of cooking, cleaning, and laundry only slightly during the 1970s. Studies did find that employed women began putting in fewer hours themselves, so that men's proportionate contributions to family work rose slightly (Fenstermaker-Berk, 1985; J. Pleck, 1983; Thompson & Walker, 1989).

What difference does it make that women do most of the everyday family work? One consistent finding has been that psychological distress is greatest among wives with husbands who contribute little (Kessler & McRae, 1982; Ross, Mirowsky, & Huber, 1983). Family work can be fulfilling, but most women have been responsible for virtually all of the most time-consuming and less pleasant tasks such as cleaning and washing. The obligatory, relentless, and lonely nature of this work has been suggested as one reason for American housewives' high levels of depression in the 1950s and 1960s (Collins & Coltrane, 1995; Warren, 1987).

Men's household chores, in contrast to women's, have tended to be infrequent or optional. Men normally concentrate their efforts on relatively fun activities such as playing with the children and barbecuing on weekends, and when they perform inside chores, they often receive help from others (Baruch & Barnett, 1986a, 1986b; Fenstermaker-Berk, 1985; Robinson, 1988). Because of the timing, type, and context of men's household labor, it is not surprising that most studies find no relationship between the amount of family work that men do and their own depression levels (Thompson & Walker, 1989).

Although no radical shifts in housework have occurred, things do seem to be changing. Since the 1970s, the household division of labor has become a little more balanced. Women still retain responsibility for assigning domestic tasks and continue to do the bulk of the work, but men are doing more than they used to. Men's average hourly contributions to inside housework have almost doubled in the past 20 years, and women's contributions have gone down by about a third, so that men now do about a quarter of the inside chores. Husbands of employed wives are most likely to do child care, shopping, and meal preparation, followed by washing dishes, cleaning up after meals, and cleaning house. Laundry is still men's least frequent housework task, although women now do about seven times as much as men, rather than more than 20 times more as they used to (Coltrane, 1996; Ferree, 1991; Gershuny & Robinson, 1988; Shelton, 1992).

We are living in an era when things seem to be changing quite rapidly at the same time that they appear to be staying about the same. This is especially so for the division of paid work and family work. Recent studies show that the total time men and women spend on both paid employment and unpaid housework is converging. When hours on the job and hours spent doing housework are added, men's and women's total hourly contributions are now almost equal (Fenstermaker-Berk, 1985; Ferree, 1991; Pleck, 1985). Other studies find that women's total time on all forms of work exceeds that of men, especially when the time spent caring for children is considered (Hochschild, 1989).

Although men contribute more hours to family work than they used to, they have been slow to assume responsibility for noticing when tasks need doing or setting standards for their performance. In the majority of families, husbands notice less about what needs to be done, wait to be asked to do various chores, and require explicit directions if they are to complete the tasks successfully. Most couples therefore continue to characterize husbands' contributions to housework and child care as "helping" their wives (Coltrane, 1989; Fenstermaker-Berk, 1985; Thompson & Walker, 1989).

Most studies have also concluded that even if couples share some of the housework before they have children, they shift toward more conventional gender-based allocations of family work when they become parents (Cowan & Cowan, 1992). Having children has thus increased women's family work, whereas men's family work has remained about the same. On average, men and women also adjust their paid work time differently when children are involved. Having a child means working about three more hours on the job per week for men, but for women, it is associated with spending about an hour less in the paid labor force each week but putting in more time on housework (Shelton, 1992). Work and gender are thus linked through family membership and family practices. Being in a family means more housework for wives and more paid work for husbands.

Stability and Change

The increase in women's labor force participation in the past few decades has been the result of a restructuring of the national and global economies. Dramatic growth in the service sector and a decrease in the relative importance of agriculture and manufacturing led to increased demand for secretaries, typists, clerks, and related support services. Most of these positions gradually became stereotyped as "women's jobs" (England & Browne, 1992). Today, occupations with especially high concentrations of women include secretaries and other office workers, retail clerks, maids, electronics assembly line workers, schoolteachers, nurses, real estate agents, and social workers. Despite some entry by women into traditionally male occupations in recent years, men continue to predominate in management, higher-status professions (e.g., doctors and lawyers), skilled crafts (e.g., carpentry and plumbing), manufacturing, and jobs involving outdoor labor. Although men's and women's jobs require roughly equivalent amounts of formal education prior to entry, women's occupations have less on-the-job training, offer fewer opportunities for advancement, and are less likely to entail supervising other workers (Miller-Loessi, 1992).

Occupational segregation by gender has weakened somewhat during the past several decades as more women have become professionals and managers. Jobs such as reporter, bus driver, bartender, pharmacist, and insurance adjuster have opened up to women, but the jobs women hold are still typically less prestigious than corresponding men's jobs. For example, school buses (the old yellow ones) tend to be driven by women, whereas metropolitan transit buses (the big silver or blue ones) tend to be driven by men. Transit or long-distance bus drivers make much more money than school bus drivers. Although there are more female doctors and lawyers than ever before, the more prestigious specialties, such as surgery and corporate law, continue to be dominated by men (Reskin & Roos, 1990). Decreasing job segregation is therefore both real and illusory (Miller-Loessi, 1992). Approximately 60% of men or women would have to change occupations for the workforce in the United States to become gender balanced (England & Browne, 1992).

Not only do men and women tend to work in different industries and to hold different jobs within an industry or organization, but women's jobs continue to pay less than men's. White women's median annual earnings in the United States are still between 65% and 75% of white men's (differing depending on whether the calculations use hourly or weekly median earnings; see England & Browne, 1992; Reskin & Padavic, 1994). Both African American and Latina women earn less, on average, than white women, but they earn closer to men's earnings within their same ethnic group. In 1992, the average Latina worker earned $15,756 per year, whereas the average white male worker earned $29,936 (Reskin & Padavic, 1994).

Inequality in the United States is increasing. Since the mid-1970s, African American and Latino earnings have decreased as a proportionate share of the earnings of whites. Similarly, the overall amount of income earned by the richest 20% of the U.S. population has been increasing, while the amount earned by the bottom 80% has been decreasing (DeVita, 1996; O'Hare, 1996). African American men, like white women, still earn between two thirds and three quarters of what white men do. Latino men earn only about two thirds of white men's earnings.

More optimistically, the gender wage gap appears to be narrowing. Women's wages in the United States have shown steady increases since the 1970s, at the same time that men's wages have remained stagnant or declined. Similarly, in most other modern industrialized democracies, women have been able to substantially increase their earnings relative to those of men. For example, in the industrial and government sectors of the Swedish economy, women workers earn about 90% of what Swedish men earn (Haas, 1992). Thus, although the gender gap in pay remains, there has been a narrowing of that gap, especially among minorities and younger adults.

Why does the labor market remain biased against women? The most frequent justification is that it is natural for women to care for children and tend homes. This separate spheres assumption is usually accompanied by claims that women are paid less or assigned to "female" jobs because they are not temperamentally suited for the competitive business world or that they are poor risks for job training because they exert less effort on the job and are likely to quit work to have babies (England & Browne, 1992). In contrast, most empirical studies find that if there are differences between men's and women's efforts on the job, it is women who expend more effort than do men, in part to overcome stereotyped notions of female incapacity (Bielby & Bielby, 1988).

Others argue that occupations are segregated because of self-selection, that is, women prefer "female" jobs because they are less demanding and allow more time off for family responsibilities. There is more support for this hypothesis, especially regarding the management of child care, but only for some women, and only under certain conditions (Moen, 1985). Although women do tend to work part-time more often than do men, the general trend is toward more women working full-time, and evidence suggests that most women's jobs have closer supervision and less schedule flexibility than do men's jobs (Miller-Loessi, 1992). The claim that women earn less because they frequently quit work to have babies is contradicted by the finding that women do not have higher turnover rates than men when the wage level of the job is considered (England & Browne, 1992). Others suggest that women favor lower-paying gender-typed jobs because they like the work involved. Self-selection into "helping" occupations such as nursing and teaching may indeed occur because the work bolsters one's self-image as a caring woman. I discuss the linkage between women and caring in the next chapter (see also Cancian & Oliker, forthcoming).

Job segregation and unequal pay, along with women's unemployment, are associated with marriage bargains that include wives' obligation to perform domestic labor and husbands' sense of entitlement to receive unpaid domestic services. Although families in the United States seem to be moving away from the separate spheres ideal, it still operates in many subtle (and not-so-subtle) ways. Few Americans admit that job discrimination against women is acceptable, yet most feel uncomfortable with women as combat soldiers or airplane mechanics. More women have been elected to public office than ever before, but most of them still sit on local school boards and city councils, rather than in state legislatures or in Congress. Most Americans say they would vote for a woman for president, but no woman has ever been nominated for that office by a major party.

Americans are even more ambivalent when it comes to women's jobs interfering with marriage and family life. Although women now are encouraged to be independent and professional, they are still expected to be generous and self-sacrificing with their families. For example, a recent Gallup Poll found that two thirds of those surveyed disagreed with the statement "women should return to their traditional role," but 87% of the same sample claimed to have "old fashioned values about family and marriage" (Skolnick, 1991, p. 189). It seems that Americans want to have it both ways. As discussed in the next chapter, although more women are going to college, taking jobs, and pursuing careers, they are still held accountable for what was once called women's work. If their houses are a mess, their children are left alone, or worse, if they forgo marriage altogether, they are subject to blame (Schur, 1984).

Similar equivocal feelings emerge about fathers and paid work. Although 8 of 10 Americans now believe it is OK for women to hold jobs, half still think that men should be the *real* breadwinners (Wilkie, 1993). By definition, men's jobs are supposed to be more important than women's jobs, and most people get uncomfortable if a wife makes more money than her husband (Gerson, 1993; Hochschild, 1989). As we will see in the next chapter, Americans want fathers to be more involved with their children, but most still feel uncomfortable if a man takes time off work "just" to be with his kids. Employers, too, are ambivalent about men's desires to be home instead of on the job. When men take advantage of parental leaves or part-time work, they are often considered unreliable or not serious, and most work-family programs in the United States are tacitly designed to be used only by working mothers (Pleck, 1993). It seems that the ideal of separate work spheres for men and women is still around, even though the economic and social factors underlying it are in the midst of change.

Note

1. In 1994, the official poverty threshold was $11,940 for a single-parent family of one adult and two children and $15,029 for a family of two adults and two children.

CHAPTER 4

Mothers, Fathers, and Family Care

Letter From Mahatma Gandhi to His Son

The following letter was written by Mahatma Gandhi in 1909 to his second son, Manilal, then 17 years old. The 40-year-old Gandhi wrote from a South African prison, in which he was allowed to write just one letter per month. In the letter, originally written in English because the prison censors would not allow him to use his native Gujarati, Gandhi tells his son how a true education is to be gained through serving family members, tending a garden, attending to detail, and being patient. As you read these excerpts from the letter, notice what is similar to or different from the father-son relationships you know.

March 25, 1909
My dear son,

... How are you. Although I think that you are well able to bear all the burden I have placed on your shoulders and that you are doing it quite cheerfully, I have often felt that you required greater personal guidance than I have been able to give you. I know too that you have sometimes felt that your education was being neglected. Now I have read a great deal in the prison. I have been reading Emerson, Ruskin and Mazzini. I have also been reading the *Upanishads*. All confirm the view that education does not mean a knowledge of letters but it means character building. It means a knowledge of duty. Our own word literally means "training." If this be the true view and it is to my mind the only true view, you are receiving the best education—training—possible. What can be better than that you should have the opportunity of nursing mother and cheerfully bearing her ill temper, or than looking after Chanchi and anticipating her wants and behaving to her so as not to make her feel the absence of Harilal, or again than being guardian to Ramdas and Devdas? If you succeed in doing this well, you have received more than half your education.

... I was much struck by one passage in Nathuramji's introduction to the *Upanishads*. He says that the *Brahmacharya* stage—i.e., the first stage—is like the last, i.e., the *Sanyasin* [monk] stage. This is true. Amusement only contin-

AUTHOR'S NOTE: Excerpted from M. K. Gandhi, *The Collected Works of Mahatma Gandhi*, 1963, pp. 205-209; originally cited in Fischer, 1950. Copyright 1950 by Louis Fischer. Used here by permission of Harper-Collins Publishers, Inc. Jessie Bernard's letters are excerpted from K. Payne (Ed.), *Between Ourselves: Letters Between Mothers and Daughters 1750-1982*, 1983, pp. 270-272; used with permission.

ues during the age of innocence, i.e., up to twelve years only. As soon as a boy reaches the age of discretion, he is taught to realise his responsibilities. Every boy from such stage onward should practise continence in thought and deed, truth likewise and the not taking of any life. This to him must not be an irksome learning and practise but it should be natural to him. It should be his enjoyment. I can recall to my mind several such boys in Rajkot. Let me tell you that when I was younger than you are, my keenest enjoyment was to nurse my father. Of amusement after I was twelve, I had little or none. If you practise the three virtues, if they become part of your life, so far as I am concerned you will have completed your education—your training. Armed with them, believe me, you will earn your bread in any part of the world and you will have paved the way to acquire a true knowledge of the soul, yourself and God. This does not mean that you should not receive instruction in letters. That you should and you are doing. But it is a thing over which you need not fret yourself. You have plenty of time for it and after all you are to receive such instruction in order that your training may be of use to others.

. . . Do give ample work to gardening, actual digging, hoeing, etc. We have to live upon it in the future. And you should be the expert gardener of the family. Keep your tools in their respective places and absolutely clean. . . . In your lessons you should give a great deal of attention to mathematics and Sanskrit. The latter is absolutely necessary for you. Both these studies are difficult in after life. You will not neglect your music. You should make a selection of all the good passages, hymns and verses, whether in English, Gujarati or Hindi, and write them out in your best hand in a book. The collection at the end of a year will be most valuable. All these things you can do easily if you are methodical, never get agitated and think you have too much to do and then worry over what to do first. This you will find out in practise if you are patient and take care of your minutes. I hope you are keeping an accurate account, as it should be kept, of every penny spent for the household.

. . . And now I close with love to all and kisses to Ramdas, Devdas and Rami.

from
Father

Although Gandhi was among the holiest of men and the greatest hero of Indian independence, his actions rarely directly benefited his family. He was notoriously hard on his sons. According to the author of a biography of Gandhi (Fischer, 1950), Gandhi "expected . . . [his sons] to be chips off the old block, but the block did not chip" (quoted in Jones, 1960, p. 27). Gandhi refused to use his influence to help his children. When Harilal was attempting to become a businessman in Calcutta in 1916, his brother Manilal (then 24 years old) lent him some Gandhi funds under his management. When Gandhi discovered the loan, he ordered Manilal to stop using the Gandhi name and to apprentice himself to a hand spinner. After this penance, Manilal was sent to South Africa and was allowed back to India to see his family only for short periods. When a wealthy investor backed one of Harilal's business ventures out of respect for the Mahatma, Gandhi denied any responsibility for his son: "Men may be good, not necessarily their children" (quoted in Jones, 1960, pp. 30-31).

Gandhi is certainly not your average father figure, but we can use his letter to begin to explore how gender affects family commitments and helps shape patterns of love and care. Several things about Gandhi's letter suggest that duty and obligation were central to his conception of being a virtuous person and a good father. His instructions to his son focused on caring for his family, tending a garden, and keeping track of finances—all related to the duties of a family protector and provider. Gandhi's dedication to abstract moral principles is demonstrated by the high goals he set for Manilal and the harsh punishment he doled out to him when, years later, he violated one of those principles. Later in this chapter, I review how being a stern moral teacher was a central part of being a good father in past times. Although Gandhi loved his sons, he demonstrated that love in an emotionally detached way. His moral absolutism and allegiance to abstract principles can be seen as an ethical stance common to men and his emotional detachment as a masculine personality trait (see, for example, Chodorow, 1978; Gilligan, 1982). I discuss related issues when I look at gendered patterns of family care in this chapter and return to the topic in a discussion of childhood gender development in Chapter 5.

Although Gandhi's letter can be seen as a blueprint for some conventional patterns of gender, his instructions also depart from stereotypes of fathers in Western culture. His fathering style includes being a stern disciplinarian, but unlike Western patriarchs, he was unwaveringly nonviolent. Unlike modern dads, he did not try to be a pal or playmate to his children. He did not indulge them, telling Manilal that amusement for boys ended when they turned 12 and later refusing to help Harilal. He was definitely a role model and teacher to his sons, but unlike modern Western fathers, he valued the type of everyday care and service that most 20th-century American fathers have avoided. For example, he talks of taking great pleasure in nursing his own father when he was a young boy and tells Manilal that nursing his mother and "cheerfully bearing her ill temper" is a worthy endeavor. He tells Manilal that he should anticipate his sister's needs, coaches him to act in a way that will keep her mind off his absent older brother, and tells him to watch over his younger brothers. These activities require a sensitivity to others' feelings and subservience to their needs that has more often been expected of American mothers than of American fathers. Gandhi's letter thus raises issues about family care and who should provide it.

Families and Care

Care is the activity of attending and responding to others. We say that people care for others when they are sensitive to the suffering, desires, and needs of those persons and when they attempt to meet others' needs and prevent harm to them. We think of children and persons who are sick, frail, and disabled as especially in need of care, but everyone needs to be cared for in essential ways. As this chapter will show, women are the primary care providers both inside and outside families.

Caring for others is an enormously important activity, and the type of care we receive tends to define the quality of our lives. Although love is more than care, care is a central component of love (Abel & Nelson, 1990; Cancian, 1987; Cancian & Oliker, forthcoming; Finch & Groves, 1983; Thompson, 1993).

Because of the legacy of separate spheres in Europe and America, we assume that the only natural place for care to be given is within families. In actuality, families do not have a monopoly on care. For example, many people get more care and appreciation from friends than from family members. Most people also pay for a good deal of care, including meals, grooming, medical care, laundry, cleaning, entertainment, recreation, and other personal services. Large institutions such as schools, hospitals, churches, and government agencies also provide much of the care and human services that people receive. Families provide substantial amounts of care, but they are definitely not the only social institution providing it, and home is not the only place where people get it.

The loving care and emotional support we think of as essential to family life today were not expected of family members in the past. Even now, we do not always expect or get the love and care we need from other family members. Families can be decidedly *un*caring. People are more likely to be physically and sexually abused by family members than by others (Finkelhor, Gelles, Hotaling, & Straus, 1983; Straus, 1991). Most families do not have extreme forms of violence, but all families have conflicts, and all family members feel angry from time to time. Family members get mad at each other and say or do hurtful things fairly frequently and, in many cases, simply ignore the needs of other family members. Idealized family imagery aside, the home environment is as much a source of suffering and hardship as it is a source of love and care. Most families come out on the plus side in the balance between care and suffering, but we cannot assume that families automatically protect and nurture their members. Families *do* provide a huge amount of support and care, especially for younger children, but it is wrong to assume that they provide only positive support or that they are people's main source of emotional support and physical care. Although mothers provide most of the care and support to family members, it is a mistake to equate family care only with maternal care, and although women provide more care and support to friends, kin, and strangers than do men, it is a mistake to assume that caring is only women's work.

Letter to an Unborn Child:
Jessie Bernard to Dorothy Lee

Jessie Bernard was an eminent sociologist, scholar, and teacher who was born in 1903. As a rare career woman in the 1930s and 1940s, her studies of women, marriage, and social psychology influenced social scientists around the world. In 1941, at the age of 38, she gave birth to her first child, Dorothy Lee. The following letter was written by Jessie Bernard to her unborn child when she was six months pregnant, and the war in Europe was growing more ominous. Below the first letter are excerpts from a letter Jessie wrote to Dorothy Lee when she was one month old.

4 May 1941
My dearest,

Eleven weeks from today you will be ready for this outside world. And what a world it is this year! It has been the most beautiful spring I have ever seen . . . aglow with color. The forsythia were yellower and fuller than any I have ever seen. The lilacs were fragrant and feathery, and now the spirea, heavy with their little round blooms, stand like wonderful igloos, a mass of white. I doff my scientific mantle long enough to pretend that Nature is outdoing herself to prepare this earth for you. But also I want to let all this beauty get into my body.

I cannot help but think of that other world. The world of Europe where babies are born to hunger, stunted growth, breasts dried up with anxiety and fatigue. That is part of the picture too. And I sometimes think that while my body in this idyllic spring creates a miracle, forces are at work which within twenty or twenty-five years may be preparing to destroy the creation of my body. My own sweet, the war takes on a terrible new significance when I think of that. I think of all those mothers who carried their precious cargoes so carefully for nine long months—and you have no idea how long nine months can be when you are impatient for the end—lovingly nurtured their babies at their breasts, and watched them grow for twenty years. I think of their anguish when all this comes to naught.

. . . To me the only answer a woman can make to the destructive forces of the world is creation. And the most ecstatic form of creation is the creation of new life. I have so many dreams for you. There are so many virtues I would endow you with if I could. First of all, I would make you tough and strong. And how I have labored at that! I have eaten vitamins and minerals instead of food. Gallons of milk, pounds of lettuce, dozens of eggs . . . hours of sunshine. To make your body a strong one because everything [depends] on that. I would give you resiliency of body so that all the blows and buffets of this world would leave you still unbeaten. I would have you creative. I would have you a creative scientist. But if the shuffling genes have made of you an artist, that will make me happy too. And even if you have no special talent either artistic or scientific, I would still have you creative no matter what you do. To build things, to make things, to create—that is what I covet for you. If you have a strong body and a creative mind you will be happy. I will help in that.

Already I can see how parents long to shield their children from disappointments and defeat. But I also know that I cannot re-make life for you. You will suffer. You will have moments of disappointment and defeat. You will have your share of buffeting. I cannot spare you that. But I hope to help you be such a strong, radiant, self-integrated person that you will take all this in your stride, assimilate it, and rise to conquer.

Eleven more weeks. It seems a long time. Until another time, then, my precious one. I say good-bye.

Your eager mother

24 August 1941

My dearest daughter,

Now that I have held your earthy little body in my arms and felt that voracious tug of your hungry lips at my breast, the earlier letters I wrote to you in the spring seem rather remote and academic. Now I am so completely absorbed in your physical care that the more abstract values in your development are crowded out.

. . . You nursed with much energy, although there was little milk for you. . . . I wanted very much to nurse you completely, but alas I did not have enough milk. So we compromised. I nurse you and then give you a bottle. So far you have shown no objection. Your positive, experimental approach showed up again the other day when we first gave you orange juice from a spoon. You took it joyfully, eagerly. No rejections. No objections. We were delighted with the ease of the new adjustment.

The first few weeks at home have been most difficult for you and for us. I am so terribly inexperienced with babies, I had to learn everything from the beginning. And even yet you baffle me completely. You are not at all a scientific object. A practice which at one moment will cause you to stop crying will have no effect at all the next time. You will be crying violently and then in an instant you stop and all is forgiven. It puzzles me immensely. I wish I understood you better.

You seem to have an insatiable curiosity about the world. You love to look at things. Your eyes open very wide and you hold your head up over our shoulders and drink in all the sights. I find you utterly adorable. I sit for hours just watching you sleep, or lie awake in your bed. Just the sight and touch of your little body gives me intense pleasure.

. . . Caring for you has absorbed me so completely that I have not been able to think or do anything else. I hope now, however, to get better control over myself. For your sake, as well as for mine. I must not allow you to absorb me completely. I must learn to live my own life independently, in order to be a better mother to you.

All my love to you, sweet daughter

The tone of these two letters from mother to daughter contrast sharply with the letter from father to son. Of course, the time of writing is separated by 32 years, and the former are to a new baby, whereas the latter are to a teenage son. But the contrast is also appropriate, insofar as mothers have usually been the ones to care for babies, and fathers, when directly involved with children, have often become more engaged as they get older.

In Jessie Bernard's letters, there is no mention of duty or obligation but rather an emphasis on wondrous beauty, creativity, and vulnerability. There is a moral concern about the war, but it is expressed in close personal terms, rather than as abstract principles of right and wrong. Bernard identifies with the mothers in Europe who carry children inside them for 9 months, raise them for 20 years, only to see them sent off to war and possible death. In a violent world run by men, this is a mother's anguish, and it contrasts sharply with the moral certainty and absolutism of men such as Gandhi (although he was committed to nonviolence).

Bernard focuses on the physicality of pregnancy and baby care: the discomfort, the vitamins and dietary worries, the nursing, the sleep. These are infant care concerns that have always been borne by mothers but sometimes, after birth, shared by men. The *we* in Jessie's letter (probably) refers to her husband, Luther Lee Bernard, who was twice Jessie's age and died of cancer when Dorothy Lee was nine years old, and her younger brothers just six and one. Thus began Jessie Bernard's life as a single mother, continuing as a professor and researcher and trying to balance the concerns of job and family (Payne, 1983, p. 20). Jessie Bernard, like Margaret Mead and a few other women academics of her time, were unusual, but the dilemmas they faced have now become commonplace.

Bernard's letters show a close emotional connection to her child, even before she was born. She had extremely high aspirations for her daughter, but she also conveys a sense of unconditional love that is much less evident in Gandhi's letter to his son. Another fascinating contrast between the two revolves around issues of confidence, authority, and sources of information. Gandhi, although most humble, is supremely sure of himself and relies on the teachings of the masters to guide his actions in parenting and in all other matters. Bernard, in contrast, finds that her scientific training can get in the way of learning how to be a good mother. She feels vulnerable and inexperienced and learns how to care for her baby girl by trying new things and learning from and with her daughter. Finally, she idolizes her daughter and falls hopelessly in love with her, wants to meet her every need, but is afraid of spoiling her. This is not the style, to be sure, of a spiritual master who lectures and serves as a distant role model. It is the style of a mother in the 20th century—a mother, as you will see below, who is expected to be able to meet everyone's needs cheerfully and endlessly.

Gender and Care

Throughout the 20th century, Europeans and Americans have harbored unrealistically high expectations for mothers (Chodorow & Contratto, 1992; Glenn, 1994). According to sociologist Ann Oakley (1974), modern images of motherhood rest on three myths that are assumed to be eternal truths: (1) All women need to be mothers, (2) all mothers need their children, (3) and all children need their mothers. Although people tend to accept all three without question, Oakley shows how they are not literally true. Not all women want to be mothers, or can be; this is becoming increasingly clear as more women remain childless. Not all mothers need children—especially multiple ones—as seen by observing how women all over the world have attempted to limit the number of children they bear. Finally, although children need regular care, it is not necessary that the biological mother provide all, or even most, of it. I return to these issues below when I describe how the separate spheres ideal shapes public perceptions about the meaning of childhood and parental care.

Motherhood myths are so pervasive that we tend to generalize from them to all women. As potential mothers, women and girls are assumed to be more kind and caring than men and boys. Women *do* provide more care and emotional support to other people than do men (Abel & Nelson, 1990; Finch & Groves, 1983; Gerstel & Gallagher, 1994; Umberson, Chen, House, Hopkins, & Slaten, 1996; Ungerson, 1990). But these conventional expectations and behaviors, like our views about love and romance, are socially constructed and subject to change. We need to look at some of the reasons for this and be alert to cases that run counter to conventional expectations. History provides many examples of mothers who have murdered their babies (infanticide) or ignored their children's needs (Langer, 1972; Skolnick, 1987). Cross-cultural studies show that in some societies, men participate in "mothering" activities (Coltrane, 1996), and contemporary observational studies show that men are capable of caring for even the youngest infants (Briesemeister & Haines, 1988; Parke, 1996; Pruett, 1987).

Humans are not programmed for fixed behaviors as are birds, bees, and butterflies. Sex-linked biological traits in humans, such as X or Y chromosomes, do not determine how kind or supportive people will be, nor do they determine how masculine or feminine individuals are (Connell, 1995; Epstein, 1988; Kessler & McKenna, 1985; Lorber, 1994; see also Chapter 5). Although it is not the typical case, some men are more sensitive and caring than most women. Similarly, some women are more independent and assertive than most men. In popular culture, everyday life, and even academic studies, people usually focus on the differences between men and women (Spence, Deaux, & Helmreich, 1985). In reality, the similarities between them far outweigh any differences (Lorber, 1994; Rubin, 1975).

As noted in the first chapter, most social scientists conclude that gender is socially constructed (for reviews, see Bem, 1993; Epstein, 1988; Lorber, 1994). In other words, global differences in behavior and disposition between men and women are learned through repeated interaction with other people who share similar views about gender. Much of this learning takes place in family settings or through family rituals, and as I discuss in Chapter 5, much of it also occurs when children are socialized. The gender differences that develop seem so entrenched in our personalities that they feel natural to most people. Nevertheless, they are not instincts, and they are subject to modification, as countless social psychological experiments and studies have shown (Bem, 1993; Howard & Hollander, 1997; Huston, 1983; Spence et al., 1985). Even in the area of emotional support and caregiving, in which women do more than men, the differences tend to be significantly reduced or disappear when researchers control for the structural conditions under which people live (Umberson et al., 1996). For instance, when women's jobs are similar to men's, the amount and type of care they provide family members, extended kin, and friends become more similar (Gerstel & Gallagher, 1994). When women and men experience similar conditions of support and caring, they have similar psychological reactions, including levels of depression and alcohol use (Umberson et al., 1996). In other words, similar social conditions elicit similar psychological reactions from individuals. Although most people believe that things such as maternal instinct, feminine intuition, and male aggressiveness are built into humans by nature, these characteristics are actually attributed to individuals because of the social roles they play.

The obvious biological differences between males and females—such as women's ability to bear children and nurse infants—do play into the social roles for women and men but in a less decisive way than most people think. As Judith Howard and Jocelyn Hollander (1997) suggest, "the pervasive cultural belief in the significance of biology may be as important a determinant of behavior as biology itself" (p. 156). In other words, people's belief about natural gender differences is at least as important as any actual underlying physiological differences between the sexes. Even if underlying biological differences promote certain traits or behaviors (a hotly debated topic among social scientists), for the traits and behaviors to survive, they must also be supported by the culture and continually reproduced through the rituals of daily interaction (Kessler & McKenna, 1985; Lorber, 1994; West & Zimmerman, 1987).

When social scientists have conducted careful experimental studies on the workings of gender in social interaction—such as asking a mixed-sex group to complete a complex task—they find that men and women respond in remarkably similar fashion to similar social circumstances (Bem, 1993; Howard & Hollander, 1997; Ridgeway, 1991; Spence et al., 1985). Given the same sorts of resources, pressures, demands, and concerns, men and women act pretty much the same. The catch is that women and men rarely face the same resources, pressures, demands, and concerns, especially if they get married and have children together (Lorber, 1994).

Biological sex differences are obviously important when we consider men's and women's roles in pregnancy and nursing, but beyond the basic physical facts of bearing children and breast-feeding, parenting and other caregiving behaviors are learned. As the letter from Jessie Bernard to her daughter Dorothy Lee reveals, women, like men, have to learn how to take care of babies. New mothers report that despite their hope for a maternal instinct to show them how to parent, their mothering skills actually develop through trial and error (Cowan & Cowan, 1992; Glenn, 1994). They read parenting books, talk to other parents, and figure out what to do by interacting with their children. In general, women have been more likely to learn how to care for children and other family members because of the many personal, cultural, and economic circumstances that shape their lives (Abel & Nelson, 1990; Cancian & Oliker, forthcoming; Gerstel & Gallagher, 1994).

Historical Views of Family Care

Shifting Images of Children

We can learn about expectations for mothers and fathers by paying attention to patterns of child rearing in the past. In earlier times, caring for children was a more collective enterprise, and most children spent less than half their waking hours in the presence of their biological mothers (Coltrane, 1988). Although societies differed greatly from one another, most were small-scale, and the boundary between the family and the outside world was much less distinct than it is today. In most societies, the entire community participated in virtually every aspect of an individual's life, including most of those things we now consider private family matters. In this older and more communal pattern, parent-child relations were constantly regulated and monitored by relatives and other community members, and what happened inside the home was relatively public (Shorter, 1975; Stone, 1977). A microcommunity of close-by adults and older children usually acted as surrogate parents, and plenty of people were always around to offer advice on what to do in specific situations. This meant that individual mothers and fathers had less control over child-rearing practices, but they also had substantial help from others (Skolnick, 1987).

The last chapter discussed how the growth of capitalism and the gradual shift from home-based production to wage labor, industrialization, and a market economy altered the dynamics of marriage and home life in Europe and America. These same social and economic developments also encouraged changes in overall ideas about children and how they should be treated. In the earlier era, children were valued mostly for their economic contributions. They usually worked on farms or labored in their parents' trade, and, by doing so, provided a type of insurance policy for their parents. Childhood was not considered such a special time of life, and children were not as sentimentalized as they are today (Ariès, 1962; but see Pollock, 1983).

Death was much more visible in those days, which probably limited intense emotional dependency between family members, or at least hardened people to the inevitability of death. Adult life expectancy was much shorter, and diseases such as tuberculosis killed many people before they grew old. Without an understanding of infection, many women also died in childbirth. In London during the 17th century, the maternal mortality rate is estimated to have been 15 per 1,000 births (Towler & Bramall, 1986) and five times that in Paris hospitals during epidemics of puerperal fever a century later (Gélis, 1991). Maternal mortality rates remained more than 5 per 1,000 until well into the 20th century (Lewis, 1980; Michaelson, 1988; Wertz & Wertz, 1977). Because birth control was largely ineffective, women who survived childbirth tended to have many children, but many of the children died young (Anderson, 1994). Demographers estimate that before 1900, half of all parents would lose at least 1 child, compared with only about 1 in 20 today (Uhlenberg, 1980).

Because of these harsh conditions, and because the sentimental individualism of the modern era had not yet blossomed, emotional involvement with children was considerably more limited than it is today (Ariès, 1962; Shorter, 1975; Synnott, 1983). In the elite upper classes, death was a less constant threat, so children had more sentimental value but still much less than now. In addition, prevailing images of children were different from modern ideas about the innocence and purity of children. Religious teachings, particularly those of the American Puritans and Methodists, stressed the "corrupt nature" and "evil dispositions" of children, and fathers were admonished to demand strict obedience and use swift physical punishment to cleanse children of their sinful ways (Muir & Brett, 1980).

As productive work became separated from the home in the modern era, the image of children shifted dramatically, especially among the more privileged classes in Europe and America. No longer sinful creatures valued for their work efforts, children came to be seen as precious "little angels" (Synnott, 1983). Relying on insurance company records and court cases, historical sociologist Viviana Zelizer (1985) shows how the economically useful child of previous times was transformed into an economically worthless yet emotionally priceless child as we moved into the 20th century. Traditional forms of child labor came to be seen as harmful and inappropriate for those of "tender years" (although working-class children, African American children, and immigrant children, like their mothers, still had to work to survive). In 1870, if an American child died in an accident and the courts concluded that another party was negligent, the parents were compensated for the value of the child's labor. By 1930, however, in cases of wrongful death, the parents were compensated for incalculable emotional pain. This period saw a remarkable increase in the emotional value of the youngest children. In the earlier era, older boy orphans were the first to be adopted because of their productive labor power. By midcentury, however, young children, especially baby girls, were the first to be adopted. The middle-class family came to be idealized as the only place where innocent and pure children could and should be protected. No longer considered evil creatures whose will had to be broken by their fathers, children had become precious creatures who needed nurturing and support from their mothers.

As in the case of past images of romantic love and of the Victorian family, this historical ideal of childhood innocence was attainable by only a minority of the population in Europe and America. In non-Western countries, of course, other cultural ideals of children predominated and were transformed as various social and economic changes unfolded. Among subgroups of the U.S. population, these childhood ideals often remained severely out of touch with everyday reality. For example, scholars debate how much white middle-class family norms and child-rearing ideals actually affected the lives of African Americans during the past 200 years (Burgess, 1995; McDaniel, 1990). Images of children among the rich white Southern gentry in the 19th century were certainly much different from those held by the slaves who were forced to work on their plantations (Griswold, 1993). Turn-of-the-century immigrant children in New York were not granted the opportunities to seem as innocent as their wealthier contemporaries. In addition, important historical events, such as war and economic depression, can change the way that people conceive of children, encouraging us to view them as potential soldiers or additional breadwinners (see, for example, Elder, 1974; Elder, Modell, & Parke, 1993; Hareven, 1982).

Shifting Images of Fathers

Although historical family and childhood research has blossomed in recent years, researchers have rarely focused their attention on what fathers did with children, and even more rarely have they distinguished between fathers from different cultural or ethnic groups (Parke & Stearns, 1993). Images of fathers among subgroups of the population undoubtedly varied immensely, but historians have yet to delineate most of those differences (for a notable exception, see Griswold, 1993). In the rural agricultural era, American fathers were supposed to serve as moral overseers, as well as masters, of their families. According to the leading middle-class ideals of the time, men performed their civic duty and developed themselves by emphasizing their home-based family roles. Although mothers provided most of the direct caretaking of infants and young children, men were active in training and tutoring children, especially as the children grew older. Before the 19th century, most parental advice was addressed to fathers, rather than to mothers. Because they were moral teachers and family heads, fathers were thought to have far greater responsibility for, and influence on, their children than did mothers. Not only were middle-class fathers involved in the direct moral and practical instruction of older children, but they were also generally held responsible for how the children acted outside the home (Degler, 1980; Pleck, 1987; Rotundo, 1993).

Before the modern era, father-child relationships were ruled primarily by duty, and although fathers' associations with their children were not devoid of emotion, they were characterized by obligation. Men were a visible presence in children's lives because their work—whether farming, artisanship, or trade—occurred in the household context. Furthermore, most work in the household economy of the agricultural era was directed by the fathers. Men introduced sons to farming or craft work, oversaw the work of others, and were responsible for maintaining harmonious relations in the household. The home was thus a system of control as well as a center of production, and both functions tended to reinforce the authority of fathers (Degler, 1980; Griswold, 1993; Pleck, 1987). Of course, different fathers faced different pressures, depending on the local economy and the part their households played in that economy. Researchers know little about the details of what fathers did with their children or how they felt about them. Some interesting debates have emerged about the distinctions between Western European and colonial American styles of fathering and about whether harsh patriarchs also showed warmth and affection toward their children (e.g., Demos, 1986; Erickson, 1958; Greven, 1970; Parke & Stearns, 1993; Pollock, 1983).

As the market economy took over from home-based production, the father's position as head and master of the household and moral instructor of his children was transformed. As men were increasingly called on to seek employment outside the home, they spent less time in interaction with their families, and their direct authority over family members declined. Only after the wage labor economy developed in the 19th century did men's occupational achievement outside the family take on moral overtones. Men came to be seen as fulfilling their family and civic duty not by teaching and interacting with their children but by being good providers. In a fundamental way, men's moral obligations shifted from family activities to work activities, and a father's duty shifted to one of financial support. The home, previously the normal site of production, consumption, and virtually everything else in life, was slowly transformed into a nurturant child-centered haven set apart from the impersonal world of work, politics, and other public pursuits. Perhaps most significant, the home became the mother's domain (Coontz, 1992; Lasch, 1977; Skolnick, 1991). As historian Mary Ryan (1981) suggests, the center of the middle-class household was shifted "from patriarchal authority to maternal affection" (p. 102).

Shifting Images of Mothers

In hunting and gathering societies that constituted most of human history, a delicate balance was achieved between ecological carrying capacity and fertility (Mintz, 1996). Because of low levels of protein intake, low ratios of female body fat, and late weaning, women exercised a sort of natural birth control and typically spread the births of their children more than four years apart. Life expectancy was short, people did not accumulate much wealth, there were relatively few distinctions between groups of people, and men and women cooperated in subsistence activities and some aspects of child care. There was much variation among the various hunter-gatherer societies from around the world, but in general, women were valued for more than just their childbearing and child rearing, and most had some control over their own fertility (see Blumberg, 1984; Coltrane, 1988; Coontz & Henderson, 1986; Whyte, 1978).

In traditional agrarian societies (e.g., ancient China, Egypt, and medieval Europe), life was harsh for the peasants who made up the majority of the population. Rural landlords took most of the surplus crops and pressured peasant women to have many babies, who, if they survived, became child laborers and field hands. In many of these societies, women had little power (as described in Chapter 2), so despite the difficulty of childbirth under poverty conditions and high maternal death rates, women were treated as breeders—their sexuality was tightly controlled and they were encouraged to bear many children. In societies in which women had more power, they took whatever measures they could to keep the birthrate more under their own control. The same is true today in many less developed countries of the Third World. When women acquire more economic resources, they tend to reduce their own birthrates by gaining access to contraceptives or abortions, sometimes in opposition to their husbands (Blumberg, 1984).

In colonial American society, there were elements of these agrarian practices, as well as a need for more children to help work the land that was usurped from the more nomadic Native Americans who preceded the colonists. Early American women were valued for both their fertility and their labor, but as noted above, in the home production era, fathers tended to get the blame or credit for how children turned out as adults. As the United States turned to a commercial economy in the 19th century and eventually to urban industrial production in the 20th century, the moral responsibility for children shifted from fathers to mothers (Demos, 1982; Ryan, 1982). Maternal responsibility for home and children was accelerated by the "cult of domesticity" as sketched out in the last chapter. As men increasingly left the home to go to work for wages, the cult of domesticity glorified motherhood and reassured middle-class women that their natural place was in the home. Motherhood was placed on a pedestal, and the contrast between the outside world and home came to be seen as a contrast between Man and Woman.

The development of separate work and family spheres thus entailed a moral war between the sexes. Men's public activities in business and politics were suspect for being greedy and corrupt, and the men came to be seen as in need of redemption via the grace and purity of the womanly home. Domestic tasks assumed a spiritual importance as the middle-class home was transformed into a private place in which women were expected to comfort and civilize both men and children. Homemaking became exclusively the woman's domain. But as outlined in the last chapter, running the middle-class household was still dependent on outside help. As Mary Romero (1992) notes, "Rather than make women's lives more similar to each other through the gender-specific activity of homemaking, social class accentuated their differences" (p. 52). Middle-class women relied on domestic servants, and poor women were forced to make ends meet by taking in boarders, growing their own food, bartering, and doing work for others.

Although working-class women continued to struggle just to get by, middle- and upper-class women transformed homemaking into a profession. The rise of scientific mothering and the home economics movement promoted the idea that the home was a private haven under women's control (Cott, 1977; Griswold, 1993; Pleck, 1987; Skolnick, 1991; Welter, 1966). The growth of the middle class meant that many more "mistresses" demanded the help of maids and nannies to perform the work required in cooking, cleaning, and raising children. During the early part of the 20th century, African American women were most likely to be servants and laundresses, especially in the South, but in the North as well. In the Southwest, Chicanas were disproportionately concentrated in domestic service, and in the Far West (especially in California and Hawaii), Asian men were most often household servants (Glenn, 1992). As the hiring class expanded, middle-class homemakers came to think of themselves as supervisors whose superior knowledge allowed them to manage and oversee the manual labor of the servants they employed (Romero, 1992). Turning the middle-class home into the woman's domain and treating homemaking and motherhood as a profession gave some wives managerial control over day-to-day domestic activities, but it also subordinated women's needs to those of their husbands and families (Bose, 1987; Skolnick, 1991).

According to the ideal of separate spheres, middle-class women were supposed to realize their "true" nature by marrying, giving birth, and most important, tending children. Motherhood was elevated to a revered status, and wives' homemaking came to be seen as a moral calling and a worthy profession. The True Woman was supposed to be inherently unselfish, and her moral purity, nurturant character, and gentle temperament were seen as uniquely qualifying her to rear young children (Coontz, 1992; Lasch, 1977; Skolnick, 1991). Arlene Skolnick notes that the development of the modern private family brought new burdens for middle- and upper-class women because they were supposed to create a wholesome home life, which, in turn, was seen as the only way to redeem society. Under the previous agricultural economy, the community regulated most family functions and repaired any moral defects of families. In the newer industrial model, however, families, and especially mothers, were supposed to compensate for the moral defects of the larger society. This general belief in the moral purity of the domestic realm was used by suffragists to claim that giving women the vote would create stronger families and a more humane society (Coontz, 1992).

Women had been involved in the everyday aspects of child care to begin with, but as the middle-class home was separated from work and morally elevated, women came to be seen as the ones most capable of training children and instilling proper values in them. As women became more responsible for children's overall well-being, they were also charged with preparing them to become proper adults. Mothers were supposed to treat sons and daughters differently (even more than they do today; see Chapter 5). In line with prevailing ideas about appropriate gender roles, mothers encouraged girls to develop domestic sensitivities and encouraged boys to be competitive and industrious (Davidoff & Hall, 1987; Ferree, 1990; Ryan, 1981).

As with the ideal that paid work was only for men, the ideal that only women belonged in the home gained widespread popularity through time. It remained a myth, rather than an everyday reality, however, for many families because most working-class fathers could not earn enough to support the whole family. African American, Latino, Asian American, and many immigrant men were not able to earn the family wage that the separate spheres ideal assumed. This meant that women in these families had to either work for wages, participate in production at home, or figure other ways to pool resources and make ends meet. Although the romantic ideal held that women should be sensitive and pure keepers of the home on a full-time basis, the reality was that women in less advantaged households had no choice but to be workers and mothers at the same time. Many working-class and minority women had to leave their own homes and children to take care of other people's children and houses (Dill, 1994; Glenn, 1992; Rollins, 1985; Romero, 1992). Motherhood ideals, like other cultural myths, did not mean the same thing to everyone and did not influence all people in the same way.

Moving Into the 1950s

A variety of economic, social, political, and technological changes combined to transform the idealized images of mothers, fathers, and children as the United States moved into the mid-20th century. As noted in the last chapter, from the late 1940s to the middle 1960s, a "fifties" version of separate spheres gained widespread popularity, fueled by the rapid growth of the middle class. The ideal father continued to be seen as a "good provider," who "set a good table, provided a decent home, paid the mortgage, bought the shoes, and kept his children warmly clothed" (Bernard, 1981, pp. 3-4). As they had during the earlier Victorian era, middle-class women were expected to be consumed and fulfilled by their "natural" wifely and motherly duties. Isolated in suburban houses, many mothers now had almost sole responsibility for raising children, aided by occasional reference to Dr. Spock or some other child-rearing manual. Television shows such as *Father Knows Best* and *Ozzie & Harriet* presented images of the ideal family—beautiful, loving, and subservient housewife; kindly, authoritative, breadwinner husband; suburban home with sprawling lawn; and at least two wholesome, intelligent, and well-meaning children. This model of family life enjoyed unparalleled popularity during the 1950s.

In the United States, by the 1950s, the traditional collective style of child rearing common throughout most of human history seemed a thing of the past. The ideal was now for biological mothers to be the sole caretakers for their children. They were supposed to be materially rewarded and emotionally fulfilled by raising two or three children alone in their own homes using the latest techniques developed by pediatricians and child psychologists. This style of isolated, indulgent, and exclusive parenting by biological mothers is an all-your-eggs-in-one-basket approach to child rearing that can produce unique stresses and strains for both mothers and children (Skolnick, 1987). When mothers are responsible for all the child care, they have few opportunities for taking breaks, and their feelings become overwhelmingly important to their children. Sole-caretaker mothers have few opportunities to derive self-worth from alternate activities, and they are often judged by how their children turn out. This can set up a hothouse environment in which mothers and children feel responsible for each other's actions and emotions, sometimes leading to confusion over ego boundaries, communication problems, and mental illness (Coser, 1964; Laing, 1971; Warren, 1987). Studies of parenting practices in different societies and in different historical eras show that mothers who are unable to escape the intensity of continuous interactions with their children are more likely to reject them than mothers who can get away from time to time (Rohner, 1975). In contrast, when women can parent under more supportive circumstances—when they receive help with the monotonous routines of housework and the constant burdens of child supervision—the love and caring they provide to family members can be intensely fulfilling (Lynch, 1994; Thompson, 1993).

Modern Parenting

Compulsory Motherhood

The idea that all women should be mothers and that they should gain intense satisfaction from it has been characterized as *compulsory motherhood* (Pogrebin, 1983). According to this view, a woman's ultimate purpose is to be a mother, and everything else she does is secondary. A woman's well-being is so tied up with mothering that her identity is sometimes assumed to be tenuous and trivial without it. Ironically, researchers have found that mothers of young children in the United States have lower levels of well-being than other women, primarily because in the absence of substantial help and support, the day-to-day activities of mothering small children are isolating, tedious, and unrelenting. When children grow older, and especially after they move away from home, mothers' well-being tends to improve (Glenn, 1991). The caring ideals associated with motherhood continue to influence women's behavior after children move away from home. Older women continue to provide large amounts of practical and emotional support to family members, as well as to friends (Gallagher & Gerstel, 1993).

Compulsory motherhood implies that women should find total fulfillment in having children and taking care of them. Although most women do gain profound satisfaction from caring for children, research shows that in overall comparisons using national samples, U.S. women without children have about the same level of personal well-being as women with children (Callan, 1987; Thompson & Walker, 1989). Motherhood is rarely the sole basis for a woman's identity, especially because most women are spending less time as mothers of young children than any time in recent history. About one in five American women never becomes a mother, and the average U.S. woman now spends only about one seventh of her adult life either pregnant, nursing, or caring for preschool children.

Recent Fertility Patterns

Birthrates fell gradually throughout most of the 20th century, but the United States continues to grow. From 1990 to 1995, the U.S. population grew an average of about 1% per year to more than 262 million people. By 2010, the U.S. population is likely to exceed 300 million. Although immigration accounted for about a third of the population growth in the 1990s, new births accounted for the rest. The United States continues to be one of the world's fastest growing industrialized countries with birthrates well above those of Japan or the countries of Western Europe.

The "baby boomlet" of the early 1990s saw the annual number of U.S. births break the 4-million mark for the first time since the 1946 to 1964 baby boom. During this time, the total fertility rate (the average number of births a woman will have in her lifetime) rose to 2.0, its highest level since 1972 (DeVita, 1996). One of the reasons for the "echo boom" was that baby boomers were having children near the end of their childbearing years. Figure 4.1 shows that the birthrate for women in their 30s has increased dramatically since about 1980. At the same time, the birthrate for women in their late 20s has remained fairly steady, but the birthrate for women under 24 has fallen. This trend has many causes, but these stand out: More younger women were avoiding or postponing marriage, attending college, and staying in the labor force; and women in their 30s began deciding to have children, whether or not they were married. Although contrary to some media reports, the teenage birthrate has fallen for four consecutive years, with the rate for African American teens dropping 17% from 1991 to 1995.

Although baby boomer women in their 30s accounted for about a third of the births in the early 1990s, two thirds came from younger women. The birthrates among minority women were particularly high during this time. Although African American women constituted about 12% of all women, their births were 16% of all births. Similarly, Hispanic women constituted 10% of all women, but their births were also 16% of the total. Even the birthrate of Asian American women, who traditionally have fewer births, exceeded the rate for non-Hispanic whites (DeVita, 1996).

Figure 4.2 shows how the 1995 birthrates for Hispanic women were higher than for any other group (103.7 births per 1,000 women). These Hispanic rates are driven primarily by the high levels of childbearing among Mexican American

FIGURE 4.1

Birthrates for Women Over 30 Are on the Rise
SOURCE: U.S. Bureau of the Census, Current Population Surveys, 1976-1994; U.S. Bureau of the Census, 1994a.

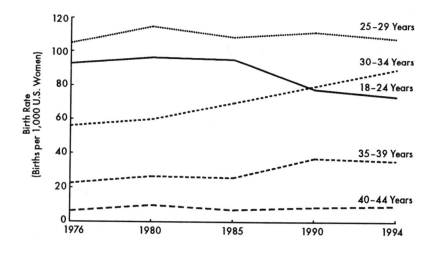

FIGURE 4.2

Birth Patterns Differ by Race and Ethnicity
SOURCE: U.S. Department of Health and Human Services, National Center for Health Statistics, 1996, Tables A and 2.

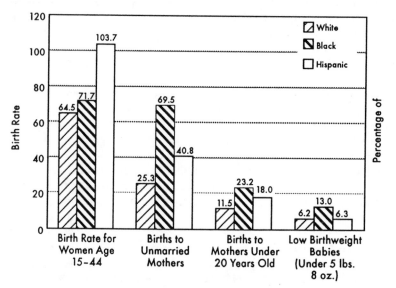

1995 Birth Data by Race/Ethnic Group

women. African American rates were also well above those of non-Hispanic whites (71.7 vs. 64.5 births per 1,000 women). These high levels of fertility among minority women are expected to continue in the future and, coupled with the youthfulness of the minority population, will lead to even more overall diversity in the U.S. population (see Figure 1.2).

Motherhood has often taken on an almost sacred quality in American society. For example, the popular phrase "mom and apple pie" suggests that nothing is as saintly as motherhood. But in the 19th and for most of the 20th centuries, only certain types of motherhood were considered worthy of being granted this sacred status. Unmarried women who gave birth to babies were a different matter. Having a baby out of wedlock used to bring shame to "respectable" women and their families. Single women who became pregnant often lost their jobs and were forced to move away to have their babies in secret, especially if they were poor. In other cases, pregnant women or their families would ensure that the couple got married before the baby arrived. "Shotgun" weddings were much more common, and social pressures were brought against the father and his family to "make an honest woman out of her."

A double message here fits with the Victorian ideal of separate spheres. The general idea is that motherhood is sacred—but only if it happens to the right type of woman. If a woman is married, then motherhood reflects the height of moral purity. If she is not married, however, then motherhood is the most shameful thing that can happen to her. This ideal is being transformed in the face of increasing levels of nonmarital births. Like other aspects of Victorian morality, the motherhood ideal applied most to women in privileged families. African American families, in contrast, have a long tradition of women having children outside marriage and of living in nonnuclear households. In 1910, for example, African American children were twice as likely as European American children to live with a single mother and more than three times more likely to live with a foster parent (McDaniel, 1994). Since the 1940s, when accurate records were compiled, black women have had nonmarital birthrates that are at least twice as high as those of white women (U.S. Department of Health and Human Services, National Center for Health Statistics [DHHS], 1995).

Figure 4.2 shows that African American women continue to be much more likely than whites to give birth outside marriage. In 1995, more than two thirds of births to African American women were nonmarital births, up from about half during the 1970s. Hispanic women are also more likely than non-Hispanic whites to have babies outside marriage, with more than 40% having nonmarital births in 1995, a proportion that has doubled since the 1970s. The proportion of births to white mothers that occur outside marriage now stands at one in four, also double the proportion from the 1970s. The overall U.S. percentage of births to unmarried women is now 32%, three times higher than in the 1960s (DeVita, 1996; DHHS, 1996).

Although the number and percentage of births to unmarried women increased rapidly in the 1980s, they have risen more slowly in the 1990s and seem to have leveled off (DHHS, 1995). In 1995, the total number of nonmarital births declined 3% from the previous year to 1,248,028. In addition, the proportion of all births to unmarried mothers declined 2%, and the birthrate for unmarried women dropped 4%. That was the first year that all three indicators of nonmarital birth had dropped since 1940 when national data were first compiled (DHHS, 1996). The high number of births to unmarried women is partially the result of there being more unmarried women. In 1960, there were fewer than 9 million unmarried women of childbearing age (15-44 years), but by 1995, there were more than 20 million. In addition, however, women who are unmarried are about twice as likely to have a child than they were in 1960 (DHHS, 1995).

The high proportion of nonmarital births (along with the high divorce rate and dropping marriage rate) is interpreted by some analysts as a sign of family decline because they assume women are being selfish or self-indulgent (for example, see Blankenhorn, 1995; Popenoe, 1993). On the other hand, sustained high birthrates among U.S. women, both inside and outside marriage, show that they continue to be committed to children and families. To understand the recent trends, it is helpful to compare U.S. patterns with those of other countries. As was shown in Chapter 2, the U.S. marriage rate is still much higher than that of other industrialized countries (see Figure 2.1). The percentage of births occurring outside marriage in the United States is still only two thirds of the percentage in Sweden or Denmark. The U.S. nonmarital birthrate is also still just below the levels in France and the United Kingdom, and only slightly more than the percentage in Canada. In contrast, proportions of births occurring outside marriage in Germany and the Netherlands are less than half the U.S. level, and in Japan and Italy, the percentages are only a small fraction of what they are in the United States (U.S. Bureau of the Census, 1995b). Regardless of where a country stands in comparative perspective, the trend in births outside marriage has been the same—more of it. Nonmarital birthrates in the U.S. are now falling slightly, but it is difficult to predict future trends. One thing is certain: We will not return to old-style Victorian practices of ostracizing a woman when she has a baby just because she does not have a husband.

Although marriage and birth patterns are changing, vestiges of the old Victorian motherhood ideal remain in popular culture, in political rhetoric, and in public policies. Since the late 19th century, middle-class white women have been encouraged to have babies, but women who are poor, immigrant women, and women of color have been discouraged from becoming mothers (although evidently not successfully because immigrant and minority birthrates have continually exceeded those of whites; see DeVita, 1996, pp. 14-15). Leaders of the eugenics movement in the early 20th century advocated sterilizing "undesirable" women to preserve racial and genetic "purity." More recently, sterilization proposals have been renewed, poor African American and Latina mothers have been forced off welfare, and young unwed mothers have been denied various health, nutrition, and housing benefits (Pogrebin, 1983; Sonestein & Acs, 1996; see Chapter 6).

Educated white women, in contrast, have been bombarded with pro-pregnancy propaganda labeled "maternity chic" by one social critic (Pogrebin, 1983, p. 180). When privileged women do not have babies, they are often criticized for being selfish. This is especially true for those who purposefully choose to forgo children. The proportion of childless women is increasing, although it is difficult to determine how many made this decision purposefully. Becoming childless is usually not a once-and-for-all decision. Women have tended to delay the decision because they were not married, were not in a secure living arrangement, could not afford to quit a job, or some other practical reason. As noted above, however, an increasing number of women who are not married have decided to go ahead and have a child without having a husband when they approach the end of their safest childbearing years. When a couple is making the decision, the major reasons for not having children include commitment to careers or to one's partner and wanting to avoid the burdens or responsibilities of child care (Campbell, 1985).

Although more women are postponing the decision or deciding to remain childless, others want children but are unable to have them. About 8% of women who wish to have children are not able to bear them (Westoff, 1986). Because of new treatments for infertility, it sometimes seems as if there are more infertile couples than in the past, but the infertility rate has actually declined since the 1960s. The infertility rate is higher for those who delay childbearing. Because people are waiting longer to have children, and older people have more money to spend on such things, more people are going to infertility clinics than ever before. Because of the ideal of compulsory motherhood, and because women have traditionally been defined by their caretaking roles, those who are involuntarily childless because of infertility sometimes feel that they are not "real women" (Houseknecht, 1987; Miall, 1987). Nevertheless, norms are changing, and women who remain childless are less likely to be hounded by relatives to have children than they were in the past.

According to conventional wisdom, something is wrong with women who do not want to have babies, and something is wrong with mothers who are not always and forever willing to put the needs of their children ahead of their own. Expectations for mothers are so extreme that they are literally impossible to fulfill. Mothers are supposed to be constantly life-giving, self-sacrificing, and forgiving. Not only are they seen as pure and altruistic, but their goodness is so profound that they are often granted an all-powerful mythical status. According to popular ideals stemming from separate spheres ideology, mothers hold the fate of their children and the future of the entire society in their hands (Chodorow & Contratto, 1992; Skolnick, 1991). At the same time, mothers are also portrayed in popular culture as powerless because they are supposedly driven by deep underlying biological forces. Their own needs are subordinated to the dictates of nature, instinct, and mythological forces beyond their control (Glenn, 1994).

Mothers are both idealized and blamed, especially if they are members of disadvantaged or marginalized groups. African American women, for example, have been stereotyped by the popular culture either as ignorant welfare moms in need of protection or as all-powerful matriarchs who almost effortlessly nurture, protect, and provide for their children. Both stereotypes are misleading. As noted previously, being married has not been a prerequisite to becoming a mother in the African American community for a long time. Poor, unemployed women have developed patterns of coping that include exchange of aid between family members, friends, neighbors, and fictive kin and their provision of mutual aid (e.g., Abel, 1990; Stack, 1974). Because of inequities in the labor market and larger society, African American and other minority women have been forced to be strong parents and workers, but the idealized images of them often exceed what is humanly possible (Wong, 1994). The new image of the (usually white and middle-class) supermom is a similarly unrealistic ideal of a woman who can "have it all" by combining career and mothering almost effortlessly.

Although these popular images are far-fetched, women are creatively forging new ways to combine mothering with basic survival, especially in marginalized communities. In the middle-class neighborhoods and barrios of Southern California, for example, mothers were responsible for organizing one of the largest grassroots political coalitions to emerge in recent decades. Sociologist Mary Pardo (1990, 1995) studied the activities of groups such as Mothers of East Los Angeles and Concerned Parents of Monterey Park, who mobilized thousands of people to fight against the placement of prisons, parole offices, and toxic waste incinerators in their neighborhoods. Rather than conceiving of these public activities as separate from their family roles (as most political theories would have it), these Latinas considered their political organizing and demonstrations as a logical and natural extension of being mothers. According to Pardo (1990), "the women in 'Mothers of East L. A.' have transformed the definition of 'mother' to include militant political opposition to state-proposed projects they see as adverse to the quality of life in the community" (p. 4). Such examples remind us that the social, political, and economic contexts of our lives continually shape and reshape our inherited notions of gender and family.

Realities of Parenthood

Becoming parents today is both joyful and stressful. Most studies show that having a baby brings on a sort of crisis, with individual well-being and marital satisfaction plummeting (Cowan & Cowan, 1992). New parents are unprepared for the huge time demands that having a baby entails, and few people adjust easily to the lack of sleep and constant vigilance that infant care demands. For couples, as the Chris and Pat story in the last chapter showed, having a baby often precipitates a shift toward a much more conventional gender-based division of domestic labor.

Young people in the United States do not receive much training for being parents. Some girls and a few boys learn about child care through baby-sitting, watching younger siblings, or taking classes in school. Compared with most other societies, however, American families require little from children and teach them even less about how they can be good parents. Although parenting skills are something that must be learned, we somehow assume that parents, especially mothers, will automatically acquire these skills. Our idealized view of motherhood assumes that a dormant maternal instinct will naturally emerge and guide women's parenting because mothering is their destiny. As Jessie Bernard's letter to her baby daughter shows, however, women must learn how to mother.

We train people for other adult roles in our society. For example, we do not expect that people will know how to perform a job without first learning about it, practicing it, and getting guidance from skilled people during an apprentice phase.

We anticipate that people will gradually work their way into gaining mastery and will be rewarded with the assignment of increasingly complex duties. Parents, in contrast, are thrown into parenthood and expected to be experts (at least the mothers are). There is no real training period because pregnancy and the medical birthing classes that prospective parents attend do little to prepare them for the day-to-day realities of infant care. Parenthood comes all at once and is irrevocable. One day you don't have a baby, and the next you are on duty 24 hours a day with few breaks in sight for years.

In the 1950s, people got married in their early 20s and had babies right away. If women worked before they were wed, they typically quit their jobs when they married, or perhaps when they got pregnant. As summarized in the last chapter, the ideal—and the practice for most women who could afford it—was to stay out of the labor force until after the children had grown up and left the home. Today, most people wait longer to get married and also wait longer to have babies. But even more important, most women keep working after they get pregnant and return to work soon after having babies. The rapid entry of mothers (not just women) into the paid labor force will probably be seen as the most important social change of the late 20th century (see Figure 3.3).

Because there are many more single-parent families than in the past, and because most families with two parents must rely on two incomes, the typical transition to parenthood is more stressful than ever. Most employers do not offer paid maternity leave programs, so few mothers are able to take much time off from work around the birth of a child. Leave for fathers is even more rare, and paid paternity leave is usually only for a few days and typically must be taken from sick leave.

Other countries, including virtually all northern European nations, have made a much larger commitment to helping new parents (Haas, 1992). More than 100 countries throughout the world have legislated coverage that allows a mother to leave work for at least 6 weeks at the time of childbirth, guarantees that her job will be there when she returns, and provides a cash benefit to replace all or most of her earnings (Kamerman, 1989; Klinman & Kohl, 1984). Canadian workers, for example, receive 15 weeks of family leave at 60% pay after the birth of a child (Etzioni, 1993). Swedish workers receive 90% pay for 36 weeks and prorated paid leave for the next 18 months (Haas, 1992; see Chapter 6).

In the United States, in contrast, most new parents tend to rely on their own resources and take advantage of sick leave, unpaid leave, and part-time work to make it through the transition of having a new baby. Pregnant employed women are increasingly likely to keep working as long as they can and to return to work as soon after the birth as is practical (U.S. Bureau of the Census, 1990). A few model companies in the United States have instituted generous family leave policies on their own during the 1980s, and more than 70% of mothers who receive some form of maternity benefits return to their jobs within six months of the birth. The Family and Medical Leave Act of 1993 (U.S. Department of Labor, 1993) mandated that companies with more than 50 employees grant *unpaid* leave for up to three months, but fewer people have taken advantage of the unpaid leaves than anticipated, and many have used them to extend their own sick leaves when ill. Without leave policies that provide some income for new parents, and without job protections so that they may return to their old jobs, American parents experience high levels of stress and economic uncertainty. Mothers carry an inordinate amount of the burden. Because of expectations that mothers should do it all, and because women's wages are usually much less than men's, a sharp division of family labor based on gender tends to develop after couples have babies.

After the Baby Arrives

Several decades of research show that women take over most domestic work and become the experts at love and care once children arrive. More than fathers do, mothers provide the continuous care that babies require, often sacrificing any free or downtime they might otherwise have (LaRossa & LaRossa, 1981). As discussed in the previous chapter, women end up doing more of the overall cooking and cleaning, but they also assume major responsibility for meeting children's other needs. They spend significantly more time than fathers do feeding, dressing, cleaning, and keeping infants and toddlers safe. Studies have consistently found that mothers spend double or triple the time fathers do in these activities, although men did increase their time with children slightly during the 1970s and 1980s, especially in conventional gender-typed activities such as physical play (Baruch & Barnett, 1986a, 1986b; Lamb, 1981; Parke & Tinsley, 1984). Although most fathers do more as children get older, mothers still perform most of the direct and indirect child care.

Other people also spend significant amounts of time caring for children. In many families, but especially among African Americans, grandmothers regularly care for children. In many larger households, and especially in Mexican American families, older children play a major role in caring for younger siblings and cousins. Many children are cared for in family day care homes, usually run by a working-class mother who watches several children in addition to her own. Almost a third of preschoolers of working mothers are cared for in organized and licensed child care facilities, including day care centers, child development centers, and preschools. As discussed in Chapter 7, this form of paid care is the fastest growing care arrangement for children when mothers are on the job. Smaller, but still significant, numbers of children whose parents are well-off continue to be cared for by nannies or in-home baby-sitters. As in the past, these caregivers tend to be immigrant or younger working-class women.

Figure 4.3 shows the child care arrangements used in 1993 for preschool-age children when their mothers were working. The type of care used is shaped, in part, by the mothers' job-scheduling requirements. For example, if the mothers have full-time jobs or work day shifts, their children are most likely to be in organized care or watched by relatives. If the mothers have part-time jobs or work nonday shifts, then the children are likely to be cared for by relatives or the fathers. Who watches the children depends on whether the mothers are married, whether the fathers or other relatives live in the home or are working, how much money is available to pay for care, the availability of care facilities, and many other factors. As children get older, many end up being on their own until their mothers, fathers, or other relatives get home from work.

FIGURE 4.3

Who Takes Care of Preschoolers When Mothers Are Employed?
SOURCE: U.S. Bureau of the Census, 1996b, Figure 3.

■ Organized Facilities (Includes day care centers, nursery schools, and preschools.)
▨ Non-Relative
◨ Other Relatives (Includes mothers, siblings, grandparents, and other relatives.)
□ Father

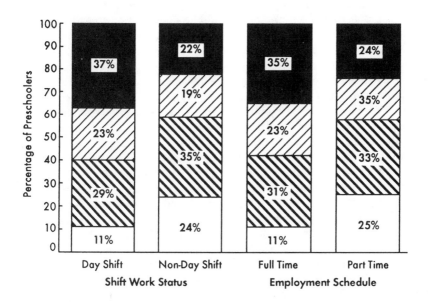

Getting someone to watch the kids is getting harder because more people than ever must work just to make ends meet. That means grandmothers or aunts who might have been available to look after the children just a few decades ago are now likely to have their own jobs. Having someone to watch the kids while parents are at work is only part of the job of parenting. The physical and material needs of the children must be met, and most mothers and fathers also want to play with their children. Effective parenting also includes setting countless limits, tending to children's emotional needs, anticipating any communication or self-esteem problems, and working to provide them with optimum learning environments. Most studies demonstrate that mothers are primarily responsible for these psychological supports, as well as for the physical aspects of child care (Ehrensaft, 1987; Hochschild, 1989; Parke, 1996). Mothers are also most likely to schedule and manage their children's social lives and to supervise child care by others. If they are around, most fathers participate in some aspects of everyday parenting, but their wives typically play a gatekeeper role, initiating and regulating the amount and type of contact children have with them.

Most research on parenting and children has focused on mothers. Guided by the ideal of separate spheres, social scientists, like the general public, assumed that understanding mother-child interaction was the key to understanding how children develop. As the next chapter shows, in the early part of the century, Sigmund Freud stressed the importance of mother-infant bonding for psychological development, leading to the popularity of concepts such as *maternal deprivation*. Freudian psychologists argued that young children needed continuous, unbroken, intimate contact with mothers or else they would become emotionally unbalanced. By the 1950s, hardly anyone bothered to ask who took care of the children. Not only did everyone assume that mothers would be solely responsible for the kids, but the concept of maternal deprivation was so thoroughly entrenched that most people assumed that severe consequences would follow if mothers were unavailable to their children on a full-time basis. As women subsequently entered the paid labor force in record numbers, however, researchers had to rethink the inherited wisdom of several decades of research. Although some early research found negative effects on children if mothers worked outside the home, most of this research failed to control for social and economic factors.

With the rapid influx of mothers into the labor market, there have been plenty of opportunities to study the effects of women's jobs on children's development. Studies of children with employed mothers show few negative effects of employment and some positive ones (Bianchi & Spain, 1986; Hoffman, 1989; Spitze, 1988). Developmental outcomes for children with employed mothers and stay-at-home mothers are roughly equivalent (Gottfried & Gottfried, 1994). Daughters with mothers who were employed when they were growing up tend to be more independent, have a stronger sense of competence, plan careers for themselves, and hold less rigid gender stereotypes (Hoffman, 1989; Moore, Spain, & Bianchi, 1984). Findings such as these support the idea that good parenting is always the product of specific social circumstances. What was good parenting in the 1920s or 1950s will not necessarily meet children's needs today.

If women enjoy their employment, they tend to be at least as good at mothering as full-time homemakers. This may be because employment generally improves women's psychological well-being. Outside employment gives women breaks from the drudgery of parenting and housework and breaks the isolation of being stuck in the home. In married-couple households, women's employment provides resources so that the power balance in the marriage is more equal. If women do not want to be employed, in contrast, or if their husbands or children voice strong opposition to it, then employment does not lead to better mental health for women (Ross, Mirowsky, & Huber, 1983). There is no evidence, however, that children must have only full-time mother care to turn out all right.

Cross-cultural studies show that women are best able to perform mothering if other people are around to help care for the children, and families in the United States seem to be moving in that direction. The Victorian ideal leads to the assumption that all children need two parents, one father and one mother, but research does not necessarily support this view. Some studies show that children of single parents turn out about the same as children of two parents, provided that the other factors influencing health and well-being are taken into account (money,

FIGURE 4.4

Single-Mother Households With Children Are Most Likely to Be Poor
SOURCE: DeVita, 1996, Table 9.

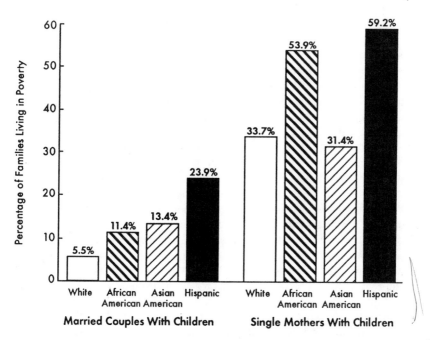

education, neighborhood, social experiences, etc.). Because so many single-parent households are poor and live under adverse circumstances, however, these sorts of comparisons are difficult to conduct. Being a mother-headed single-family household is the single best predictor of whether that household will be living in poverty (see Figure 4.4).

Most studies using large-scale surveys find that children of single mothers (and those with divorced parents) have a harder time of it than children who have two parents around to guide, teach, support, care, and pay for them (e.g., Amato, 1993; McLanahan & Booth, 1991; McLanahan & Sandefur, 1995; Seltzer, 1994). One factor that seems to make a big difference is how much time the parent (or parents) can spend with the child, which is obviously also influenced by having enough money to not have to work all the time.

Infants do need stability in their environments and some regularity in their care arrangements, but there is no evidence that the mother has to provide most or all the care. Other caregivers can be fathers, grandparents, siblings, other relatives, friends, neighbors, or paid helpers. As long as the caregivers are affectionate and consistent and meet the children's needs, children seem to turn out all right. Having several persons who regularly care for the child also seems to be an enriching experience.

Bringing the Fathers Back In

In the 1960s, a companion perspective to maternal deprivation developed that reinforced the notion of separate spheres for mothers and fathers. Researchers began to include fathers in some of their studies but focused on father absence. The idea was that families without fathers created unhealthy environments for children. Fathers were supposed to provide masculine role models for their sons, and some researchers worried that children without fathers in the home would not develop an appropriate gender identity. Others worried that without fathers to challenge them or set firm limits, children would not develop academic competence or morality. These studies have been criticized for confusing father absence with other social conditions, such as living in a bad neighborhood or being poor. Father absence studies also adopted a rigid and narrow view of appropriate gender development, assuming that social standards for masculinity that called for aggressiveness and unemotionality were normal. Many of these studies, like the new traditionalism of the 1990s, assume that teenage boys need fathers to discipline them or else they will turn out to be juvenile delinquents. Implicit in this view is the idea that boys raised exclusively by women will be more likely to turn out to be effeminate "mama's boys" rather than "manly" men (Blankenhorn, 1995; Popenoe, 1996; but compare with Connell, 1995).

Contradicting this view, social scientists have more recently discovered that having fathers around is about as likely to encourage sensitivity as it is to encourage violent aggression (Coltrane, 1996). The difference is how men (or women) interact with children and the resources they bring to the household, not just whether they live under the same roof with the children (McLanahan & Booth, 1991; Seltzer, 1994). In overall child development and well-being, whether the children's parents are married or unmarried matters little. Rather, optimum development depends on having parents or others who spend sufficient time with the children and provide the children with the resources that they need.

Starting in the 1970s, psychologists and sociologists began to report that a new fatherhood ideal was gaining in popularity (Fein, 1978; Furstenberg, 1988; LaRossa, 1988; Parke & Tinsley, 1984). Films such as *Kramer vs. Kramer, Mr. Mom, Three Men and a Baby,* and *Mrs. Doubtfire* celebrated men's love for children, even if the men they pictured were initially shown as comically inept parents. By the 1980s, television comedies such as *Full House* and *Who's the Boss* began to show men as loving fathers and relatively competent housekeepers, although they routinely demonstrated their ignorance, requiring coaching from the women and children around them. By the end of the 1980s, even more fathers than mothers were on television commercials, with more men than ever shown cuddling babies and pushing strollers (Coltrane & Allan, 1994). These images provide parents with new models for father-child relationships, although some scholars argue that they create unrealistic expectations in their wives (LaRossa, 1988).

Just as contradictions are embedded in romantic images of self-sacrificing mothers and priceless children, the modern ideal of the "new" father carries some hidden messages. Some scholars suggest that the image of sensitive and involved fathers can be considered a new class icon because it sets middle-class fathers apart from working-class and ethnic minority fathers, who present a more "masculine" image (Connell, 1995; Hondagneu-Sotelo, 1994; Messner, 1993). Other commentators suggest that images of new fathers are more widespread than actual practice (LaRossa, 1988) or that sensitive men's androgynous parenting styles may lead to gender identity confusion in their sons (Blankenhorn, 1995).

During the 1970s, when the new fatherhood ideal came on the scene, developmental psychologists began to focus on what fathers actually do in families. Until that time, following the old separate spheres ideal, virtually everyone assumed that men would not want to participate directly in child care and that most men were not capable of daily hands-on parenting. Most research focused on infants and preschoolers, and results showed that men were interested in and capable of caring for young children (Parke, 1981, 1996). Following an individual differences research tradition in psychology, many studies also focused on sex differences in parenting style. Fathers were found to be more likely than mothers to engage in rough-and-tumble play, to give more attention to sons than daughters, and to treat boys and girls differently. In addition, fathers tended to be more directive in their interactions with children than were mothers. Mothers tended to give more frequent verbal encouragement and fewer direct orders and interacted more similarly with boys and girls (Lamb, 1981; Parke, 1988, 1996; for more on how parents socialize children, see Chapter 5).

Another difference that emerged from later studies of fathers and mothers was that men and women perform child care in different settings and in conjunction with different activities. Women often perform child care in the home and are frequently engaged in multiple household tasks while simultaneously attending to children's needs or keeping track of them. Fathers, in contrast, are more likely to watch children in public settings and to take care of them as a sole activity. When American fathers talk about what they do for their children, they often talk in broad platitudes about "being there," serving as role models, promoting family values, and setting limits. When they talk about specific activities, they often mention playing with their kids, joking with them, taking them to the park, driving them to practice, helping them with homework, and teaching them skills. Sometimes, too, they will mention that they watch the kids to give their wives a break. The conventional pattern is thus for child care to be a continual and taken-for-granted task for mothers, albeit an emotionally satisfying one, that they must fit into their other obligations. For men, in contrast, child care tends to be a novel and fun distraction (Thompson & Walker, 1989).

Most parenting studies, however, have focused on households in which the father is the primary breadwinner, and the mother, even if she is employed, is the primary parent. This has tended to conflate parenting style with gender, reinforcing the notion that women and men naturally do it differently. More recent studies show that parenting is a complex and contradictory endeavor, no matter who does it. To decide if most of the observed differences in caretaking style between fathers and mothers result from biology, personality, social constraints, or something else, social scientists have begun to conduct more detailed studies (Coltrane, 1996; Parke, 1996).

As noted above, mothers have assumed responsibility for the day-to-day feeding and supervising of younger children and usually provide all children with emotional and physical comfort. But men are capable of doing these tasks, even for the smallest infant, and when they do, they develop the skills necessary to be successful parents. Even the care and attentive love that we think of as "mothering" can be performed by fathers, but it is less common to see men doing these sorts of nurturing activities (Coltrane, 1989; Risman, 1986; Ruddick, 1989). Regardless of who "mothers," the experience of everyday parenting generates a contradictory mix of emotions. On the one hand, everyday parenting is monotonous, irritating, and stressful. This is because the tasks associated with parenting are repetitive and never ending and because children's dependency and self-centeredness can be vexing. At the same time, interacting with children and helping them develop can be the most profoundly rewarding job in life. Caring for children on a regular basis makes one feel needed and can provide a sense of fulfillment rarely available through other activities. Thus, because parenting is simultaneously frustrating and meaningful, it is a unique source of ambivalence for most mothers. It is also increasingly a source of ambivalence for fathers, who were once expected to stay aloof from everyday tasks but who are now expected to participate more directly in parenting.

Although the results of most large studies looking for changes in men's assumption of family work have not matched the new fatherhood ideals, a few smaller-scale studies described men who were nurturant, caring, and emotionally attuned to their children (e.g., Coltrane, 1989; Pruett, 1987; Radin, 1982; Risman, 1986; Russell, 1983). Survey research using large representative samples also reported small, but significant, increases in the average amount of time contemporary American fathers spent with their children in the late 1980s and early 1990s (Goldscheider & Waite, 1991; O'Connell, 1993; J. Pleck, 1983). Because of increasing levels of female labor force participation, married-couple parents are increasingly likely to work different shifts and to alternate routine child care between them (Presser, 1986, 1988, 1989). As Figure 4.3 shows, when mothers are on the job, fathers (and other relatives) are increasingly likely to watch the children (Hoffman, 1989; Moen, 1992; O'Connell, 1993; U.S. Bureau of the Census, 1996b). Some studies show that when married women with children are employed regularly, their husbands contribute about a third of the total child care hours (note that Figure 4.3 shows a lower percentage of father caregiving because it includes many nonmarried households; see Goldscheider & Waite, 1991; Pleck, 1987). Some reviewers suggest that men's increased time with children is still spent in direct interaction or as helpers, rather than as equally responsible caregivers, but the trend is toward more time with their children (Lamb, 1981; Marsiglio, 1993; Pleck, 1987).

When husbands share child care and other aspects of family work with their wives, employed women escape total responsibility for the "second shift" (Hochschild, 1989) and enjoy better mental health (Kessler & McRae, 1982; Ross, Mirowsky, & Huber, 1983). When fathers assume responsibility for children, they grow emotionally and develop sensitivities that have been assumed to come with being mothers (Parke, 1996). If men are routine caregivers of young children, they emphasize verbal interaction and use subtle cues as mothers do rather than engaging in rough-and-tumble play and giving orders as conventional fathers do.

Perhaps even more important, they begin to treat sons and daughters more similarly. In addition, most studies show that children with actively involved fathers thrive intellectually and emotionally and develop more balanced gender stereotypes and expectations (Biller, 1993; Chodorow, 1978; Radin, 1994). Sharing the parenting is also associated with less discrimination against women in legal, political, and economic matters (Chafetz, 1990; Coltrane, 1988).

At the same time that some men are spending more time with their children, a growing number of men never see their kids. This results from the rise in nonmarital childbirth and continuing high levels of divorce. Because many men do not marry the mothers of their children, get divorced, move out, or fade away without making regular child support payments, the United States also has an epidemic of "deadbeat dads." Like the image of the new father, the symbol of the deadbeat dad gained swift acceptance because of widespread media coverage, although both images probably outpaced men's actual behaviors. The incidence of both "good dads" and "bad dads" is expected to continue to rise (Furstenberg, 1988). This is because both are responses to the same underlying sociological trends, including women's increased labor force participation and the changing nature of marriage (Coltrane, 1996).

Prospects for the Future

In the last part of the 20th century, the United States has seen the development of new family forms and practices and will see even more changes as we move into the new millennium. The loving but stern and distant moralist father, exemplified by Gandhi in his letter to his son, is no longer the dominant ideal in American society. As the economy continues to restructure, the family wage is becoming a thing of the past. The good provider role is getting harder to fill, and more men are realizing that they cannot be sole breadwinners and paternalistic family protectors. As a result, more men will forsake marriage altogether. Others will continue trying to enact the old ideals in a changing world. Insofar as they continue to enjoy access to wealth and prestige, they will be able to continue being on the receiving end of women's care and concern. For others, however, the marriage bargain will become a more equal enterprise. Many men will react to the recent social and economic changes by taking on more of the family work and becoming playmates to their children. Some will share more completely in providing the care that was formerly done by women. New ideals will coexist with the old as men struggle to get their needs met and to meet the needs of other men, women, and children.

Similarly, the isolated homemaker ideal is no longer dominant. The idea of compulsory motherhood is weakening as more women remain in the labor force, postpone marriage, choose not to marry, and elect to remain childless. Even more important, the relationship between marriage and childbearing has loosened, as increasing numbers of women are deciding to become parents without husbands. In the face of continued high levels of divorce, custody and stepparenting arrangements are becoming more common and more complex (see Chapter 6). We will not see a wholesale retreat from caring by women, however. They will continue to provide the majority of care to children, husbands, the sick, the frail, and each other. At the same time, as their earnings and attachment to careers come to resemble those of men, women's patterns of giving and receiving care will move closer to those of men, as men's will to theirs.

The overall trend is thus for gender to become less of a prescription for family roles and life chances. The move is toward uncoupling gender from caring. This uncoupling will be neither swift nor complete, but even if it were, it would not mean that the family would necessarily become less important to most Americans or that children would not be cared for. Following long-term trends, people will continue to expect more from families and close relationships than in the past. This is because the family is our most highly valued social institution and because we will continue to depend on it for our sense of identity and security. Before we hastily conclude that gender differences will disappear, however, we need to take a closer look at how children learn about gender in the first place and at the social and psychological consequences of gender differentiation.

CHAPTER 5

Engendering Children

The vast majority of American parents in the 1950s earnestly believed that the world was naturally, inevitably, and beneficially divided into two mutually exclusive categories—male and female. Because the notion of complementary sex difference was so taken for granted, most parents did not stop to question that there might be negative impacts associated with turning their sons into manly men and their daughters into girlish women. This was the way things were supposed to be.

Because they loved their children and wanted them to fit in, parents dressed their boys in pants and their girls in dresses. They gave their boys trucks and balls to play with and gave their daughters dolls and tea sets. If, as often happened, a boy played with dolls, he could be chastised and called a "sissy" or, alternately, steered away from such activities under some pretense. Pretty soon, he would get the message. If a girl wanted to wear pants, climb trees, and play ball, she was often tolerated—up to a point. It was OK to be a tomboy as long as she still dressed up in her fancy dress for church on Sunday. But if she tried to carry such activities beyond her childhood years and into her teens, she was likely to get a good talking to. The advice she got was often about the difficulties of getting a boy to notice her unless she made herself pretty and started acting "like a lady."

But, you might protest, that was many decades ago, and we are way past the days of telling girls to act dumb so that boys will feel smart. The women's movement changed all that, . . . didn't it? In this chapter, I will begin to address that question by exploring how children are raised today. Does gender just naturally develop in children, or do they acquire it in interaction with their parents? It will probably come as no surprise that parents' actions make a big difference, and you already know that gender is socially constructed. But you might be surprised to learn that even people who believe strongly that women and men are equal often end up paying more attention to their sons than to their daughters. For all their good intentions, parents are still part of the larger culture, and they often unwittingly pass on ideas about gender inequality via subtle and indirect actions. Children develop ideas about gender through observation and imitation, by doing the little things children do in their daily lives, and by noticing parents' and others' reactions to them. In this chapter, I explore how these processes work and ask what might happen if we changed the way we raised children.

Images of Childhood Gender Difference

Differences between boys and girls are assumed to be natural, but most of these differences must be taught. Later in the chapter, I review studies that describe what parents are doing today to teach children about gender. First, however, I focus on some old messages about gender from the popular culture and outline psychological and sociological theories of gender acquisition.

Fairy tales are stories that are told to young people for their enjoyment and education. All cultures have different versions of such stories, and similar tales have appeared in different countries of Europe, Asia, and North America dating back several centuries. Most fairy tales work with polarities of good and bad, beautiful and ugly, and tell of the adventures of a hero or heroine who overcomes supernatural forces to reach a lofty goal. In the modern, sanitized versions of such tales (most produced by Walt Disney Studios), the hero also wins the girl and they live happily ever after. Most children know about *Cinderella, Snow White, Beauty and the Beast, the Little Mermaid,* and so on through animated movies, whereas tales such as *Jack and the Beanstalk, Little Red Riding Hood,* and *The Three Little Pigs* are more often read aloud to children or recited from memory as in past times. These morality tales teach about good and evil, but they also carry implicit messages about gender. By paying attention to who gets to be the hero and who needs rescuing, we can see that men and women are rarely interchangeable in such tales and that the boys generally get the good parts. Although these tales are not presented as true, children take them much more literally than do adults, primarily because young children are less able to distinguish between what is real and what is fantasy.

Nursery rhymes are an even older form of oral tradition containing implicit messages about gender. These short poems are recited or sung to entertain young children (in repeated, ritual fashion). They often contain a single verse, sometimes more, and are usually anonymous. Some of the earliest published nursery rhymes in the English language appeared in a collection called *Mother Goose's Melody* in 1760. Many other versions of Mother Goose have appeared since then in Europe and America. Often, the original intent or specific social meaning of the rhyme have been lost, but they live on through repetition. Like fairy tales, however, they provide a template for seeing and thinking about gender.

The World According to Mother Goose

Boys	*Girls*
What are little boys made of, made of?	*What are little girls made of, made of?*
What are little boys made of?	*What are little girls made of?*
Frogs and snails	*Sugar and spice*
And puppy-dog tails,	*And all things nice,*
That's what little boys are made of.	*That's what little girls are made of.*

Boys

*Little Jack Horner
Sat in the corner;
Eating a Christmas Pie;
He put in his thumb;
And pulled out a plum;
And said, What a good boy am I!*

*Georgie Porgie, pudding and pie;
Kissed the girls and made them cry;
When the boys came out to play;
Georgie Porgie ran away.*

*Ding, dong, bell;
Pussy's in the well.
Who put her in?
Little Johnny Green.
Who pulled her out?
Little Tommy Stout.
What a naughty boy was that
To try to drown poor pussy cat;
Who never did him any harm;
And killed the mice in his father's barn.*

*When I was a little boy
My mama kept me in;
Now I am a great big boy
I'm fit to serve the king;
I can handle a musket;
And I can smoke a pipe;
And I can kiss a bonny girl
At twelve o'clock at night.*

Men

*Peter, Peter, pumpkin eater;
Had a wife and couldn't keep her;
He put her in a pumpkin shell
And there he kept her very well.*

Girls

*Little Miss Muffet
Sat on a tuffet,
Eating her curds and whey;
There came a big spider,
Who sat down beside her
And frightened Miss Muffet away.*

*There was a little girl,
and she had a little curl,
Right in the middle of her forehead;
When she was good,
she was very, very good,
But when she was bad she was horrid.*

*Mary, Mary, quite contrary,
How does your garden grow?
With silver bells and cockle shells,
And pretty maids all in a row.*

*Little Polly Flinders
Sat among the cinders,
Warming her pretty little toes;
Her mother came and caught her
And spanked her little daughter
For spoiling her nice new clothes.*

*Polly, Dolly, Kate, and Molly,
All are filled with pride and folly.
Polly tattles, Dolly wriggles,
Katy rattles, Molly giggles;
Whoever knew such constant rattling,
Wriggling, giggling, noise, and tattling.*

Women

*There was an old woman
who lived in a shoe,
She had so many children
she didn't know what to do;
She gave them some broth
without any bread;
She whipped them all soundly
and put them to bed.*

Excerpted from *The Real Mother Goose*, 1916, pp. 13, 20, 26, 32, 39, 84, 90, 98, 108.

What messages do children get about gender from these ritualized rhymes? Girls are sweet, cute, and prone to wriggle, giggle, and tattle. They need to remember to keep their clothes clean, are easily frightened, and although generally good, can be very bad. Boys, on the other hand, are rough, tough, and mischievous. They are proud of themselves, take risks, want to be grown up, and like to kiss girls (sometimes against their will). As for grown men, besides smoking a pipe, handling a musket, and serving the king, like Peter, they need to keep their wives, even if they have to lock them up in a pumpkin to do it. Mothers, if the old woman in the shoe is any guide, are too busy worrying about their many children to do much else.

Like the characters in fairy tales (or even those in modern cartoons, movies, and comic books), these nursery rhyme personalities are more stereotyped by gender than most real people. But that is intentional. These stories teach young people the cultural standards for masculinity and femininity. Many are cautionary tales about what happens when one violates those cultural standards. Most portray conventional heterosexual relations, but there are a few exceptions. Consider, for example, the following *Mother Goose* rhyme about two young men:

> *Robin and Richard were two pretty men,*
> *They lay in bed till the clock struck ten;*
> *Then up starts Robin and looks at the sky,*
> *"Oh, brother Richard, the sun's very high!*
> *You go before, with the bottle and bag,*
> *And I will come after on little Jack Nag."*

Excerpted from *The Real Mother Goose*, 1916, p. 20.

Although these "brothers" get to lounge in bed together until midmorning, there is a cautionary element to their gay tale. After they realize that it is late, they devise a plan to depart separately—presumably so they will not be seen together and identified as lovers. This example reminds us that popular culture, like real life, does not necessarily conform to conventional standards for gender relations, sexuality, or other social practices. Literature, songs, and theater, from Shakespeare and Mother Goose to modern rock music and performance art, frequently expose and exploit the contradictions between social norms and human lives. For ironic art forms to work, however, the audience needs to be aware of the conventional taken-for-granted social expectations. Instilling conventional expectations in boys and girls is what gender socialization is all about.

Theories of Gender Socialization

Social scientists have long been concerned with how children grow and develop and how they become fully functioning adult members of society. This process of socialization happens in many ways and in many different contexts, but it is generally assumed that the most important processes begin in the family. Children also develop and learn about life through other means, but most theories assume that parents, or other regular adult caregivers, are the major socializing agents for developing children. This reflects the idea that although people continue to change and learn throughout life, it is during childhood that they acquire enduring personality characteristics, interpersonal skills, and social values (Maccoby, 1992).

In the early part of the century, little attention was spent on documenting how and why children developed specific gender-linked traits, but during the 1950s and 1960s, social scientists began to pay more attention to the role of parents in shaping childhood gender (Maccoby, 1992). As noted in the previous chapter, researchers were primarily interested in figuring out how parents could make sure that boys would turn out masculine and girls feminine. In other words, the social theories and psychological studies of the day were concerned with helping children occupy their "proper" or "natural" place in the family and in society. These theories and studies about gender, like all forms of knowledge, were products of cultural understandings prevalent at the time. Not surprisingly, the 1950s suburban ideal of separate spheres shaped how researchers, doctors, social workers, religious leaders, and parents thought about children's needs. In general, there was a consensus among the experts that boys and girls should be treated differently, that this differential treatment was normal, and that it would benefit the entire society.

Since the 1970s, a new set of ideas about gender have entered into popular and scientific debates about how children should be raised. As a result of social movements focusing on equal rights for minorities and women, people began to question how child-rearing techniques might promote prejudice and perpetuate inequality. The new ideas about gender that emerged focused on how rigid and polarized stereotypes prohibited boys and girls from developing their full human potential. This was a switch from the earlier idea that boys needed manly role models and girls needed stay-at-home moms, or else they would be misfits in society. It also reflects a shift toward valuing individualism and emotional expression in children as well as in adults. The movement toward more gender-neutral child rearing continued to gain popularity throughout the 1980s and 1990s, although some conservative countermovements advocated the continuation of corporal punishment and sex segregation in schools.

Because the old ideal of separate spheres has not disappeared, debates about the proper way to raise children continue to be heard within individual families, in churches, and in political campaigns. Hoping to gain support for the political agendas they support, some social scientists focus on a "decline in family values" to argue that boys and girls should be raised differently and that only married heterosexual couples should raise children. The underlying assumption of such arguments is that boys and girls need different things, that women are better at raising children than are men, that women need husbands, and that all children need to be raised by their biological parents. These separate spheres arguments are predicated on the false assumption that anatomical sex is the same thing as gender (e.g., Blankenhorn, 1995; Popenoe, 1996; but compare with Stacey, 1996).

In contrast, a general consensus has developed among social scientists that sex and gender are not the same thing and that both men and women are capable of performing almost any task. Sexual identity and the choice of sex partners may be somewhat shaped by biological factors, but they are also influenced by the cultural categories available for describing, experiencing, and understanding such things. Gender, on the other hand, is almost wholly a social and cultural creation and is therefore subject to change. The most recent research on sex and gender suggests that the relationship between the two is far more complicated and malleable than was previously assumed by more biologically based models of human behavior (for reviews, see Bleier, 1984; Butler, 1990; Epstein, 1988).

Despite any biological predispositions that males and females might have, and despite the religious convictions or political beliefs that people hold, everyone is subject to the larger cultural and economic shifts that have been occurring throughout this century. The changes that have moved U.S. society toward more equality between men and women have also moved us toward more gender-neutral styles of child rearing. Experts continue to argue about whether true shared parenting is possible, and how much difference it would make if parents began to treat sons and daughters similarly, but most agree that families are slowly moving in that direction (Coltrane, 1996; Ehrensaft, 1987; Segal, 1990).

Child Socialization

To evaluate conflicting arguments about gender acquisition in the family, one needs to understand how parents and others influence their children's development. Older individualized models of childhood socialization provided by Freud, Piaget, and their followers from the earlier part of the 20th century were both social and biological, and although they differed from each other, most included the basic idea that individual children passed through a set of predetermined stages of increasing competence and self-regulation. More social theories, such as those of Durkheim and Mead, focused on how the structure and functioning of society were maintained because children eventually internalized common norms governing thought, emotion, and action. Whether socialization theories were focused on the individual or on the social structural level of analysis, they described how young people gradually become competent members of a specific culture (see Bem, 1993; Goodman, 1985; Peterson & Rollins, 1987).

Virtually all theories of socialization have agreed that the major experiences shaping children's identity occur within families, although most recognize that children are also socialized by schools, churches, the media, peer groups, and other social institutions. As a microcosm of society, families locate children within a social structure and provide a first exposure to culture. The simple fact of being born into a family provides a particular set of socialization experiences for children. These experiences include where they live, what they eat, whom they see, what they wear, how they talk, what type of medical care they get, what type of work they do, and a host of other small and large things. These experiences are important because to a large extent, they determine children's living conditions and life chances as they grow up. Sociologists summarize these types of influences on socialization by talking about the social class, ethnicity, or composition of the families into which children are born (Collins & Coltrane, 1995; Peterson & Rollins, 1987).

Families are also important because they provide the children's first exposure to interaction with other humans. Compared with other animals, all humans are born premature, insofar as they are born with awkwardly functioning bodies and only partly developed brains. Consequently, human newborns need significant amounts of care and attention to survive. Many other animals have the ability to learn how to live in the world in a matter of days or months, but human babies need to grow and develop for many years before they can be self-sufficient and assume their place in society. Although different cultures expect children to do different things at different ages, human children cannot survive without the care of their parents or other adults for the first few years of their lives. Children's extreme dependence on others makes the socialization that occurs in families particularly salient and is one of the major reasons that adult-child relationships remain emotionally charged well into adult life (Maccoby, 1992).

Not all families look alike, of course, and most societies have had families that are larger and less isolated than the American version (mostly contained in smaller and more collective dwellings). This means that children have typically grown up interacting with more people and observing more adults than contemporary American children do. Regardless of how living arrangements differ, however, babies have usually developed the capacity to roll over, sit up, crawl, walk, and run in family settings. Similarly, children learn how to recognize faces, make gestures, and eventually to talk by interacting with family members and other people in the immediate household. Not only do most developmental processes unfold in such contexts, but children also first learn the meaning of authority and gain awareness of what is acceptable and unacceptable behavior within the family and in other daily caregiving situations. As children grow, the importance of the family decreases somewhat, and the importance of the peer group, schools, and other socializing agents increases. Most researchers agree, however, that the family (or more precisely the household in which the children spend the most time) remains the primary socializing agent for children at least until the teenage years (Maccoby, 1992; Peterson & Rollins, 1987).

Socialization can be seen as a holistic process of turning children into "cultural natives" (Bem, 1993, p. 139). Children (and adults) end up feeling as if they belong in their culture because their daily lives are organized in similar ways and because they use the same frameworks for seeing the world. Becoming a cultural native is a subtle process that happens with little effort. As individuals grow and develop and participate in similar types of social rituals, they adopt culturally approved cognitive lenses and emotional capacities that allow them to "see" and "feel" the same social reality (see also Berger, 1963; Geertz, 1973; Shweder & Levine, 1984).

Children are not socialized primarily through direct and explicit instruction. Rather, ways of understanding and thinking are transmitted in a continuing and unconscious way, so that preferred cultural understandings are the only ones that seem possible. The culture does not get transferred directly into the heads of passive children as if they were empty vessels waiting to be filled with knowledge.

Instead, they learn culturally appropriate ways of thinking and being as they follow routine rituals and respond to the everyday demands of the world in which they live. Because they are active, pattern-seeking beings, children both create and assimilate the culture around them as they grow and develop. They do not learn how to be cultural natives all at once but gradually decipher the meanings embedded in social practices a little at a time, eventually establishing a set of behaviors and an identity that allow them to fit into their social surroundings (Bem, 1993).

Socialization is thus a delicate interplay between how daily life is structured, how people perceive it, and how they react to their circumstances. The same can be said for gender socialization. Because everyday practices are based, to a large extent, on a gendered division of labor and on culturally accepted notions of appropriate gender behavior, children assimilate and shape the meaning of gender as they go through normal steps in their development. What they do, how they feel about themselves, and what they become are influenced in important ways by the organization of gender in the family and in the larger society.

Separating Boys and Girls

There is not room in this chapter to cover all that researchers know about how baby boys are turned into men and baby girls into women (for more complete reviews, see Bem, 1993; Huston, 1983). Nevertheless, a few of the most influential ideas about how children acquire gender deserve attention. The most important insight from research on gender socialization is that because boys and girls are treated differently and put into different learning environments, they develop different needs, wants, desires, skills, and temperaments; in short, they become different types of people—men and women—who hardly question why they are different or how they ended up that way.

Although the specific social and psychological processes through which gender socialization occurs are the subject of much debate, the basic underlying model is that of the self-fulfilling prophecy (Bem, 1993; Merton, 1948; Rosenthal & Jacobson, 1968). Because people think boys and girls are supposed to be different, they treat them differently and give them different opportunities for development. This differential treatment promotes certain behaviors and self-images that re-create the preconceived cultural stereotypes about gender. The process repeats itself over and over in an unending spiral across the generations, so that although gender stereotypes are being constantly re-created and modified, they seem natural and impervious to change.

The self-fulfilling prophecy is more complicated than this simple summary suggests, but the basic idea remains the same: Treat boys and girls differently, and they become different. This fits nicely with the social constructionist idea of doing gender introduced earlier in this book. It is not just that boys and girls are naturally and fundamentally different in some unchanging way. Rather, to be considered competent members of society, they must learn how to fit in as appropriately gendered individuals. This is not an optional process. Because gender is so important to the adults in our society, children are called on to conform to the gender standards currently in force. For children to develop identities, they must also develop gender identities, and they must work to make their actions and thoughts conform to what the people around them expect. Children literally "claim" gender identities as they interact with adults and other children (Cahill, 1986; Thorne, 1993). This concept of doing gender, which is something that both children and adults are required to do, helps us see that gender is not something innate but rather something that must continually be re-created (West & Fenstermaker, 1993; West & Zimmerman, 1987).

The doing gender concept alerts us to the idea that gender is not a single fixed thing. There are now, and have always been, multiple forms of masculinity and multiple forms of femininity (Connell, 1995; Lorber, 1994). What it means to be a man will be different in various types of families, depending on the family members' needs, desires, and experiences. Masculinity in a two-parent household with a Marine drill sergeant father will look different from masculinity in a fundamentalist minister's home, a gay couple's home, or a single mother's home. It will look different in an inner-city African American household from what it is in an affluent African American household in the suburbs. Masculinity will not mean the same thing in a Mexican immigrant family as it does in a fifth-generation middle-class Chicano family. The dominant popular cultural ideal of a "real" man, whether from action movies or fairy tales, will undoubtedly be at odds with actual men's experiences. As a consequence, boys (and men) end up constructing a private and personal manhood from their own experiences and the images, ideals, and expectations of their social surroundings.

To describe gender as socially constructed in this way does not mean that most people believe they have choices about it, or even that they give it much thought at all. We rarely question how our identities are tied up with the meaning of gender, and most of us are unaware of how gender shapes our expectations for children. But in countless little ways, beginning before babies are even born, we make gender so important that it is impossible for children to ignore. I recently asked a newly pregnant woman I had just met if she was going to have her doctor perform a test (amniocentesis) to determine the sex of her baby. She replied that she always thought she would want to be surprised at the birth, but for practical reasons, she was going to have the test done. I asked what was practical about it, and she said, "If I know the sex, then I can get all the right kinds of clothes and work on setting up the nursery, and all of that." She reasoned that she could not get started acquiring physical things for the baby until she knew the baby's sex. To her, girl babies had to be dressed in pink frilly outfits right from the start, and everything from her crib, to her toys, to the paint on the wall had to be for a girl. She explained that this would save money and time because people could give the "right" baby gifts, she could buy the "right" items, and she would not be bothered with returning the "wrong" stuff. Although the needs of newborn girls and newborn boys are identical, this mother-to-be took for granted that they *must* be treated differently. Her belief in gender difference was so central to her thinking that she was willing to undergo a painful medical procedure—one that significantly increases the chances of a miscarriage—all for decorating purposes!

Our gender prescriptions (what boys should do and what girls should do) and our gender proscriptions (what boys shouldn't do and what girls shouldn't do) become so habitual that we rarely concern ourselves with them. So, although doing gender is a constant and continuing process, it does not seem that way. Our sense of gender is so built in to our everyday activities that it takes on a life of its own. In a basic sense, it becomes a lens through which we see the world. This gender lens gets transmitted to children without parents even noticing.

Although I am focusing on babies and young children in this chapter, socialization is not limited to childhood. Socialization never stops because adults continue to be faced with social pressures to adopt appropriate behaviors and thoughts. Still, the dependence of children on adults and their need to develop a sense of self in interaction with others make them especially likely to internalize messages about gender from the larger culture. How does this internalization come about?

In the following discussion, I focus on two social psychological theories that attempt to explain how gender understandings structure feeling and thinking: one psychoanalytic and one cognitive. These two explanations focus attention on different aspects of the process of acquiring gender lenses and maintaining gender differences. They show how gender can be simultaneously socially constructed and deeply embedded in personalities. The theories also remind us that the internalized psychic structures that make gender seem so fixed can change as the social, economic, and family conditions that shape them undergo their own transformations.

Psychoanalytic Gender Theory

In the late 1800s and early 1900s, Dr. Sigmund Freud treated his patients' physical and emotional ailments through a radical new talking therapy called psychoanalysis, which used free association and the interpretation of patients' dreams. According to Freud, it was necessary to look below the surface of normal everyday talk and activity to uncover unconscious mental processes. For example, most people have heard the term *Freudian slip*, referring to times when persons embarrass themselves by mistakenly using the wrong word (usually one with a sexual meaning). For instance, a person might be making small talk, trying to ask whether the attractive waiter or waitress was making much money in tips that evening, but instead blurt out, "How are your *lips* tonight?" According to psychoanalytic theory, the lips slip reveals a desire that the conscious mind did not want to reveal or maybe did not even realize it had. Freud focused on these sorts of hidden thoughts, emotions, and sexual urges that people usually try to keep submerged below the surface of consciousness. According to Freud, we must understand these deep psychological workings if we want to understand how children develop into adults with a normal sexual identity.

Many of Freud's (1905/1938, 1924) theories about child development and the unconscious originated during the prudish Victorian era when sex was a taboo subject. His early ideas focus on the importance of repressed sexual feelings in the developing child. According to Freud, every child has unconscious emotional needs and erotic feelings that emerge in relation to the mother and develop in interaction with others. Because many of these thoughts and feelings threaten to overwhelm the child, Freud said that the child represses them into the unconscious during normal stages of development. Infant sexuality, in Freud's terms, was *polymorphously perverse*, meaning that it took many forms, was not focused on one body part, and was not necessarily directed toward a heterosexual partner. The theory did not assume that just because a boy infant has a penis, he would automatically develop a male sexual identity and be sexually attracted to females. According to Freud, such things are formed in the interplay of sexual attractions between child and mother and go through various stages or complexes that must be successfully resolved. In the oral stage, for example, the child's sexual urges are focused on the act of sucking, whereas in the anal stage, they are focused on the withholding and expelling of feces. During the phallic stage, the normal child is supposed to recognize genital differences and develop feelings of attraction toward the mother (or father). In the so-called Oedipus complex, boys renounce their erotic love for the mother because they come to fear the father's jealousy. According to Freud, this process helps boys develop a superego (a sort of moral conscience) and allows them to transfer their sexual urges toward adult women. Freud had much more trouble explaining the psychosexual development of girls, who were supposed to transfer their early sexual urges toward the mother to the father and men.

Many of the specifics of Freud's developmental framework have been challenged and discredited through the years. For example, both psychoanalysts and feminists have pointed out not only that things such as "penis envy" and the "castration complex" are relatively rare among girls but that Freud's whole analytic scheme treated boys and men as normal and girls and women as deficient. Nevertheless, Freud's basic insights about the unconscious mind and sexual or erotic impulses have become part of our cultural stock of knowledge, and many psychologists and even feminist theorists have used them to try to understand the psychology of sex and gender (Chodorow, 1978; Erikson, 1950; Mitchell, 1974).

Psychoanalytic ideas are now so integrated into modern ways of thinking that many people do not even realize that Freud popularized them. For example, terms such as *unconscious, subconscious, repressed, neurotic, hysterical, id, ego, superego,* and *Oedipus complex* are commonly used throughout the Western world. Although it was not necessarily true during Freud's day, the medical profession now even acknowledges that the mind can cause a range of emotional and physical symptoms—called psychosomatic illnesses. In addition, modern versions of talking therapies that originated with psychoanalysis are now common treatments for many family problems and psychological disorders. Freud's ideas are not necessarily popular with psychologists who work in university settings today, however; most research-oriented psychologists reject psychoanalysis in favor of more rational models of human behavior and scientific experiments that isolate specific causal variables.

Freud's ideas are too complex and debates about them too numerous to cover in detail here, but one offshoot of Freudian theory can help us think about how modern children learn about gender. Newer versions of psychoanalytic theory are especially helpful in figuring out why gender identity seems so fixed and stable. Freud said that children had innate sexual urges and that they learned to direct these urges toward appropriate others in the context of family interactions. Freud's theories assumed that the important interactions happened early in the child's life, that these early childhood experiences shaped the gender identity of the child, and that they set the emotional tone and shaped the psychological dilemmas faced after the child becomes an adult. Most of this happens at an unconscious level.

According to Freud, infants do not have a firm sense of individual self. At first, their sense of self is merged with the mother, and only later do they develop an autonomous self by separating from her. Because infants are usually cared for by the mother, she is symbolically and unconsciously incorporated into both boys' and girls' psyches. Because she provides suckling and care, the mother is also the first erotic love object for children of both sexes. For the child to mature and develop in sexually appropriate ways, Freud speculated that this early erotic attachment to the mother must be broken and directed outward.

Nancy Chodorow (1976, 1978, 1985) extended this part of Freudian theory, as did some other women psychoanalysts (e.g., Deutsch, 1944; Horney, 1967) and feminist theorists (Dinnerstein, 1976; Johnson, 1988; Mitchell, 1974), by placing more emphasis on early infancy and correcting for Freud's relative neglect of girls' psychological development. According to Chodorow, because girls are the same sex as their mothers, they do not need to sever the deep primary attachment to mothers in the same way that boys do. Girls are given more permission to be close and affectionate with mothers for a much longer time than are boys, and because their identity is not dependent on being different from them, they stay much closer to mothers both physically and emotionally. This means that girls can form a self without severely separating from mothers and from the internalized unconscious image of mothers that develops within them. Consequently, girls tend to develop a personality that allows them to intuitively experience the world in connection with others. According to Chodorow, girls thus retain more of the sense of merging with the world that all infants experience in the original love relationship with mothers. The "feminine" personality that subsequently develops in girls tends to direct their attention toward other people and instills in young women the desire and emotional capacities to mother in later life.

Boys, on the other hand, end up with "masculine" personalities that are more separated and independent than those of girls. This is because they are also raised by mothers but must reject them in the normal course of establishing a sense of self. Because boy babies realize that they are not like their mothers, and because they are treated differently by mothers, they establish an identity based on being different from mothers. According to the theory, because boys have internalized mothers in early infancy and experienced them as the first erotic love object, they must distance themselves from a deep part of their own psyches as well as from the actual mothers. This results in boys and men who experience the world as fundamentally separate from others. They develop more rigid ego boundaries, tend to be more distant from others, are less focused on their own and others' emotions, and are therefore more prone than are women to be instrumental and domineering. Finally, Chodorow (1976) believes that for boys to separate from mothers, they must devalue both women and what is feminine. According to other social theorists, this routinely produces men who fear their own sensitivities and makes them likely to engage in warfare and aggression (Balbus, 1983; Easlea, 1981). It also encourages men to fear anything feminine and leads directly to sexual exploitation and the rape and abuse of women because men can so easily objectify others (Benjamin, 1988; Dinnerstein, 1976; Lisak, 1991).

Chodorow's (1978) Freudian psychoanalytic theory gives a social explanation, on the basis of who does the parenting, of why men and women seem so different in a deep psychological sense. They seem to have quite different personalities and to have different emotional perceptions of the world. Men (at least stereotypically) seem to focus on things instead of people, preferring the world of action, competition, sports, machinery, work, science, and power. This preference seems deeply ingrained in their very being. Women, on the other hand, seem to focus on people and emotions, and especially on romance, family, and babies. Stereotypical women are more "relational" with more fluid ego boundaries and a greater ability and desire to merge with those around them. They prefer intimacy and warmth in personal relationships, and their identity comes more from how others receive them than from solitary pursuits or accomplishments. As with the men, this temperamental difference feels deep-seated and is resistant to change. According to Chodorow, it also provides the best explanation for why women continue to be the ones who take primary responsibility for raising children.

Chodorow's (1978) theory is a general view of how mothering is reproduced from generation to generation and how parenting practices perpetuate personality differences based on gender. The theory also suggests how current patterns might change. If men began to take on more of the parenting duties while children were still young, boy and girl babies would both start out by psychologically merging with both the mother and the father. Hypothetically, boys' and girls' paths toward independence would be more similar, and both would develop more balanced ego structures. According to the theory, the average girl would end up more assertive and independent than today, and the average boy would end up more sensitive and emotionally connected (for more on this, see also Coltrane, 1996).

Actual gender development is influenced by much more than psychological object relations, and some social scientists reject the premises of Chodorow's neo-Freudian theory. Most scholars agree that parenting practices play an important role in the development of children's gender identities, but social psychological research shows that gender-linked personality traits are less fixed and more influenced by events later in childhood or adulthood than psychoanalytic models imply (Huston, 1983; Risman, 1986; Ruddick, 1989; Spence et al., 1985). Gender theorists argue about whether personality traits should be considered the cause or the consequence of parenting practices, and some question whether the heavy emphasis on deep psychology is appropriate (Collins, Chafetz, Blumberg,

Coltrane, & Turner, 1993; Lorber, Coser, Rossi, & Chodorow, 1981). Others agree with parts of the theory but place more emphasis on biological constraints (Mead, 1949; Rossi, 1977), cross-cultural variations (e.g., Mead, 1935/1963; Whiting, 1965), or economic and social structural elements (Chafetz, 1990; Hartsock, 1983; Johnson, 1988; Lorber, 1994). Nevertheless, psychoanalytic accounts provide a provocative explanation for how deep-seated personalities and emotional lives of boys and girls come to be different and, coincidentally, how they might be changed.

Cognitive Gender Theory

Whereas psychoanalytic theories have focused on sexuality, emotions, and the unconscious mind, cognitive theories have focused on how the developing child perceives the world, processes information, and develops the capacity for rational thought. Theories in this general area of psychology are so widespread and studies so plentiful that it is impossible to summarize them here, but I can review one important variant of the cognitive approach to gender, called *gender schema theory* (Bem, 1983).

Like psychoanalysis, many cognitive theories have assumed that children will naturally and automatically become sex-typed as the result of the unfolding of internal psychological processes. Piaget (1932), Kohlberg (1966), and other cognitive theorists argued against the assumption that children learned by passively absorbing knowledge from parents and other adults around them. Instead, they assumed that children sought information from their environment and organized it in predictable ways as they aggressively tried to make sense of the world and their place within it. In other words, children were not simply passive recipients of knowledge. They were active cognitive beings who were constantly engaged in seeking patterns and figuring out categories even if their minds could grasp only certain concepts at specified ages. According to these theories, children actively develop cognitive capacities as they spontaneously construct a sense of self and learn about social rules. For Kohlberg, the nature of children's cognitive processing and the natural perceptual salience of the male-female dichotomy lead children to choose gender as a major organizing principle for social rules. For Piaget, Kohlberg, and others (Bem, 1983; Maccoby, 1992; Martin, 1993), the childhood preoperational stage leads them to think that same-sex behavior is morally re-quired and rigidly fixed.

More recently, cognitive psychologists have found that gender development is more variable than Kohlberg and others first thought and that it must be understood in a cultural context. Although children do seem to be active partici-pants in the process of gender acquisition, psychologist Sandra Bem (1993) notes that they are motivated to match their behavior to gender stereotypes only to the extent that society demands it. Her research shows that gender is not something that is naturally prominent in the minds of children but that it reflects the gender polarization in the larger culture. Her theory about this rejects the narrow ages and stages view of Piaget or Kohlberg but retains an emphasis on how children process information about the world as they develop increasingly complex cognitive and reasoning skills.

Bem (1983) focuses on the development of a cognitive structure called a *schema*. A schema is a way of organizing information in the mind—a type of human computer program for collecting, sorting, processing, and storing information according to predetermined categories. A schema allows individuals to impose structure and meaning onto a vast array of incoming stimuli, but it is also highly selective. Bem (1993) suggests that gender *schematicity*

> is the imposition of a gender-based classification on social reality, the sorting of persons, attributes, behaviors, and other things on the basis of the polarized definitions of masculinity and femininity that prevail in the culture, rather than on the basis of other dimensions that could serve equally well. (p. 125)

It is a perceptual lens that predisposes individuals to see the world in two neatly defined opposites—male and female, masculinity and femininity.

According to gender schema theory, when the culture (language, art, customs, economy, polity, etc.) is stereotyped according to gender, children become gender schematic without even realizing it. They develop networks of associations that guide their perceptions, so that they come to see the world in gender-polarized ways. Bem (1983) notes that a gender schema is anticipatory, promoting a readiness to search for and assimilate information if it fits with the schema. Gender categories or "equivalence classes" can incorporate a variety of information and implicitly force individuals to ignore other ways of categorizing people or things. For example, terms such as *tender* and *nightingale* might spontaneously be placed in a feminine category, whereas terms such as *assertive* and *eagle* might be placed in a masculine category (p. 604).

Bem's theory forges important links between gender polarization in the larger culture, the organization of everyday life, and the child's developing view of the world. Gender polarization organizes the daily lives of children from the moment they are born: from pink versus blue to dolls versus trucks. The overriding importance of the male-female distinction is communicated to children in the different ways adults talk to boys and girls, the different social experiences adults provide children, and the different expectations adults have for them. Children learn that virtually everything in their world can and should be classified according to gender. A gender schema is not just something that people can use if they want to, according to Bem, but a culturally mandated way of viewing the world. By being programmed into the very ways of perceiving and thinking, gender becomes unavoidable (see also Kessler & McKenna, 1985; West & Zimmerman, 1987).

Gender polarization means more than just different toys or clothes for boys and girls because, ultimately, every child learns to apply gender schematicity to the self. Children evaluate their own thoughts, feelings, and actions according to the gender polarization they observe in the culture and come to see themselves according to its rigid either/or dichotomy. They tend to favor those traits and behaviors that seem to fit the gender schema and avoid those that do not. They learn that it is inappropriate for girls to desire autonomy and power and for boys to desire intimacy or have feelings of vulnerability, and they enact these stereotypical scripts in their daily lives. Thus, according to Bem's (1983) cognitive approach, children's self-concepts become gender stereotyped and "the two sexes become, in their own eyes, not only different in degree, but different in kind" (p. 604).

The idea of a gender schema organizing our perceptions and our social world is a persuasive one. Most research supports the idea that children develop cognitive frameworks and gender scripts that reflect cultural values and shape future behavior (Martin, 1993; Signorella, Bigler, & Liben, 1993). A person with a polarized gender schema is more likely than others to notice and pay attention to things that fit the schema and to quickly store that information in memory according to its link with gender. As Bem (1983) notes, "sex-typed individuals" (those with polarized gender schemata) "have a greater readiness than do non-sex-typed individuals to encode information in terms of the sex-linked associations that constitute the gender schema" (p. 607). People with polarized gender schemas are also significantly faster at endorsing gender-appropriate attributes and rejecting gender-inappropriate attributes than are others (p. 608). Bem also found that individuals who describe themselves as more gender stereotyped sort information into categories on the basis of gender, even when other categories would work better for sorting the information. This leads people to exaggerate gender differences and to ignore those things that are similar between men and women.

Other researchers have confirmed and extended Bem's work on gender schema by considering how children form gender "scripts" (Levy & Fivush, 1993). Even young children organize their knowledge of the world in scripts—time-ordered routines that they regularly see and in which they participate. For example, there are scripts for changing a diaper, going to bed, eating dinner, going to a birthday party, and so on. Scripts provide children with sets of expectations about what to expect from different people in particular situations. Scripts are like schemas because they organize perceptions and allow children to comprehend, process, and predict events and event-related information. Children use scripts to help them acquire language, develop cognitive categories, and learn logical reasoning (Nelson, 1986).

Gender scripts are particularly important to the thought processes of developing children. For younger children, an occurrence that is inconsistent with a gender script is likely to be ignored, not remembered, or distorted in memory to conform to the script (Levy & Fivush, 1993). Like a gender schema, a gender script teaches children that boys and girls are different and provides prescriptions and proscriptions for their respective behaviors. Early research shows that preschool children pay more attention to scripts for their own sex, and some researchers find that boys have more elaborate scripts and are more concerned with following them than are girls (Fagot, 1985; Levy & Fivush, 1993).

Other theories of childhood gender acquisition combine the insights of the cognitive approach with those of interactionist theories (e.g., Mead, 1934/1967), granting children even more agency. For example, Spencer Cahill (1986) suggests that children regulate their gender performance relative to the participation of parents and others. As acquiescent participants, they accept the gender investiture made by parents and other significant adults on the basis of their biological sex class. With continued exposure to gender-differential treatment and social bestowal of "gender-appropriate" traits, children begin, unwittingly, to respond behaviorally in gender-differentiated ways. Acquiring the use of language and more agency with age and maturity, children then begin to explore various gender identity options. At this stage, however, the children find, through both direct and indirect approbation and censure, that the alternatives are limited to either the derogatory category of "baby" or the alternate positive category of "big girl" or "big boy." Beginning to comprehend the boundaries of appropriate gender behavior that will lead to a favorable categorization, children typically start to incorporate a commitment to socially correct gender behavior that corresponds to their assigned sex class. Thus, "by the end of the preschool age years . . . children are self-regulating participants in the interactional achievement of their own normally sexed identities" (Cahill, 1986, p. 177; see also Coltrane & Adams, forthcoming; Thorne, 1993).

Patterns of Gender Socialization

Although the psychoanalytic, cognitive, and interactionist theories summarized above focus on different ways that children learn about gender, they all suggest that what adults do with children influences their outlook on gender. Not only do children learn at a conscious level that the world is divided into boys and girls, men and women, but they also learn this in a subconscious way. At the level of unconscious emotions and in automatic perception and memory, children develop ways of seeing the world that are deeply gendered. These ways of seeing become incorporated into developing selves as children test out gender categories in interaction with people around them. All this contributes to the sense that gender is something that is natural, fixed, and unalterable (although gender means different things in different cultures, and different forms of masculinity and femininity coexist in any particular society).

Not surprisingly, the vast majority of American children conform to the expectations of the larger culture regarding gender. Following gender schemas and gender scripts, children consider most objects and activities as exclusively appropriate for only boys or girls. Responding to deeply gendered ways of relating emotionally, boys and girls feel that they are fundamentally different. Boys and girls also prefer and enforce same-sex play for themselves and for their peers, which further reinforces gender differences (Huston, 1983). As theories and research show, this is primarily because parents insist on treating boys and girls as categorically different. In the remainder of the chapter, I review the many studies showing how boys and girls are treated differently. Keep in mind, however, that these patterns are changing as societal attitudes toward gender change and as parenting practices change. According to theories discussed above, as child socialization practices change, there should also be less rigid personality differences and less polarized gender schemas.

Gender Differences in Treatment of Infants

Male and female infants are similar to one another, but most adults go to great lengths to make them appear dissimilar. As noted above, differential treatment by gender begins as soon as parents and other adults know the infant's sex. The newborn nursery typically provides color-coded blankets and identification bracelets, with pink for girls and blue for boys. People select gifts for newborns depending on their sex, with girls receiving pastel outfits, often with ruffles, and boys receiving tiny jeans and boldly colored outfits (Fagot & Leinbach, 1993). Parents routinely dress their tiny infants in sex-appropriate clothes and attempt to style their hair in stereotyped ways so that others can quickly categorize them according to sex (Shakin, Shakin, & Sternglanz, 1985). Even the bedrooms of infants are arranged according to gender, with girls' rooms typically painted pink and populated with dolls, whereas boys' rooms tend to be blue, red, or white and contain plenty of vehicles and sports gear (Pomerleau, Bolduc, Malcuit, & Cossette, 1990).

To assess how important knowing the sex of babies is to adults, researchers have devised some ingenious tests. In one study, parents were asked to rate and describe their own babies shortly after they were born. Because they had spent little time with their newborns, one of the only pieces of information they could rely on was the child's sex. Although the boy and girl infants in the study showed no differences on any objective measures, girls were rated as littler, softer, finer featured, and more inattentive than boys (Rubin, Provenzano, & Luria, 1974).

When some of my students read about the results of this study, they told me that things had changed since the "dark ages" of the 1970s. Much to their surprise, studies from the 1980s and 1990s show the same propensity to label boys and girls differently, although some of the stereotypes are starting to weaken (Fagot & Leinbach, 1993; Stern & Karraker, 1989). In one type of labeling study, people are exposed to a baby and asked questions about the baby's personality traits or behaviors. Often, the same baby is dressed in gender-neutral clothes but labeled *male* for some people and *female* for others. People are typically given little, if any, information about the infant other than the sex. Because the baby's sex is always the same, these studies can isolate the impact of calling the baby a boy or girl.

Although specific results from two dozen such studies vary, in general they show that the actual sex of the babies makes little difference because people use gender stereotypes in rating the babies. This is especially true when the people doing the rating are children (Cowan & Hoffman, 1986; Stern & Karraker, 1989). For example, in studies using child raters, boy babies were routinely perceived as bigger, stronger, and noisier; often seen as faster, meaner, and harder; and sometimes seen as madder and smarter than girl babies (Stern & Karraker, 1989).

Studies also looked at how adults interacted with the infants. In several studies, labeled girls received more verbalization, interpersonal stimulation, and nurturance play. Similarly, labeled boys received more encouragement of activity and more whole-body stimulation. This pattern has also been observed for parents with their own children, especially for fathers (Cherry & Lewis, 1976; Fagot, 1974, 1978; Fagot & Leinbach, 1993; Stern & Karraker, 1989).

Some of the infant-labeling studies looked at toy choice as a way of measuring whether adults were using gender stereotypes in interacting with infants. No differences were found in about half of the studies, probably because most of the toys were inappropriate for infants. Nevertheless, dolls were more often given to girl babies, and a football or hammer more often given to boy babies, supporting the idea that adults encourage gender-specific toys, even in infants under a year old (Stern & Karraker, 1989).

The conclusion from these laboratory experiments with infants is that people tend to treat boy and girl babies differently, although not always. Knowledge of an infant's sex is most likely to influence adults' evaluation of an infant if they have little other information or if the infant's behavior is ambiguous. Most of these studies have been conducted on college campuses with well-educated subjects who were probably trying to avoid acting in rigidly gender-stereotyped ways (Stern & Karraker, 1989). Although it is harder to draw statistical conclusions from studies on parents in their own homes interacting with their own infants, it is here that most gender stereotyping occurs. The research suggests that even with infants under a year old, parents expect different things from girls and boys, set up their environments in different ways, treat them differently, and in many subtle ways direct them toward gender-appropriate behavior (Deaux, 1984; Fagot, Leinbach, & O'Boyle, 1992; Huston, 1983).

Because infants and toddlers develop gender schemas and gender scripts on the basis of what they are exposed to in their immediate environment, parents' and other adult caretakers' attitudes and behaviors tend to have a substantial impact on their gender development. Infants enter the world much more prepared to extract information from their environment than social scientists once thought. Indeed, infants are actively engaged in processing information from their earliest days, and they are exposed to gender-relevant messages from the beginning. By the age of seven months, infants can discriminate between men's and women's voices and generalize this to strangers. Infants less than a year old can also discriminate individual male and female faces. Even before they are verbal, young children are developing gender categories and making generalizations about people and objects in their environments, although they have not yet developed gender schemas (Fagot & Leinbach, 1993).

Gender Differences in Treatment of Children

Preschool-age children are more adept at differentiating between genders than infants. Between the ages of two and four, most children master gender labels as applied to themselves and other children, but they cannot always link gender to anatomical sex (Fagot & Leinbach, 1993). To illustrate, Bem (1993) tells a story about her son who went to nursery school one day wearing barrettes and was told by another boy that he was a girl because "only girls wear barrettes." After repeatedly insisting that he was a boy because he had a penis, he became exasperated and pulled down his pants. To this, the second boy remarked, "everybody has a penis; only girls wear barrettes" (p. 149). By the time they are two years old, 80% of American children can distinguish males from females on the basis of social cues such as hairstyle and clothing. But only half of three- and four-year-olds can distinguish males from females if all they have to go on are biologically natural cues such as genitalia and body physique (Bem, 1989, 1993, p. 114). In other words, preschool children in the United States learn that the cultural trappings of gender are more important than the underlying physical differences between boys and girls.

Children quickly incorporate new information into their developing gender schemas. Before the age of five, American children assign *bears, fire,* and *something rough* to boys and men, whereas *butterflies, hearts,* and *flowers* are associated with girls and women (Leinbach & Hort, 1989). These children are not taught directly to put bears and men together, but by this age they are able to categorize using a gender schema that associates qualities such as strength or dangerousness with males. Similarly, flowers and butterflies become associated with females through a metaphorical cognitive process that associates women with gentle qualities (Fagot & Leinbach, 1993, p. 220).

During the preschool and kindergarten years, parents provide even more gender-stereotyped toys and furnishings than they did for infants. Boys' rooms contain more vehicles, sports equipment, animals, machines, and military toys. Girls' rooms, in contrast, contain more dolls, dollhouses, and domestic toys (Bradbard, 1985; Etaugh & Liss, 1992; Pomerleau et al., 1990; Rheingold & Cook, 1975). Many children do not have all the toys and interior decorating that the upper-middle-class children in these studies enjoyed. But even when homeless children are given toys, the packages are specially marked to make sure that boys get "boy toys" and girls get "girl toys." When preschool children of all social classes ask for toys, parents are much more willing to provide them if they are the "right" type according to gender stereotype (Robinson & Morris, 1986). Different toys and furnishings promote different activities, which, in turn, reinforce rigid gender schemas and scripts. "Masculine" toys such as trucks and balls promote independent or competitive activities that require little verbal interaction. "Feminine" toys such as dolls encourage quiet, nurturing interaction with another, physical closeness, and verbal communication (Wood, 1994a).

Not only do parents provide gender-stereotyped environments, but they also interact with preschool and school-age children in different ways depending on their gender. Parents often reward gender-typical play and punish gender-atypical play (Huston, 1983; Jacklin, DiPietro, & Maccoby, 1984; Lytton & Romney, 1991). Boys are often discouraged from playing house, and girls are sometimes discouraged from engaging in vigorous competitive games. (This is changing somewhat as more girls are getting involved in organized sports such as soccer, baseball, and swimming.) Virtually all studies using preschool and school-age children find that parents engage boys in physical play more than they do girls (Lytton & Romney, 1991; Maccoby & Jacklin, 1974; Parke, 1996).

Another consistent finding is that parents assign boys and girls gender-segregated household tasks, although this is less common in all-girl or all-boy households, in single-parent households, and in African American households. In the majority of houses, however, chores such as cooking and cleaning are usually given to girls, whereas more active chores such as mowing the lawn are typically assigned to boys (Goodnow, 1988; McHale, Bartko, Crouter, & Perry-Jenkins,

1990). As with toys, different chores encourage specific ways of experiencing and understanding the world. Girls' chores usually take place inside and emphasize taking care of other people, whereas boys' chores usually take place outside and emphasize the maintenance of things.

Studies of gender socialization in other areas report more mixed results. Some studies find that parents show more emotional warmth toward girls and encourage more emotional dependence in them. Others report little difference in parents' tolerance of boys' and girls' proximity and comfort seeking (Fagot, 1978; Lytton & Romney, 1991; Maccoby & Jacklin, 1974). Although differences are typically small, research shows that parents more frequently encourage achievement in boys, discourage aggression in girls, and use more physical discipline with boys (Lytton & Romney, 1991). Researchers report that these patterns can vary by ethnic or cultural group, with African American boys and girls socialized more equally toward both autonomy and nurturing than white children and more likely to participate in household chores than other children (Albert & Porter, 1988; Bardewell, Cochran, & Walker, 1986; Hale-Benson, 1986). Research on children's task sharing in Latino families is just beginning, but anecdotal evidence suggests that children in Mexican American households, especially daughters, are called on to do more housework than are children in Anglo households (Coltrane & Valdez, 1993).

Boys and Masculinity

Bem (1993) reports that boys are more rigidly socialized to gender norms and allowed less crossover behavior than girls: She finds that it is easier for girls to be tomboys than for boys to be "sissies." In her study of children's play on elementary school playgrounds, sociologist Barrie Thorne (1993) reports similar findings. High-status girls were most able to cross gender boundaries and play in boys' games, but boys who tried this were usually ridiculed. Thorne finds that the labels of "tomboy" and "sissy" were largely replaced by labels of "fag" or "faggot." Being labeled a tomboy (i.e., like a boy) was seen as praise, whereas being labeled a sissy or fag (i.e., like a girl) was a put-down. Thorne finds considerable crossover between girls' culture and boys' culture, with girls much more likely to try to get into boys' games than the reverse. Nevertheless, gender "borderwork" on the playground—rituals such as "cooties" and chasing games—serve to reinforce the boundaries between the boys and girls.

On the playground and at home, both girls and boys learn that they should conform to gender-appropriate behaviors, but studies find that boys are encouraged to conform to masculine ideals more than girls are encouraged to conform to feminine ideals. In addition, boys tend to receive more rewards for gender conformity than girls (Wood, 1994a). In part, this is because boys tend to get more attention than girls. Children, as well as adults, generate more restrictive gender rules for young boys than for young girls (Bem, 1989). Another consistent finding across studies is that fathers enforce gender stereotypes more than mothers do, especially in sons. This is generally true across types of activities, including toy preferences, play styles, chores, discipline, interaction, and personality assessments (Caldera, Huston, & O'Brien, 1989; Fagot & Leinbach, 1993; Lytton & Romney, 1991).

The receipt of more gender restrictions by boys than by girls seems a bit contradictory because men, as a group, have more social power than do women. Men are more likely to hold positions of authority, occupy a wider range of professional roles, earn more money, and have greater freedom of movement than women. This is also true in the comparison of adolescent boys with adolescent girls. It is also true that school-age boys tend to be given more freedom of movement and are given fewer chores than school-age girls. So why do we allow young girls more gender freedom than boys? Because we have a male-dominated or androcentric cultural bias that values masculine traits over feminine traits, we are more likely to approve of those traits whether they are exhibited by boys or girls (Broverman, Broverman, Clarkson, Rosenkrantz, & Vogel, 1970). But boys are more forcefully encouraged to adopt culturally valued masculine traits and more often discouraged from adopting the lower-status feminine traits (Bem, 1993; Kimmel & Messner, 1992; Lorber, 1994). According to the psychoanalytic and cognitive theories noted earlier, masculine gender identity is also more fragile than feminine gender identity and must be continually re-created (Bem, 1993; Chodorow, 1978; Dinnerstein, 1976; Mead, 1949). Because it requires the suppression of human feelings of vulnerability and denial of emotional connection, the maintenance of a stereotypically masculine identity requires more psychic effort than the maintenance of feminine identity (Chodorow, 1978; Maccoby & Jacklin, 1974). Because masculinity is inherently fragile and defined in opposition to femininity, researchers note that men spend considerable time and energy maintaining gender boundaries and denigrating women and gays (Connell, 1995; Kimmel & Messner, 1992). For these reasons, boys are given less gender latitude than girls, and fathers are more preoccupied than are mothers with making sure that their sons are not sissies.

Although adult men are more concerned than are women with instilling masculinity in boys, a father's role in perpetuating gender difference is neither fixed nor inevitable. The finding that mothers are less apt to enforce gender stereotypes is related to the amount of time they spend with children. Because they are doing most of the child care, mothers are more realistic about both similarities and differences between children and less likely to let preconceived notions of gender stereotypes shape their perceptions of an individual child's abilities or needs. Similarly, researchers find that when men coparent or take care of children as single parents, they act more like conventional mothers than like conventional fathers (Coltrane, 1996; Risman, 1986). Like mothers, involved fathers encourage sons and daughters equally and use similar interaction and play styles for both. They avoid rigid gender stereotypes and avoid the single-minded emphasis on rough-and-tumble play common among traditional fathers (Coltrane, 1989; Parke, 1996). When fathers exhibit a close, nurturing, continuing relationship with their preschool or school-age children, boys hold less stereotyped gender attitudes as teenagers and young adults (Hardesty, Wenk, & Morgan, 1995; Williams, Radin, & Allegro, 1992).

Parenting and Gender Inequality

Perhaps the most consistent and important finding from the childhood gender socialization research of the past few decades is that parents and other adults create different learning environments for boys and girls and ask them to do different things. Girls are given dolls and stoves to play with and are encouraged to cuddle, clean house, and care for others. Boys are given balls and trucks to play with, are engaged in rough-and-tumble play, and are asked to take out the trash. In general, girls are expected to be kind and caring, whereas boys are expected to be independent and aggressive.

Differences in the ways that adults treat boys and girls have perpetuated separate spheres for men and women. By setting up different social and interpersonal environments for them, parents encourage girls to develop nurturing behaviors and boys to develop autonomy. By shaping different environments and holding different expectations for boys and girls, parents promote the formation of gender schemas, gendered personalities, and taken-for-granted gender scripts that make gender differences seem natural and inevitable (Crouter, McHale, & Bartko, 1993; Eccles, Jacobs, & Harold, 1990; Etaugh & Liss, 1992; Thompson & Walker, 1989). For example, most girls grow up more interested in babies, are more responsive to them, and take more responsibility for them than boys (Ullian, 1984). Because girls experience more contact with young children, they also have more opportunities to develop nurturing capacities, and by the time they reach childbearing age, they are predisposed to want to bear children and to take primary responsibility for their care (Bem, 1993; Chodorow, 1978).

Not all girls are subjected to these socialization pressures in the same way, however, and lately, most girls have also been strongly encouraged to do well in school and to pursue careers. Even in the past, some women have excelled at conventionally masculine pursuits, and an individual girl's disposition or personal desires have motivated her to deviate from a narrow path of conventional femininity. Because different ways of life have produced different styles of femininity, women have always had some choice in the matter. Some models of femininity have emphasized helplessness or physical beauty, but others have emphasized emotional strength and creativity. Not all feminine ideals include domestic or maternal traits. For example, compare the stereotyped images of the stoic Midwestern farmwife, the strong-willed inner-city mother, the cheery suburban housewife, the shapely Hollywood starlet, the prompt and efficient secretary, the athletic gym teacher, the serious and weathered naturalist, and the elegant lady of high society. All are images of femininity, and all have been available for girls and women to emulate during the past few decades. Not only has there been enormous variability in feminine stereotypes, but the gender stereotyping that parents do to children is never so uniform or controlling that girls have not had some choices. And the choices that women have are expanding rapidly.

Boys, in contrast to girls, have been socialized to occupy a privileged status in families and in society. There is wide variation in this, as minority men have often been granted privileges within their families but denied them in the larger society

(Taylor, 1994). In all racial/ethnic groups, however, when compared with women, men have been encouraged to be competitive, individualistic, and often unemotional. If men have access to jobs and wealth, they tend to enact masculinity through being breadwinners and providers. If they are denied access to decent jobs and earnings, they tend to enact masculinity through "cool pose," hard living, and violence (Majors, 1992; Rubin, 1976, 1994). Most boys develop into young adult men who are relatively uninterested in babies and unprepared to care for the emotional needs of others. In addition, our child-rearing practices and social ideals tend to produce young men who feel entitled to the domestic or sexual services of women, are preoccupied with reaffirming their masculinity, and are prone to use violence when they feel threatened (Connell, 1995; Kaufman, 1993; Kimmel & Messner, 1992).

As is the case for girls, however, not all boys grow up to fit this narrow masculine mold. Many men turn out to be kind, sensitive, and loving, and most men share their deepest feelings with others (although usually still with women). As with femininity, there have always been various models of masculinity. Compare the physical toughness of a construction worker with the intelligence of a rocket scientist or the arrogant authority of a rich banker—all representing a specific acceptable form of masculinity. There have always been multiple forms of masculinity whose definitions have been played off against the others and against stereotyped notions of femininity. Some have been subordinated, but still visible, as evidenced by the Mother Goose nursery rhyme about Robin and Richard. Although dominant forms of masculinity have reflected the norm among men with more power and authority, oppositional forms of masculinity have always coexisted. The suburban middle-class European American masculinity ideal of rationality and unemotionality is not the same as that found, for example, among suburban middle-class African Americans, inner-city ghetto dwellers, recent Mexican immigrants, or urban gay youth (Connell, 1995).

The choices that are open to men and boys are expanding. More emphasis is placed on being kind and loving fathers, both in the media and in real men's lives. The movement toward more active fathering is not limited to just one segment of the population, as evidenced by a rapid increase in the number of single fathers and the prevalence of pro-father groups, from the African American Million Man March to the fundamentalist Christian Promise Keepers. There are more two-job families and more two-career professional couples, a development that is turning husbands into equal partners rather than benevolent bosses. In contrast, many men, especially those who are chronically unemployed, are more likely to stay single or get divorced. As male baby boomers age, increasing numbers of men are seniors and retirees. Older men, especially those who are not in positions of authority, have always been allowed more latitude in expressing emotions and caring for other people. As the number and proportion of men of color expand in the coming decades, their unique styles of masculinity will also flourish and become more visible. Younger men, in particular, have a greater willingness to accept women as equals and to engage in more mixed-gender social activities. More men are admitting that they are gay, and despite a continuing backlash against them, it is more possible to be openly gay in this country than ever before.

Popular images of men and masculinity in the media also provide a much wider range of hypothetical options than in the past (although shoot-'em-up action heroes still predominate). Even nursery rhymes—at least most of the new ones—have become less sexist. The choices of how to be a man are considerably more varied than before, and so the narrow gender stereotyping of children described above is not necessarily a blueprint for the future.

I summarized the conventionality of past socialization practices to highlight the real, and sometimes quite large, differences in the ways that parents treat children according to gender. By raising children to be "proper" boys and girls, parents and other family members have re-created broad gender differences and prepared the next generation to occupy unequal positions in a system of gender hierarchy. But things are changing. Most families now look different from the typical family of the 1950s. Indications are that children who experienced a divorce, those raised in single-mother families, those in stepfamilies, and those excluded from material prosperity are developing new ideas about how boys and girls should be treated. Even those from stereotypical traditional families are reevaluating their past experiences and asking new questions about how children should be raised to meet the gender expectations of a new century.

You will need to refer to your own experiences to see how many of the gender socialization patterns I described apply to you or your family. You should also remember that even when you are socialized in a particular way, you always have many opportunities for changing your own actions, so that your personal gender traits, gender schemas, and gender scripts can also change. The same theories that show how gender differences have been socially constructed provide a glimpse into how they might change in the future. As I discuss in the next chapter, strong institutional forces are operating in society that limit how much things might change. But also, other institutional, cultural, and economic forces are propelling the United States toward even more possibilities for change. These conflicting tendencies will put crosscutting pressures on parents and families of the future. My prediction is that gender socialization practices will continue their movement toward equality. We may not train the next generation of boys and girls to be equally assertive and sensitive, but even small changes in that direction will have ripple effects on the rest of society. Just as inequality in the social and economic structures governing our lives produces contrasting gender cultures, so too will similarities in children's gender schemas help lessen inequalities in the society at large.

CHAPTER 6

Regulating Families and Gender

News Stories

Man Claims Right to Rape His Wife

In 1994, a Los Angeles man tried to rape his wife, claiming that marriage gave him the legal and religious right to have sex with her. Ray Eastman, a 54-year-old upholsterer, had just returned home after a short trip. He demanded that his wife, Maria, have sex with him. She was a devout Catholic and mother of 10 children, and although she had given in to his advances in the past, this time she said no.

To get away from her husband, Maria locked herself in an attic bedroom. Ray responded by opening the door with a butter knife, slapping her, ripping her clothes, and trying to force himself on her. Although she was frightened, she successfully resisted his advances.

Two years later, Ray was brought to trial. He insisted that he had religious and constitutional rights to have sex with his own wife when he wanted. Court papers filed by his attorney claimed "consent is presumed, between husband and wife, to at least fondle each other." The judge disagreed and sentenced Ray to one year in jail. (Adapted from "A Wife, Too, Can Say No," 1996; Rivenburg, 1996; actual names changed)

Wife Killer Awarded Custody of Daughter

In 1995, a Florida man convicted of murdering his first wife was granted custody of his daughter because her mother was a lesbian. James Budd fatally shot his first wife and served eight years in prison for the crime. Apparently rehabilitated, he remarried after his release, and the couple gave birth to a baby daughter. When the girl was eight years old, James and his wife, Jenny, were divorced, and child custody was granted to the mother. The girl lived with her mother for the next three years, although she visited her father occasionally.

After James had fallen behind in his monthly support payments by about $1,500, Jenny filed for an increase in the level of court-ordered child support. James, who had recently remarried, countered that Jenny had exhibited inappropriate behavior, including poor hygiene, bad table manners, and a preference for men's cologne, which warranted a change in custody. Citing the mother's lesbianism, the judge ordered that the 11-year-old girl be taken from her mother and placed in her father's custody. The judge commented that he wanted to give the girl a chance to live in a "nonlesbian world." (Adapted from Associated Press, 1996; actual names changed)

Six months later, a Florida Appeals court upheld the lower court ruling granting custody to James Budd: "Absent a showing of an abuse of discretion by the trial court, this court is not at liberty to disturb the modification of custody." The case is under appeal to the Florida Supreme Court (Navarro, 1996, pp. 7N, 7L).

Abused Husband Denied Custody of Son

Shortly after marrying, Alan Web reported that his wife, Sylvia, began to beat him. He did not fight back. When he told her he wanted a divorce, she was apologetic, initiated sexual intercourse, and conceived a child. Reluctantly, Alan stayed with Sylvia to be with his son, changing diapers and staying home when the boy was sick. The verbal, emotional, and physical abuse continued, and three years later, Alan filed for divorce and moved out. He paid half his salary to Sylvia for temporary child support, asked the New Hampshire court for custody, and claimed cruel and abusive treatment at the hands of his wife.

According to Alan, Sylvia refused mediation, denied him visitation, refused to sell the house, filed fraudulent counterclaims of abuse, and had an arrest warrant issued for him after he went bankrupt trying to pay child support. Alan moved out of the state after Sylvia smashed his car windshield. He called his son once a week, which is all the court allowed. The case dragged on for two years, with Alan blocked from attending the final hearing. In the end, the court ordered Alan to pay 40% of his salary in child support, give up the house, and pay Sylvia's attorney fees. Legal and physical custody was awarded to Sylvia. Alan committed suicide. (From a series of Internet postings: soc.men, alt.child support, http://www.vix.com/men/wells/index.htm, 5/7/96; actual names changed)

These condensed news reports are about actual legal cases. Although these stories are more dramatic than the majority of cases that come through U.S. courts, they illustrate how the state, via the judicial system, shapes family and gender relations. In most cases, judges make assumptions about what is good for families and children in the face of contradictory laws and conflicting evidence. Courts are supposed to balance the rights of the individual with the obligations of being married or being a parent, but as these cases show, this is a difficult challenge. In part, this is because the laws themselves are gender biased. But the task of adjudicating family conflict is also difficult because judges, like the rest of us, draw on taken-for-granted meanings associated with manhood, womanhood, and family well-being. Problems are especially likely to arise when family law, or the judge's understanding of it, conflicts with the views of at least one of the parties involved. That is what happened in each of the cases above. By highlighting hidden messages about gender in our laws and policy decisions, we can see how families are regulated by official state institutions. By focusing on how government laws and policies implicitly define appropriate gender behavior, we can also better understand what is happening in American families today.

The three legal cases presented above show that family law is changing but in contradictory ways. We cannot be sure that all the facts of each case were reported completely or accurately, but the stories show some important issues now confronting our courts and lawmakers. In the first case, the court was protecting a wife's choice not to have sex, even though she opposed her husband's wishes. In the second case, the court awarded child custody to a man who was a convicted wife murderer because the child's mother did not conform to a narrow view of appropriate sexual behavior. In the third case, the court refused to acknowledge that the husband was an abused spouse, instead awarding custody to the mother. In all these cases, the courts made decisions based, in part, on an evaluation of behavior as appropriate according to gender.

It is not new for courts to make assumptions about proper behavior on the basis of being a husband or wife. Neither is it new for the law to deny some rights to wives, assume that mothers should care for children, or deny that husbands could be abused. In Chapter 2, I introduced the idea that marriage is a type of market exchange involving sex and property that has traditionally been controlled by men. In Chapter 3, I suggested that the marriage bargain usually included husbands' control of wives' domestic labor, and in Chapter 4, I focused on the ways that the marital exchange entailed the wife providing physical and emotional care while the husband provided economic resources to the family. In Chapter 5, I showed how parents reinscribe notions of gender difference in their children. In this chapter, I turn attention to the ways that government policies and the legal system have defined, defended, and enforced these conventional understandings of gender and family.

Gender, Family, and the Law

The case of attempted marital rape described above would not even have been possible just a few years ago in most states. Because the courts assumed that the husband was legally entitled to have sex with his wife, he could not be tried for raping her. Until recently, the concept of marital rape was thus a legal contradiction in terms. At the same time, rape laws have prohibited men from having sex with other men's wives or daughters. Notice, however, that both types of laws protected men's interests in "their" women. Although such blatantly sexist assumptions about women as men's sexual property seem outdated, they were still part of our legal system until just a few decades ago, and they continue to influence how we think about marriage, family, and women's rights.

Many women (and men) who entered the legal profession in the 1960s and 1970s recognized that such laws were unfair to women, and they set out to change them. Feminist attorneys successfully challenged the worst inequities in the laws regulating marriage and sexuality, and some new laws with gender-neutral language were adopted by Congress and state legislatures. But changes have been slow, and some of the legal reforms created unanticipated problems of their own. Even when laws were changed, judges sometimes continued to make assumptions that perpetuated the old sexist traditions.

Even today, some women give up legal rights as individuals when they get married. In some courts, it is still not possible for a wife to bring criminal charges against a husband who rapes her (Liss, 1987; Lorber, 1994). In most states, however, a man can now be tried for marital rape, as was the case in California. But even in states with laws that allow prosecution for marital rape, it is rare for judges to find men guilty and sentence them to extended jail time. In the California case noted above, the convicted man will probably spend only a few months behind bars, rather than the full year specified in his sentence. If he had been found guilty of attempting to rape a stranger ("someone else's woman"), it is likely that he would have been sentenced to several years in jail.

Although it seems outrageous that a man is entitled to rape his own wife, this idea is consistent with the long-standing legal precedent defining marriage as a property relationship. People do not like to think of marriage in these terms, but as noted in Chapter 2 and discussed below, American legal codes have assumed that the wife is technically the husband's property. For that reason, sending a man to jail for attempting to rape his wife, if only for a few months, marks a significant break with tradition. The United States is definitely moving away from the worst gender biases in past marriage laws, although we still have a ways to go.

The other two stories recounted earlier, about judges awarding custody to a wife-killing ex-husband and to an abusive ex-wife, raise questions about whether the courts can provide truly equal gender treatment, even under reformed laws. Can the courts stop defining women and children as the legal property of men, stop assuming that heterosexuals are automatically better parents, and stop assuming that only men abuse their partners? Before we explore these and other difficult questions arising from these cases, we need to get some general historical perspective on the laws regulating marriage and family life. To better understand the significance of recent legal changes, we also need to understand some basic principles about the ways that governments regulate gender and sexuality through family policy.

Family Policy and the State

When politicians and journalists use the term *family policy*, they mean government actions that are specifically addressed to families, such as guaranteeing that a worker's job will still be there after taking time off to have a baby and allowing a tax deduction for child care. But *family policy* is a vague term that leaves out much of what governments do to shape family life. When legislators or government agencies mandate minimum wages, limit immigration, subsidize farm crops, build highways, set interest rates, enact trade embargoes, regulate health care, alter criminal sentencing rules, adjust taxes, or declare war, they are influencing how families can operate in the society. In so doing, they also indirectly shape how husbands and wives act toward their children and toward each other. How people form and sustain sexual and marital relationships is also directly affected when laws and policies governing rape, prostitution, pornography, same-gender relationships, abortion, and birth control are reformed. When lawmakers and the courts alter the formal ways they treat marriage, divorce, custody, child support, schools, and welfare, families are affected even more directly.

For these reasons, some researchers suggest that family policy should refer to everything that governments do that affects families (Zimmerman, 1988). Using such a definition, although essentially correct, makes it difficult to evaluate whether family policy is working or even who is talking about it (Haas, 1995). Some researchers use the term *family policy* quite narrowly, to emphasize the state's deliberate shaping of programs and laws to realize widely agreed-on objectives to help families (Moen & Schorr, 1987, p. 795). Others suggest that family policy does not really exist in the United States because there is no set of laws or administrative orders labeled *family policy* and because there are no high-level offices in federal or state governments that are responsible for directly overseeing government policies that affect families (Bane & Jargowsky, 1989). Many industrialized nations have specific agencies devoted to family well-being, but the U.S. government has typically taken an official hands-off policy toward families.

To study specific trends in family policy, researchers usually adopt fairly narrow definitions of it. For example, "family policy refers to objectives concerning family well-being and the specific measures taken by governmental bodies to achieve them" (Aldous & Dumon, 1990, p. 1137). Such a definition limits family policy to programs consciously undertaken to affect families in a positive way and makes it easier to study recent policy initiatives explicitly designed to help families, such as the 1993 Family and Medical Leave Act mentioned in Chapter 4 (see U.S. Department of Labor, 1993). This federal government policy allows U.S. parents who work for companies with more than 50 employees to take 12 weeks of unpaid leave to care for a new baby or seriously ill family member. The law was passed because some people were losing their jobs when they temporarily quit to take care of a newborn infant.[1] This is one of the few laws in the United States that qualifies as family policy according to the narrow definition suggested above.

Although the majority of modern industrialized nations have numerous policies and programs designed to fulfill specific family goals, most of the legislation affecting families in the United States does not explicitly spell out its goals for families (Kamerman & Kahn, 1988a; Zimmerman, 1992). For example, recent attempts by U.S. politicians to balance the federal budget, restructure the tax code, and reform welfare could also be called family policies because the reforms will have far-reaching impacts on families. In contrast, most of the political rhetoric surrounding family values since the 1980s has focused on doing away with the few explicit family policies that exist on the national level, including those welfare programs initiated in the 1930s under Roosevelt's New Deal and in the 1970s under Johnson's War on Poverty (e.g., Murray, 1984).

In an effort to improve the life chances of children, many social scientists and child advocates have defined family policies in regard to the well-being of children (Hernandez, 1993). For example, Marian Wright Edelman (1987), president of the Children's Defense Fund, suggested that instead of formulating something called family policy, the United States should fund health, nutrition, education, and housing programs aimed at directly benefiting children (virtually all of whom live in some sort of family). She has publicized the plight of children living in single-parent families, most of whom live at or near the poverty level (see Figure 4.4). Edelman (1989) focuses especially on the plight of African American children, whose life chances have been declining in recent years. When compared with white children, black children are

> *twice as likely to* die in the first year of life, be born prematurely, suffer low birthweight, have mothers who received late or no prenatal care, see a parent die, live in substandard housing, be suspended from school or suffer corporal punishment, be unemployed as teenagers, have no parent employed, live in institutions; *three times as likely to* be poor, have their mothers die in childbirth, live with a parent who has separated, live in a female headed family, be placed in an educable mentally retarded class, be murdered between five and nine years of age, be in foster care, die of known child abuse; [and] *four times as likely to* live with neither parent and be supervised by a child welfare agency, be murdered before one year of age or as a teenager, be incarcerated between fifteen and nineteen years of age. (pp. 63-64)

Similar declining life chances are evident for Latino youth (Hernandez, 1993; Pérez & Salazar, 1993; Starrels et al., 1994).

The harsh conditions faced by many American families, coupled with the lack of government attempts to alleviate them, put children in the United States at a distinct disadvantage relative to children in other developed countries. According to demographer William O'Hare (1996), "Many social scientists contend that the lack of investment in our children will put us at a competitive disadvantage in the international marketplace of the 21st century" (p. 36). Studies comparing child poverty in the United States with that in other industrial countries show that conditions are getting worse for U.S. children (Palmer, Smeeding, & Torrey, 1988; Rainwater & Smeeding, 1995). Only the poverty rates for children in Ireland and the United Kingdom exceed that of the United States, but in those countries, government assistance programs lift half the impoverished children out of poverty. The United States lifts only 17% of its poor children out of poverty, leaving it at the top of the list (see Table 6.1). After figuring in the government assistance, the level of child poverty is 50% higher than that of the next highest country (Australia) and almost 10 times higher than that of Sweden or Finland. Not only are the majority of children better off in those countries to begin with, but their governments do much more to lift the children who are poor up to a decent standard of living (O'Hare, 1996; Palmer, 1988; Rainwater & Smeeding, 1995).

The tendency of the United States to spend so little on children and to avoid creating explicit family policies stems from the common assumption that families are private and fundamentally separate from the government (or the church, schools, economy, or any other social institution). As noted above, many government laws and policies regulate, control, and shape families, even if they are not identified as explicit family policies. Does this represent a one-way process of government intrusion into the "private" life of the family? Definitely not. Chapters 2 and 3 have already shown that the idea of the family as a private domain apart

TABLE 6.1

Child Poverty in 17 Developed Countries (1980s-1990s)

The United States ranks high in child poverty to begin with, but the U.S. government does less than other developed countries to assist poor children.

Country	Percentage of Children in Poverty		Percentage of Children Lifted Out of Poverty by Government Programs
	Before Assistance	After Assistance	
United States	26	22	17
Australia	20	14	29
Canada	23	14	40
Ireland	30	12	60
Israel	24	11	54
United Kingdom	30	10	67
Italy	12	10	17
Germany	9	7	24
France	25	7	74
Netherlands	14	6	55
Norway	13	5	64
Luxembourg	12	4	65
Belgium	16	4	77
Denmark	16	3	79
Switzerland	5	3	35
Sweden	19	3	86
Finland	12	3	78

SOURCE: Adapted from O'Hare, 1996, p. 36; Rainwater and Smeeding, 1995.

from work or politics is a relatively modern invention and one that has never been literally true. As a consequence, when researchers try to analyze how governments (or businesses, or schools, etc.) affect families, it is extremely difficult to determine what causes what.

Sometimes changes in law and policy bring about direct changes in family form, such as when the government of China decided to curb overpopulation by limiting each Chinese family to just one child. But such policy actions also have unintended consequences, as when the rate of female abortions, female infanticide, and female abandonment increased dramatically in China (Croll, Davin, & Kane, 1985; Lorber, 1994). A related example in the United States concerns Aid to Families With Dependent Children (AFDC). This program, designed to ensure a minimal standard of living for poor children, actually discouraged fathers from living with their children. Early in the AFDC program, mothers and children were denied benefits if a social worker visited the home and found a man's clothes or other belongings in the house. Combined with patterns established in the previous century, and in conjunction with low wages and systemic patterns of job discrimination, this policy discouraged low-income African American fathers from marrying the mother and living in the child's home. By the mid-1990s, only about a third of African American children were living with two parents, compared with more than three fourths of white children (Mason, 1996). Ironically, many new government programs aimed at low-income children are now designed to bring men (and their limited incomes) back into the family by encouraging them to sign paternity declarations at the birth, performing blood tests to determine paternity, and directly withholding child support payments from their paychecks. The policies most likely to encourage poor men to become involved fathers or to marry the mothers of their children are based on providing them with jobs (Mason, 1996).

The examples of AFDC and the China one-child policy show that laws and policies emerge within complex cultural and economic contexts and cannot be considered in isolation. One thing is for certain: Changes in laws, economic policies, and social programs are rarely as simple or straightforward as their proponents claim. Even when government and corporate leaders do not intend it, changing specific policies and practices also affects the gender balance of power in the family. Tipping the power balance a little more toward men or women also begins to set in motion other social processes that lead to changes in the symbolic meaning of gender in the larger culture.

Shifts in laws and policies are themselves the result of larger social and historical changes, rather than the sole or major cause of changes in the family. Most changes in family organization are the result of a complex interplay of many social forces, with changes in the economy typically leading the way. A good historical example of the relationship between family law and social custom is in the area of interracial marriage. As discussed in Chapter 2, the number of interracial marriages has increased substantially since midcentury. Formerly, such marriages were prohibited by legal statutes called antimiscegenation laws. Until the 1950s, the United States was a thoroughly and openly racist society, and its legal system reflected that racism. Segregation was the norm, especially in Southern states, but discrimination against people of color, interracial couples, and multiracial children was common in jobs, housing, schools, and so on throughout the country. The civil rights movement of the 1950s and 1960s brought a rapid change in many of our legal codes (although it did not eliminate many forms of discrimination). The last of the antimiscegenation laws (in Virginia and South Carolina) were struck down by a U.S. Supreme Court ruling in 1967 (Spickard, 1989; Williamson, 1980). After that, the rates of interracial marriage went up even faster. Did changing the laws increase the rate of interracial marriage, or did the law changes simply bring the legal code into line with changed marriage practices? Each can be seen as a cause of the other, but a better way to understand them is to see both as the result of some larger social processes. Both were encouraged by growing economic prosperity, reflect a general movement toward more individual control over choice of marriage partners, and result from the increasing ethnic diversity in the population.

As we look at some of the other important changes in American families in the past three decades, such as the rising level of divorce and the increasing number of single mothers, we need to be careful about assigning a causal role to laws or government programs. For example, passing no-fault divorce laws had little impact on the rate of divorce: It had already climbed in the years preceding the legal changes (Jacob, 1988). Similarly, single motherhood increased most after welfare payments were declining, not as a result of governments giving more money to teenage moms (Jaynes & Williams, 1989). Despite public opinion to the contrary, economists report that when other relevant variables are considered, the AFDC program in the United States encouraged neither divorce nor premarital childbirth (Mason, 1996). European analyses consistently find that their more generous programs for single mothers do not result in more women having babies to qualify for social benefits, nor do couples break up to get benefits (Kamerman & Kahn, 1988b). According to the leading researchers in this area, "Social policies do not cause these developments. But once an unwed mother has a baby, and once a couple divorces, social benefits make the single-parent family possible in various ways, depending on the policy" (Kamerman & Kahn, 1993, p. 230).

Whether laws and policies cause changes in families, or whether they simply follow larger social and economic changes, they are worthy of scholarly attention. Focusing on how laws and government programs are changing can illustrate how family arrangements and gender relations are evolving together. Focusing on the *lack* of legal change or the *in*action of the government can also show how family and gender are intimately intertwined. Before turning to such an analysis, however, I introduce some general theories about governmental regulation of gender and families.

Theories Linking State, Family, and Gender

Social scientists and political theorists have been writing about "the state"—meaning government in general—for a long time, but they have only recently focused on how families, gender, and the state are deeply intertwined (Connell, 1987; Eisenstein, 1984; MacKinnon, 1989). A full review of theories about these linkages is beyond the scope of this chapter, but it is important to understand a few of the main ideas. In briefly introducing these theories, I encourage you to ask some basic questions: Why do governments exist in the first place, and whose needs do they serve? Why have some governments worried about sex and marriage, whereas others have virtually ignored them? What is the basic purpose of family law and family policy today?

These are difficult questions without easy answers. To grapple with them, however, we need to think about the overall organization of society. The theories introduced below suggest fundamentally different views of society and assume different roles for government. Most focus on issues of power and control—topics often left out of textbooks on families and often downplayed in textbooks about

American democracy. As I did earlier in the book, I have left out theories that assume that human behavior is essentially preprogrammed by biology or predestined by God. Instead, I have focused on some of the more provocative and controversial ideas about how governments and families are related. The theories suggest different reasons for how and why laws and policies about sex, marriage, divorce, child custody, and spousal abuse have been used to regulate personal lives. These ideas make some people uncomfortable, but they can help us make sense of many of the policy changes throughout the long sweep of history and will, I hope, allow us to better understand what is happening to American family policy today.

Pluralist Theories

Many theories view the state as a neutral arbitrator of various competing interests, especially in Western democracies. This is the dominant approach in American social science today and derives from a long line of pluralist political philosophers dating hundreds of years. According to this general approach, various interest groups (led by men) have been able to influence the political process in democracies, but nothing inherent in the political system theoretically prohibits women from gaining more influence. These theories suggest that women have been excluded from powerful government positions because they did not want them, because they could not gain direct access to the policy process, or because they were unable to mobilize around definable interests. Modern versions of this approach are exemplified in liberal feminism (e.g., the National Organization for Women [NOW]), which seeks to redress gender inequities by including more women in the various processes associated with making laws and running the government. Most of the reform movements surrounding women's rights are supported by this general theoretical approach, including the successful campaign for women's suffrage (voting), the unsuccessful campaign for the Equal Rights Amendment (ERA), and campaigns for policies promoting employment opportunities for women (comparable worth, equal pay, and affirmative action; Connell, 1987; Tong, 1989).

Conflict Theories

Class Conflict

Conflict and radical theories based on social class focus less on balance among competing interests and more on structured economic inequality and the role of the state in maintaining the status quo. Beginning with the writings of Karl Marx and Friedrich Engels in the 19th century, these theories suggest that the state acts on behalf of a rich, property-owning class and that everything from trade policy to criminal law is essentially designed to maintain the power of the ruling class over the working class (Hobsbawm, 1982; Tucker, 1978). Later theories have expanded this analysis to show how states also have their own autonomous interests (e.g., Skocpol, 1979), how the state controls sexuality in the general service of maintaining class interests (e.g., Marcuse, 1955), and how the state promotes individualist families that consume capitalist products (e.g., Zaretsky, 1976). Many critical scholars continue to draw on these theories to show how, as a by-product of protecting the interests of ruling elites, the state helps men subordinate women (Agger & Shelton, 1993). Although these class conflict theories help explain how laws and governments promote and sustain capitalism, they usually fail to provide a convincing explanation for why gender oppression is essential to the maintenance of class interests (Connell, 1987).

Patriarchy

A final approach draws on elements of the class conflict tradition to explain how the state perpetuates male dominance. Theories in this general category place women and gender at the center of their analyses by treating the state as an institution that has served the needs of men from the beginning (Eisenstein, 1984; MacKinnon, 1989). Although the different versions of feminist theories are too numerous to summarize here, they have some similar features (Chafetz, 1988; Connell, 1987; Lorber, 1994; Osmond & Thorne, 1991; Tong, 1989). Men have used the state apparatus from ancient times to control the lives and sexuality of women, and this has also meant regulating and controlling what people do in and for families.

Some use the term *patriarchy* to refer to any society in which there is rule by the father (the patriarch), although the label technically applies to a specific type of premodern society such as those that existed in medieval Europe or Japan. The powerful families of noblemen were the first states, so there are many theoretical and empirical links between men's control over families and their control of emerging patriarchal governments. When states first developed, they protected the property interests of a few powerful households and ensured that lords and noblemen would exercise a monopoly over weapons and the organized use of violence. As technology and production improved, elite men used governments and armies to maintain their wealth and power and used the state apparatus to maintain control over marriages and women's sexuality. Although now more subtle than in feudal agrarian societies, men's monopoly over the legitimate use of force and their power over wives and daughters have continued in various legal and political forms up to the present (see Chafetz, 1990; Collins, 1975; Coontz & Henderson, 1986; Sanday, 1981).

By emphasizing issues of power as suggested by conflict theories, we can bring some of the linkages between state and family into critical focus. Rather than assuming that state actions are necessarily beneficial for everyone, we can begin to see how they promote some interests at the expense of others. The design and passage of statutes, the interpretation of case law, the adoption of social policies, and the implementation of government programs reveal how family life is structured for the benefit of particular interests at particular times. Looking back through history, we can see how taken-for-granted gender meanings have shaped legal images of marriage and how the legal images, in turn, have shaped popular understandings of family life. Because marriage has been the primary institutional mechanism through which gender inequality is perpetuated, I focus my review on laws governing husband-wife relationships (Johnson, 1988). A more complete picture of how family relationships are shaped by the state would require a review of laws and policies governing parent-child relationships, sexuality, inheritance, labor practices, immigration, land availability, taxation, and various other aspects of inter- and intrahousehold exchange.

Family Law in Historical Perspective

The modern term *family* comes from the Latin *familia*, but in ancient Roman times, it referred to a man's household property, including his fields, house, money, and slaves. In fact, the Latin word *famulus* means *servant*. When a man took a wife, he would literally buy her, and on marriage, she became recognized by the law as part of his property—his *familia*. Although husbands and wives had feelings for each other, the marriage was not usually based on romantic love (see Chapter 2). Instead, marriages were fundamentally property relationships, and the law was primarily concerned with protecting the man's wealth and ensuring an orderly family inheritance (usually from father to eldest son). Although marriage laws and customs varied considerably during the long period of ancient Roman history, getting married always brought the wife under the legal control of her husband (Glendon, 1989).

England and the European nations inherited the most important features of Roman legal practices governing marriage, property, and family relationships. For example, laws in most Western societies defined women as inferior beings who needed to be protected by men (Weitzman, 1981). The modern custom of fathers giving away their daughters during wedding ceremonies is a holdover from the days when women were treated as the legal property of their fathers and husbands. Although most people think of such practices as normal, quaint, and harmless, they symbolically continue the legal notion that women are inferior to men and in need of protection by them.

Throughout Europe and England, traditional customs and legal procedures dictated that a woman lost rights to act on her own behalf when she married, although she usually gained the legally enforced right to be supported by her new husband. Practices varied from country to country and region to region, but even if a woman was allowed to own property or enter into contracts when single, she lost that right when she married (Basch, 1982). This is because the legal principle on which marriage laws were based merged the identities of husband and wife.

The Legal Doctrine of Coverture

The legal doctrine of coverture that took shape in the Middle Ages and was codified into English law stipulated that the unity resulting from marriage equaled the husband. In his famous *Commentaries on the Laws of England* (1765/1832), Sir William Blackstone noted,

> By marriage, the husband and wife are one person in law: that is, the very being or legal existence of woman is suspended during the marriage, or at least is incorporated and consolidated into that of the husband; under whose wing,

protection, and cover, she performs every thing. . . . Upon this principle, of a union of person in husband and wife, depend almost all the legal rights, duties, and disabilities that either of them acquire by the marriage. . . . A man cannot grant any thing to his wife, or enter into covenant with her, for the grant would be to suppose her separate existence. (p. 442; cited in Glendon, 1989, p. 94, n. 29)

Because the wife's identity was merged into that of her husband, she became a legal nonperson and lost the right to act on her own behalf (Sachs & Wilson, 1979).

Because the legal system in the United States was founded on the customs and codes of English common law, the effects of coverture are not just some remote vestige of legal history. In both England and the United States during the 18th and 19th centuries, a married man assumed legal rights over his wife's property on marrying, and any property that came to her during marriage was legally his. From the legal unity of the husband and wife, it also followed that a married woman could not sue or be sued unless her husband was also party to the suit, could not sign contracts unless her husband joined her, and could not execute a valid will unless he consented to its provisions. Because a woman was unable to act as an individual after she was married, her husband could spend her money, sell her stocks, and even appropriate her clothing and jewelry if he wanted (Salmon, 1986; Shanley, 1989). When a woman became a wife, she also lost any freedom of movement she had because she was required by law to live in her husband's domicile, or home (Baron, 1987).

In the 18th and 19th centuries, respectable women were expected to marry, and most spent their adulthood fulfilling the obligations of being wives and mothers. Because access to divorce was strictly limited, wives were literally bound to their husbands until death. Not only did coverture severely constrain women's rights within marriage, but opportunities for women outside marriage were also extremely limited. Unwed mothers and divorced women were social outcasts. As spinsters, unmarried women had few jobs open to them, and the pay was much lower than for men's jobs. Consequently, unmarried women were as economically dependent on their fathers or brothers as wives were on husbands (Degler, 1980; Hill, 1989, pp. 221-239; Lorber, 1994, pp. 260-264; Stone, 1977).

Husbands' Rights Over Wives

Common law assumptions based on the doctrine of coverture also governed other aspects of marital and family relationships in England and America. For example, because a husband was legally accountable for his wife's behavior, he was also entrusted with the power of "restraint by domestic chastisement" (Rhode, 1989, p. 238). For example, in 1862, the North Carolina Court held that

the wife must be subject to the husband. Every man must govern his household, and if by reason of an unruly temper, or an unbridled tongue, the wife persistently treats her husband with disrespect, and he submits to it, he not only loses all sense of self respect, but loses the respect of other members of his family, without which he cannot expect to govern them. . . . It follows that the law gives the husband power to use such a degree of force as is necessary to make the wife behave herself and know her place. (*Joyner v. Joyner*, 1862, as cited in Liss, 1987, p. 787)

Although husbands had the legal right to use physical force against their wives, and even though they were expected to make sure wives "knew their place," community standards usually limited more extreme forms of spousal violence (Dobash & Dobash, 1979; Gordon, 1989). In general, the legal decisions that affirmed husbands' rights to beat their wives also urged them to exercise restraint, and the common law right of husbands to physically chastise their wives weakened substantially during the 19th and early 20th centuries. Nevertheless, some judges in both the United States and England continued to rule that husbands had a right to assault their wives if wives refused to obey their husbands' orders (Edwards, 1985).

Early marriage laws also explicitly treated sexuality as a type of property. The 17th-century jurist Sir Matthew Hale suggested that when a wife marries, she permanently gives up her right to control her own sexuality:

> The husband cannot be guilty of a rape committed by himself upon his lawful wife, for by their mutual matrimonial consent and contract the wife hath given up herself in this kind unto her husband which she cannot retract. (from *Pleas of the Crown*, cited in Liss, 1987, p. 787)

According to English common law, all husbands thus maintained rights to have sex with their wives, referred to discretely by the courts as husbands' right to *consortium*. Acts that today might be considered sexual abuse were routinely excused by the courts in 18th-century England and America, especially if they were initiated by husbands against their wives or by wealthy landlords against female slaves and indentured servants. In other words, the courts considered these women's sexuality to be the property of their masters. Because women's sexual services were figuratively owned by the male head of household, the courts placed monetary value on them, sometimes compensating husbands if their wives ran off with other lovers. As late as the mid-19th century, the courts issued writs of "ravishment" or "trespass" that allowed husbands to obtain monetary damages from the men who had taken "their" wives. In this way, the courts compensated husbands for the loss of sexual services and for their wounded honor. In contrast, no such legal action or redress was available to wives (Edwards, 1985, pp. 191-192).

The idea that husbands are entitled to have sex with their wives is the argument that Ray Eastman used in the news story that opened this chapter. Although the judge did not support him, Mr. Eastman argued that he had the right to rape his own wife. Based on legal and religious principles stemming from the doctrine of coverture, Eastman figured he could do what he wanted with his wife. Because he was married to her, he assumed that he could have sex with her, regardless of her wishes. The California judge rejected Eastman's argument because the law now recognizes the individual rights of married women, but the legal precedent for treating wives as sexual property goes back hundreds of years.

Nineteenth-Century Feminist Challenges to Coverture

Marriage statutes in England and the United States came under attack during the 19th century because of their blatant treatment of women as second-class citizens. A few social activists, such as Lucy Stone and her husband, Henry Blackwell, set out to create an emancipated marriage that would allow the wife full freedom for a public career, by signing a contract in which the husband renounced his rights to his wife's services and property and in which the wife contracted to keep her maiden name (Lerner, 1977). In their "Marriage Protest of 1855," they declared that the marriage laws "confer upon the husband an injurious and unnatural superiority, investing him with legal powers which no honorable man would exercise, and which no man should possess" (Kraditor, 1968, p. 149). These sorts of individual contracts were rare, however, and were not sufficient to sustain a legal challenge against existing marriage laws (Liss, 1987, p. 769).

Two decades later, suffragist Susan B. Anthony attacked the common law notion of coverture at a trial in which she was found guilty of the "crime" of voting (U.S. woman were not allowed to vote at that time). In an impassioned line of argument, she sought protection for women under the 15th Amendment, which abolished slavery:

> I am ashamed that not one State has yet blotted from its statute books the old common law of marriage, . . . husband and wife are one, and that one is the husband. Thus may all married women, wives, and widows, by the laws of the several states, be technically included in the 15th Amendment's specification of "condition of servitude." . . . What is servitude? "The condition of a slave." What is a slave? "A person who is robbed of the proceeds of his labor; a person who is subject to the will of another." . . . I submit if the deprivation by law of the ownership of one's own person, wages, property, children, the denial of the right as an individual, to sue and be sued, and to testify in the courts, is not a condition of servitude, most bitter and absolute, though under the sacred name of marriage? (Susan B. Anthony, *United States of America v. Susan B. Anthony,* 1873, cited in Sachs & Wilson, 1979, pp. 88-89)

Susan B. Anthony, Elizabeth Cady Stanton, and other 19th-century feminists used a political discourse that equated marriage and slavery (Clark, 1993). Marriage as slavery was a powerful metaphor that helped mobilize support to reform legal codes, as did the joining of abolitionist and feminist causes. But the conditions of slavery for African Americans in this country (both women and men) produced much more brutal and direct exploitation than did the unequal marriage laws of the 19th century (Gutman, 1976; Rollins, 1985; Romero, 1992).

The 19th-century enactment of the Married Women's Property Acts removed some of the common law restrictions on the legal rights of wives, but marriage laws continued to treat women as second-class citizens into the 20th century (Speth, 1982). As the ideology of separate spheres developed (see Chapters 3 and 4), the distinction between public and private realms became the leading justification for treating men and women differently. Treating the public sphere of work as men's rightful domain and the private sphere of family as women's rightful domain provided an updated justification for sex-based laws. For example, the U.S. Supreme Court decided in 1873 that admission to the legal profession was not one of women's "privileges and immunities" guaranteed by the Constitution (Baron, 1987, p. 477). The court held that women's participation in the paid labor force could be legally restricted because "nature" intended that women remain confined to the family:

> The civil law, as well as nature herself has always recognized a wide difference in the respective spheres and destinies of man and woman. Man is, or should be, woman's protector and defender. The natural and proper timidity and delicacy which belongs to the female sex evidently unfits it for many of the occupations of civil life. The constitution of the family organization, which is grounded in divine ordinance, as well as in the nature of things, indicates the domestic sphere as that which properly belongs to the domain and functions of womanhood. . . . The paramount destiny and mission of woman are to fulfill the noble and benign offices of wife and mother. (*Bardwell v. Illinois*, 1973; cited in Otten, 1993, pp. 60-61)

The ideal of separate spheres provided justification for limiting women's rights outside marriage, but it also served as the basis for legal nonintervention in the family. At the same time that the courts were limiting women's rights in the public sphere of the economy, the private sphere of family was largely exempted from legal regulation. Citing constitutional precedents, the federal government avoided intruding into matters affecting the family, allowing individual states and the courts to define marriage, divorce, and inheritance rights. A patchwork quilt of state laws, court decisions, and government regulations arose to deal with family issues (Liss, 1987, p. 774). The complex and contradictory body of law that developed became known as family law. In it, the sanctity and privacy of the home were often invoked to exclude marriage from contract law and to exempt husbands from criminal and civil liabilities applied in other cases (such as spousal abuse and marital rape).

Invoking the concept of separate spheres and suggesting that men and women had separate destinies allowed 19th- and 20th-century law to continue to treat men and women differently, although with less outright discrimination than under the older system based on coverture. Under the older property-based system, private agreements between husbands and wives were not recognized. Under the new body of family law that has emerged, families have gained new rights to negotiate and bargain for the terms of their personal relationships, including marriage, divorce, child support, custody, and property disposition (Liss, 1987, p. 780).

These new rights have been limited, however, by state laws and by court decisions. For example, in the *Marvin v. Marvin* case of 1976, the California Supreme Court found several ways in which nonmarital cohabitation (living together without being married) could require a division of assets similar to what happens when a marriage breaks up. Although the court did open the door to the application of contract law to family relationships, it did not consider cohabitation to be the same as marriage. Although the courts and new state laws have sometimes expanded individual control over defining such family relationships, they have stopped short of making it an individual matter. For example, no state sanctions gay or lesbian marriages, and most forbid same-sex marital unions (Liss, 1987).

There are cross-cultural and historical precedents for the recognition of same-sex marriages, and gay and lesbian couples in the United States are now seeking the right to marry and the spouse benefits marriage affords (health, retirement, social security, etc.). Three Hawaiian same-sex couples applied for marriage licenses in 1990, and when their applications were denied, they sued the state, claiming they were treated unfairly. The Hawaii Supreme Court sent the case back to the Circuit Court (*Baehr v. Lewin*, 1993) where the judge, hearing evidence that gays and lesbians parent as well as heterosexuals, ruled that the state could not deny marriage licenses to same-sex couples (*Baehr v. Miike*, 1996). Because marriages performed in one state are typically recognized by the other 49, the Hawaii case prompted many legislative proposals at the federal and state levels. In 1996, Congress passed the "Defense of Marriage Act," stipulating that no state could be forced to recognize another state's same-sex marriage, and defining the marital union as between a man and a woman (104th Congress, HR3396). As of 1997, 16 states had passed anti-gay marriage measures and 20 states had rejected them. Laws banning same sex marriages are currently being challenged as unconstitutional, on the grounds that they deny certain rights to a particular group of people.

Modern Vestiges of Marriage as Property

Although things have changed considerably during the past century, conceptions of marriage based on Roman law, coverture, and the ideal of separate spheres continue to shape views about marital relationships. The ideal of marriage as property was carried forward in four essential provisions of the legally binding marriage contract: (1) The husband is the head of the household; (2) the husband is responsible for financial support; (3) the wife is responsible for domestic services; and (4) the wife is responsible for child care (Weitzman, 1981). Through the years, these essential provisions have been the legal bases for adjudicating marital disputes and the distribution of property on divorce.

People might think of these marital contract provisions about who is the family "boss" and who has to provide services to whom as overly formalized relics of the past, especially because so many American wives are now employed. Nevertheless, U.S. courts were still explicitly relying on these central assumptions about marriage during the 1970s, and most states continued to treat wives and their earnings as the property of their husbands. Legal provisions assumed that wives were supposed to tend house for their husbands, who were the rightful heads of their families. For example, many courts refused to enforce written or verbal contracts stipulating that the husband should pay his wife for housekeeping, entertaining, or other "wifely" duties. Even if the wife performed services outside the home, such as working in her husband's business, many courts voided the contracts requiring the husband to pay her because they assumed that he had rights to her labor and property because she was his wife (Weitzman, 1981).

People usually do not think about the legal obligations and property rights inherent in the marriage contract until they get divorced and divide up the property. In the 1960s and 1970s, many American women got a rude introduction to these patriarchal legal principles when their marriages ended. In some cases in which wives worked at their own jobs and saved money for their children's college during the marriage, courts awarded all the college savings to husbands on divorce. These courts reasoned that because the husband had the legal responsibility to support the family, any money left over after paying bills was legally his. In states with strict "head and master" rules, husbands were able to sell houses out from under their wives, even when the wives had purchased the houses entirely with money they had earned from their own jobs. Because the duties of cooking, cleaning, child care, and home upkeep were an expected part of the legal marriage bargain, when couples got divorced, the courts sometimes refused to let wives share any increase in the monetary value of house, farm, or other investments (Weitzman, 1981).

Although these examples show how many women lost out during marriage or after divorce, other cases show much more equitable distributions of property between husbands and wives, and some even show that men were discriminated against because of legal principles based on coverture or the ideal of separate spheres. For example, some judges made assumptions about men's superior earning capacity and women's superior parenting skills that favored women at the time of marital dissolution. Marital property rights differ, depending on whether one lives in a separate property or community property state and on the different laws passed by each state to govern what happens when two people get married. Legal decisions also depend on the case law that is used as precedent in each trial, on the attitudes and understandings of the judges and attorneys, and to some extent, on the normative expectations that exist in the community in which the trial is occurring. Other customs and practices governing marriage also come into play in divorce trials, including assessing blame for the marital breakup, awarding alimony, assigning child custody, and ordering child support. Divorce trials pose complicated questions for the courts, especially because the norms surrounding marriage and divorce are changing rapidly and because states are constantly reforming the marital contract laws.

Marriage and divorce laws have changed significantly since the 1970s, and most states now have laws that treat husbands and wives similarly. The most obvious inequities that occurred in the past relating to women's lack of control over marital property have been minimized, but debates continue about whether the new laws create as many problems as they solve (see, for example, Chesler, 1986; Jacob, 1988; Weitzman, 1981). Although marriage laws throughout the nation have become more gender neutral in the past two decades, the idea that women belong in the home, or that wives are the property of husbands, has not entirely disappeared from legal proceedings. As noted below, many judges continue to evaluate men and women differently, and women in some states still lose rights to own property or enter into legal contracts on the same basis as unmarried women (Freed & Walker, 1988; Liss, 1987; Lorber, 1994; Rhode, 1989). Even where the marriage and divorce laws have become more gender neutral, inequities remain because the labor market, family life, and other aspects of society are not gender neutral. To address these inequities, some have advocated going back to the old gender-differentiated laws that protected women (while treating them as second-class citizens). A more progressive solution would be to focus on making the other institutions of society as gender equitable as some of the new laws. For example, if women had the same job prospects, earnings, and chances for occupational advancement as do men, then gender-neutral laws governing postdivorce property dissolution and support would seem more equitable to women. If fathers took more responsibility for the day-to-day aspects of raising children, then gender-neutral laws for deciding child custody would seem more equitable to men. I return to these issues below.

Marriage Customs and Laws Change Together

Although legal reforms change the formal rules and regulations governing marriage, most people are affected more immediately by the informal customs surrounding marriage. When the laws change, social customs begin to change, but it is also true that when taken-for-granted practices associated with marriage begin to change, pressure mounts to change marriage laws. Although customs and laws are reciprocally linked in this fashion, they are not perfect mirrors of one another. Thus, some older legal assumptions about marriage survive in symbolic form.

For example, older marriage laws, following the principle of coverture, required that the wife take her husband's name when she got married. Although this legal requirement has changed, a vestige remains in the common practice of the wife taking her husband's name at marriage. If Miss Amy Jones marries Mr. Robert Smith, she becomes Mrs. Amy Smith, or more formally, Mrs. Robert Smith. The husband stays Mr. Robert Smith, just as before he got married. Symbolically, the wife is still being merged into the husband.

This custom is being transformed as marriage comes to be seen as a more equal institution. Some women now prefer to use the label *Ms.*, both before and after marriage, instead of using *Miss* before they get married and *Mrs.* after they get married. Nevertheless, changes have been slow, and the old customs still prevail, especially among families with more resources. More attention is given to naming offspring and tracing lineage when families have wealth to pass on to future generations. Even in such families, however, there have been complicated and long-held traditions of assigning names and retaining the mother's "maiden" name in a long string of ancestral labels.

New naming practices are gaining popularity among all segments of the population. Some women do not change their name when they marry or remarry. Instead, they maintain their birth name ("maiden name"). Others choose to hyphenate the last names of the husband and wife (although there are practical limits to the number of times this could be accomplished in succeeding generations). Others select an entirely new last name when they get married or assign the mother's last name to girl children and the father's last name to sons.

No new system has been developed to replace the old. Although some novel approaches are emerging, women continue to feel considerable social pressure, mostly from older family members, to adopt the husband's name when they marry. Not only are wives still much more likely to give up their old names than are husbands, but women are also more likely to use a hyphenated name than are men. The old assumptions about women being merged with their husbands on marriage are still present in this symbolic form. Perhaps even more influential in the modern context, however, are gender ideals and customs surrounding who should take care of children. In the following sections, I use changes in child support programs and child custody laws to show how old assumptions about gender, although changing, still shape public policies relating to family life.

Government Child Support

With nonmarital birth and divorce rates remaining at consistently high levels, there is increasing public concern over what happens to the children. Most live with their mothers, and because women continue to get paid less on the job than do men, recent studies show that in the aggregate, children in America are worse off than they have been since the federal government began keeping track of such things (Hernandez, 1993; see Figure 4.4). One study of poverty in the United States found that 1 in 3 children born around 1970 was poor for at least 1 year before reaching the age of 11; 1 in 3 was poor for 1 to 3 years; 1 in 12 was poor for 4 to 6 years; and 1 in 13 was poor for 7 to 10 years (Ellwood, 1987). Children who live in single-mother households for their entire childhood are much more likely to spend some of those years in poverty than are children in other family situations (O'Hare, 1996).

The racial/ethnic gap in poverty for both adults and children remains large and is increasing. Despite civil rights laws and sporadic attempts at affirmative action, the poverty gap between whites and minorities was the same in 1994 as it was in 1959. African Americans and Latinos are three times as likely to be poor as are whites, and Asian American poverty rates are more than one third higher than those of whites. When one considers assets as well as income, minority families are even worse off. White families with incomes under $12,000 per year had almost $8,000 in assets (median net worth) in 1993. In contrast, African American families of the same income level had a net worth of only $250, and Latino families of only $499 (O'Hare, 1996, pp. 24-25).

Thirty years ago, the percentage of older people (65 years and older) living in poverty was almost double the percentage of children (under age 18) living in poverty. In 1994, the percentage of children who were poor (22%) was nearly double the percentage of older persons who were poor (12%; O'Hare, 1996, Table 3). The implementation of social security and Medicare, plus a shift in the overall age of the population, has reduced the level of poverty for older people to less than half of what it was in the 1960s. The trends for children have gone in the

FIGURE 6.1

AFDC Is a Small Part of Federal Assistance Payments: Federal Social Assistance Payments to Individuals by Program, FY 1996 (Projected)
SOURCE: O'Hare, 1996, p. 32; U.S. Office of Management and Budget, *Budget of the United States Government FY 1997*, Table 11.3.

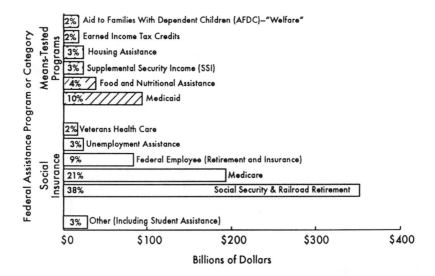

other direction, primarily because the level of government assistance to children has been declining. The largest government direct aid program for children has been AFDC, and its payments declined by nearly 50% between 1970 and 1994 (after adjusting for inflation; see O'Hare, 1996). It is likely that cash assistance to children will continue to decline; recent efforts to reform welfare have targeted AFDC for restructuring and massive cuts (see Chapter 7).

Although the American public has been frustrated by what appear to be soaring welfare costs, there is a common misunderstanding about what programs are driving those costs. Direct assistance to the poor constitutes a shrinking percentage of government expenditures. In 1996, the federal government was projected to spend more than $900 billion to provide benefits directly to individuals, about 58% of the total budget. Three out of four federal social assistance dollars will go to programs that are not targeted to persons who are poor. Figure 6.1 shows that social insurance (including programs such as social security, railroad retirement, federal employee retirement, veterans' health care, Medicare, and employment assistance) will consume almost three fourths of this money, or about $670 billion. Means-tested programs directed to the poor will account for $217 billion, or 24% of the total, with AFDC accounting for only about 2% of the total (O'Hare, 1996).

The recent decline in the well-being of children is linked to both family structure and poverty. Although some politicians and social scientists have suggested that women are frivolously walking away from marriages out of selfishness, recent studies show that most mothers who divorce their children's fathers are avoiding violent or unhealthy situations and trying to improve their children's life chances (Arendell, 1986; Kurz, 1995). Divorce is not a choice that is made lightly by most mothers because it is associated with increased chances of living in poverty. Children who live in single-parent households tend to be at greater risk than other children for delinquency, teen pregnancy, low educational achievement, and eventual poverty when they become adults. Nevertheless, economic differences between single-parent and two-parent households explain most (but not all) of the differences between the two groups (McLanahan, 1985; McLanahan & Booth, 1991; McLanahan & Bumpass, 1988; Seltzer, 1994). This suggests that many of the risks confronting children today could be alleviated by raising their standard of living.

Child Support and Child Custody Reforms

Rather than acting to increase direct assistance to children at risk, most recent government efforts have been directed toward reforming laws and policies regulating child custody determinations, the setting of parental child support levels, and the collection of child support payments from noncustodial parents. In an unusual convergence of interests during the 1980s, liberal feminists joined new right conservatives in reaffirming divorced fathers' obligations to provide financial support to their children. Organizing around the issue of "deadbeat dads" and from a desire to reduce child poverty and welfare dependency, several child support reforms were instituted.

In 1984, 1988, and 1993, the U.S. Congress passed legislation regulating how the courts award and collect money from noncustodial parents. Most of these changes were designed to ensure that the custodial parent (usually the mother) gets an award that is adequate to support the child and that the absent parent (usually the father) can be found and made to pay. In response to high levels of nonpayment, the federal government began to help states locate missing parents, monitor efforts to collect delinquent child support payments, and establish paternity at birth or conduct blood tests later. These reforms were aimed at three major weaknesses of the child support enforcement system: (1) Not all custodial families have child support awards (only about half); (2) existing awards are not fully paid (half receive full payments and a quarter receive partial payment); and (3) existing award levels do not generally reflect the noncustodial parent's ability to pay (most noncustodial fathers could pay three times more) (Sorensen & Turner, 1996).

Progress in getting absent parents to pay has been slow, primarily because efforts were initially directed toward recovering monies from parents (mostly fathers) of children receiving AFDC. Not surprisingly, people without steady work cannot afford to pay much. In 1995, the average amount of child support paid in an entire year was still only $530, and about half of absent parents were still paying nothing at all. Nevertheless, by standardizing award levels, computerizing tracking systems, and using automatic wage withholding, most states are now showing improvement in the amount of child support collected.

During the 1980s, family professionals, researchers, and the media showed renewed interest in children's needs for continuing close relationships with both parents. Although the ideal of keeping both parents involved in their children's lives had been around for some time, it received increased attention, especially from lawmakers. Championed by the fathers' rights movement, this ideal became institutionalized in joint custody statutes in state after state. In 1979, only five states had joint custody statutes, but by 1988, 34 states had adopted some form of joint custody (Ferreiro, 1990; Folberg, 1984; Freed & Walker, 1988). The courts in many states also began to make two distinct custody awards: legal custody and physical custody. Physical custody refers to which parent the child will live with on a day-to-day basis, and legal custody refers to the parental power to decide such things as a child's religion, education, and medical treatment. Although the courts continue to award physical custody to mothers in most cases, the trend has been toward more joint legal custody determinations. In some states, the majority of both mothers and fathers now request joint legal custody when they divorce, and courts routinely award it. For example, in California, the first state to enact a joint custody statute, about 20% of divorce decrees provide for joint physical custody, but more than three fourths provide for joint legal custody (Little, 1991; Mnookin, Maccoby, Depner, & Albiston, 1990).

Gender Politics in Custody/Support Reforms

Although issues of child custody and child support are closely intertwined for individuals involved in a divorce, legislative action and advocacy to change divorce laws tended to occur in relatively distinct arenas. Individual states modified their divorce laws to allow for joint custody, and the federal government changed the ways that it assisted in child support enforcement. In a study of grassroots custody and support organizations, I discovered that the joint custody advocates were almost all men, and the child support enforcement advocates were almost entirely women (see Coltrane & Hickman, 1992). The two movements used similar strategies: They both relied on individual horror stories (such as those presented in the news stories at the beginning of this chapter) to typify the injustices that they faced. They also offered huge numbers about the extent of the problem and argued for the moral superiority of their own position.

Gender was central to the custody and support reforms because activists claimed that the needs of (a) men or (b) women were being ignored. Although on opposite sides of the issue, both the fathers' groups and mothers' groups used gender bias as their rallying cry, but only the fathers' rights groups advanced claims using a language of rights and entitlement. Echoing the Roman and English common law notions of family as property, the men argued that fathers should have rights of access and control over their children. The mothers' groups, in contrast, were rarely referred to as rights groups by themselves or in the media. Instead, they usually advanced their claims through a separate spheres rhetoric of "needs," claiming that children needed to live with their mothers and that they needed the financial support of their noncustodial fathers. Mothers' claims often employed a language of loss, relying on notions of purity and innocence and calling for altruism and social responsibility by lawmakers. Images of benevolence or social control were typically invoked when women's "problems" were discussed, in stark contrast to the language of rights and sense of entitlement invoked when men's custody issues were presented (see Edelman, 1987; Ibarra & Kitsuse, 1993).

Both fathers' and mothers' groups claimed that the other gender enjoyed unfair advantage during adjudication of postdivorce parental rights and responsibilities. Both complained that judges, attorneys, mediators, psychologists, social workers, and other professionals used double standards when evaluating their fitness as parents or their obligations to pay child support. In other words, men and women activists claimed that judges and other professionals let normative expectations about mothers' and fathers' abilities influence judicial determinations about parental fitness and the best interests of children.

Fathers' rights groups argued that men were discriminated against in custody cases because both laws and judges assumed that mothers were better child caregivers. The men's groups claimed that bitter ex-wives routinely made false accusations about child abuse to limit the men's contact with their children, whereas their own claims about abuse by wives were ignored (as in the Alan Web case presented earlier). The men's groups also wanted the courts to enforce their rights to visit their children, even if they failed to make child support payments. Many fathers' groups advocated making joint physical custody a preference in state law, so that postdivorce child care would have to be shared unless one parent convinced the court that such an arrangement was unworkable.

In contrast to the fathers' groups' claims that judges automatically preferred mothers over fathers, the mothers' groups argued that expectations for mothers were so high that even minor transgressions called a mother's fitness into question (Chesler, 1986; Chodorow & Contratto, 1992). Conversely, expectations of fathers as child caregivers were so low that even minimal involvement was seen by judges as evidence of fitness for award of child custody. Mothers' groups also suggested that a double standard was used when considering employment. A man's superior earning power was considered by the courts as evidence of ability to provide a good home, whereas a woman's need to work long hours to earn minimal wages was seen as detracting from her ability to mother.

Feminist legal scholars also argued that a postdivorce sexual double standard was applied because judges interpreted single fathers' romantic involvements as potentially leading to the presence of a stepmother, whereas single mothers' romantic involvements were interpreted as evidence of moral decrepitude (Chesler, 1986; Fineman & Opie, 1987; Girdner, 1986; Smart, 1984). The Florida case cited in the beginning of the chapter—in which the judge removed a daughter from the care of her lesbian mother in favor of a heterosexual wife murderer— reflects such a double standard. This double standard follows from the cultural ideal of separate spheres for men and women. The movement for more strict child support enforcement paradoxically reinforces the ideal of separate spheres, insofar as it attempts to make the absent parent (usually the father) fulfill his duty as provider. But there are also ways in which the new reforms begin to transcend the separate spheres ideal because the language is usually gender neutral, so that occasionally the mother must pay child support if she has higher earnings and the child is residing with the father.

Although both fathers' and mothers' groups alleged that judges inappropriately used gender-linked stereotypes to decide custody and support, it was the fathers who vehemently promoted gender-neutral laws. Adopting the rhetoric of equal rights, the fathers' groups insisted that custody statutes should make no reference to a parent's gender. Mothers' groups countered that this sometimes ignores structural inequities faced by single mothers because they are women. For the most part, states quickly adopted the gender-neutral legal provisions promoted by the fathers' groups and thus stripped the old laws of some of their gender-linked protections for women, at the same time that they eliminated some of the sexist assumptions inherent in the laws. Because gender neutrality came faster to family law than to other legal areas, some interpreted divorce and custody reforms as a backlash against women's modestly expanding opportunities outside the home (Faludi, 1991; Lemon, 1981).

Should Laws and Policies Be Based on Gender Differences?

As the custody and support reforms show, the issue of whether the law should recognize differences between men and women has become hotly contested. In custody law reform, some women's groups advocate a maternal preference on the basis of the belief that children need mothers more than they need fathers. Fathers' rights groups oppose this as biased against men, and some feminists agree. As an alternative, others have proposed a gender-neutral primary caretaker provision, giving custody preference to the parent whose previous child care activities have been more extensive. This would treat men and women similarly, but in the typical case in which the mother did most of the child care, she would be a more likely candidate for becoming the custodial parent. In the more rare case in which the father did more of the child care, his contribution to the child's well-being would also be given paramount consideration. Such reforms are likely to increase the court's emphasis on determining who has been, and who is likely to be, the better parent. Unfortunately, the courts have proved to be better at adjudicating contracts than in determining what children need or what makes a good parent (Mnookin, 1975).

The general direction of reform in custody law, as in most other areas, has been toward more equal treatment of men and women. This is normally accomplished through the use of gender-neutral language, but many questions remain about whether gender neutrality in the law actually improves women's living conditions. The move to no-fault divorce laws symbolically reduced husbands' power over wives but at the same time reduced husbands' obligation to support their ex-wives after divorce. As the courts have come to expect both spouses to be employed after a divorce, they have been less willing to grant spousal support (alimony). Under the old laws, the assumption was that wives needed protection and that husbands should continue to be financial providers. The new gender-neutral language of most no-fault divorce laws can thus be seen as a blow against the patriarchal assumptions of the old laws and a victory for gender equality. Nevertheless, studies show that the actual financial condition of divorced women declined after the new laws went into effect (Duncan & Hoffman, 1985; Kurz, 1995; Seltzer, 1994).

Because some women have suffered under the gender-neutral legal reforms, feminists, as well as conservative traditionalists, have called for government attempts to acknowledge women's differences from men and to reinstate laws to protect them (Hauserman, 1983). Protective legislation, based on women's unique physiology (e.g., the capacity for menstruation, pregnancy, childbirth, and menopause) has been considered in health care, family leave, workplace safety, and exposure to hazardous substances. The conservative argument for special treatment assumes that women's first obligation is to be mothers and that they should be prohibited from performing certain dangerous jobs, such as military combat (Gilder, 1973; Schlafly, 1981). The feminist argument for special treatment focuses on substantive inequality rather than formal equality. This position assumes that gender neutrality is not equality in practice because it ignores the special needs of some individuals (MacKinnon, 1989).

Despite continuing debate on the issue, most feminists continue to reject attempts to treat women differently from men because of their special biological needs. The problem, according to Judith Lorber (1994), is that the biology that supposedly makes women "real women" simultaneously turns them into second-class citizens (p. 46). Following the ideology of separate spheres, laws and government policies tend to use women's procreative physiology to limit their access to work and thus to confine them to the home.

As noted above, the courts have used the principle of protection to exclude women from various male-dominated occupations (Baron, 1987). In *Muller v. Oregon* (1908), the U.S. Supreme Court justified placing women in a separate legal classification defined by their reproductive and social roles as mothers and wives. On the one hand, the court assumed that male employees could take care of themselves and that the state should not infringe on their inalienable right to contract their own labor (Baron, 1981). On the other hand, the court decided that women were a special class in need of protection because they were potential mothers and had always been dependent on men (Justice Brewer writing for the majority, cited in Rhode, 1989, p. 41). Ironically, the *Muller* decision has been used to exclude women from relatively well paying traditional male jobs but has not been used to protect women from toxic substances in traditional female jobs such as hairdressing or housecleaning (Baron, 1987; Wright, 1979). Even in nonemployment-related cases, U.S. courts have relied on *Muller* to justify unequal treatment of women, leading some legal scholars to assume that an Equal Rights Amendment would be required to overturn its assumptions (Baron, 1987, p. 487).

In contrast to the strategy of protecting women on the basis of biological difference, most feminists continue to advocate implementing more gender-neutral laws and policies. Some (e.g., Lorber, 1994) suggest that law and policies should be used to minimize the influence of gender, thereby making women and men interchangeable in both jobs and family work. To move in this direction, Lorber emphasizes the need to change more than people's attitudes:

Women and men at present are rarely interchangeable because the social order is structured to advantage men and disadvantage women. In the micropolitics of everyday life and the macropolitics of laws and state policies, dominant men are so privileged that they continue to dominate without much conscious effort. Women and subordinate men have to show that they are as good as dominant men to succeed economically, politically, or artistically—the burden of proof is on them. Social policies that ignore this structure of gender inequality and assume that remedies can take place on the individual level are doomed to failure, and the failure will be attributed to the attitudes, competencies, and motivations of the individuals concerned, both dominant and subordinate, not to the social structure. (p. 298)

Lorber's point is that gender bias is so embedded in our social institutions that it is not just an individual problem. Gender equity is not simply a matter of changing people's attitudes and trying to guard against being prejudiced. We must change the underlying structure of the institutions so that the microstructures of social interaction will allow for more equitable gender relations (Risman & Schwartz, 1989). If we want individual men and women to be able to choose who or what they want to be on an equal basis, then we need to change the opportunities and rewards available to them.

Linda Haas (1992) makes a similar point in suggesting that social policy initiatives promoting equal parenting must begin in the workplace:

As long as women's and men's job situations remain different, with women being channeled into part-time, low-status, and lower-paying jobs, women will remain uninterested in relinquishing their monopoly over child care. . . . As long as employers see men as less dispensable than women, consider women to be responsible for early child care, and value short-term profit over long-term productivity gains, men will be discouraged from reducing their involvement in paid employment to be more involved in active child care. (p. 228)

The Larger Social Context

My concern in this chapter has been to examine how most government policies can be seen as family policies and how family policies are also gender policies. These policies and laws, whether explicitly about families or not, have been tied up with issues of power and control, as suggested by critical theories of gender and the state. I have illustrated this with reference to the history of laws regulating marriage, as well as with reference to recent legal reforms in divorce and child custody. Because the legal system is only one of many social institutions, this analysis has necessarily been incomplete. One could also examine other social institutions, such as education, medicine, religion, media, business, and politics, to see how assumptions about gender enter into the definition and regulation of families.

I referred to some of the public programs that attempt to serve families directly but did not cover the many areas in which government action helps to shape social contexts within which families operate. In a more extended policy analysis, one could examine the gender assumptions inherent in the government's involvement as provider or regulator of prisons, health care, job training, unemployment, social security, or welfare. Moving from public to private organizations, one could examine the gender meanings inherent in the church's policies about sex, birth control, abortion, child discipline, or divorce or corporate policies relating to work scheduling, parental leave, day care, and so on. There is no room for these analyses here, but I would be surprised if such analyses produced results that were much different from those presented for the law. Whether the focus was on schools, hospitals, churches, or factories, gender meanings would undoubtedly shape the definition of families and the delivery of services to them. Tracing the history of these institutions' treatment of families would show patriarchal beginnings, an emergent ideology of separate spheres, and some recent movement toward gender neutrality. The analyses would also probably show that patriarchy, separate spheres, and gender neutrality continue an uneasy coexistence in official policies up to the present.

Equally important, the individuals responsible for implementing various programs and policies would undoubtedly treat families according to their own conventional understandings of appropriate gender behaviors. Judges and lawmakers have done this in the past, and the news stories at the beginning of the chapter show that this continues today. It is hoped that those responsible for helping families of the future and those framing new family laws and policies in the coming decades will be able to examine their own gender biases and learn from the mistakes of the past. It is impossible to anticipate all the consequences of a particular law or policy and to avoid having preconceived notions about what families should be and what mothers and fathers should do within them. Neither is it always possible to enact policies that affect men and women the same. But by becoming aware of preconceived notions and by considering the gender implications of family policies, policy makers and family professionals will be better able to serve the needs of all family members in the future. When they can see the gender implications of various policy proposals, lawmakers, public officials, religious leaders, and business executives will be in a better position to make subtle changes in the structural conditions under which we live. This is an enormous challenge, but one that must be faced to create a more just and equitable world.

Note

1. The Family and Medical Leave law has not been operating long enough to evaluate fully how it is working, but preliminary reports suggest that fewer people have taken advantage of it than anticipated, probably because they feel that they cannot afford to. Because the leave is unpaid, most people take it when they have used up the rest of their sick leave but cannot yet return to work.

CHAPTER 7

Where Do We Go From Here?

In this book, you have seen how family life is influenced by gender and how families re-create the meaning of gender. You have also seen how gender and family are social constructions shaped by specific historical and economic conditions. Unlike biological sex, gender is produced through routine social interactions, many of which are linked to family life. Some are formalized ceremonies, such as weddings, baby showers, birthdays, and family holidays, but most are common everyday practices that people take part in without giving them a second thought—such as talking, making dinner, and watching television. Until reading this book, you probably didn't think that controlling the TV clicker or doing the family laundry had the potential to create gender difference and sustain gender inequality. You may not have considered how you might change the family and gender patterns you see around you, but the social constructionist theory presented in this book offers you a way to do just that. One of the nice things about this theoretical approach is that it takes what people think and do seriously. It says that you create your own reality. Of course, you don't get to create your reality out of nothing, and plenty of other people are running around trying to create their own version of reality, which might be at odds with yours. Although you are always involved in creating and re-creating the social meaning of things, it takes many actions and countless people to transform social customs and change economic structures. Nevertheless, the social constructionist framework shows you how the little things you do in your everyday life will inevitably influence some of the larger structures that govern society. Ultimately, you have the power to change the world!

Scholars have only recently begun to study how gender and families are socially constructed, but we are now beginning to understand some of the primary processes involved. We are learning more about how an analysis of power and inequality is essential to knowing how gender and families are interrelated. There are now many books and articles on the topic from a variety of academic disciplines and political perspectives. (As a starting point, consult the list of references at the back of this book.) In this volume, I have been able to touch on just a few of the different approaches, primarily focusing on the sociological, historical, and social-psychological aspects of links between gender and families. I have attempted to defend the assertion that we cannot understand families without reference to gender, nor gender without reference to families, and that both must be understood within larger social and historical contexts and with reference to important differences based on class, race, and ethnicity.

In Chapter 1, I suggested that family rituals such as Thanksgiving carry hidden messages about gender and contribute to our common everyday understanding about who men and women are and what they should do in and for families. In Chapter 2, I described how love and marriage are linked to gender, with patterns of courtship and romance shaped by different opportunities on the marriage market and different approaches to sex and intimacy. In Chapter 3, I showed how the ideal of separate spheres developed in response to changing economic conditions, with men becoming identified with paid work and women identified with housework. In Chapter 4, I turned to a description of how parenting and family life have been affected by the ideal of separate spheres, with women assuming primary responsibility for raising children and taking care of family members' emotions. In Chapter 5, I explored how parents and other adults have socialized children to conform to rigid gender expectations and how some of those practices might be changing. Finally, in Chapter 6, I looked at how laws and government policies have reinforced conventional gender expectations but also at how they have struggled to keep pace with the realities of life in American families today.

In most of these chapters, I focused on historical examples because they are the most compelling way to show how things change when the social, political, and economic contexts change. I imagine that most of you are more concerned with the present than the past, but reviewing the history of families and gender gives us a glimpse into some of the underlying dynamics of social change and into the social processes that sustain gender inequality. History also gives us an idea of what might be possible in the future. I focused on the ideal of separate spheres in family rituals, courtship, work, caring, child rearing, and the law to bring modern linkages between gender and families into focus. The ideal of separate spheres is not fixed or unalterable—quite the opposite. In the future, we are likely to see the ideal transformed in profound ways.

In this final chapter, I reflect on issues now confronting families and describe the direction in which families might be headed. I review some of the findings from the earlier chapters as I highlight the most important trends that will influence families and gender in the coming decades. In addressing our future prospects, I ask some questions that do not have easy answers. That means that you need to draw on your own insights and developing knowledge about families and gender to make your own predictions about the future. The issues involved include many that you will face in your personal lives as family members and in your professional lives if you are going to work with families. I hope you can generate some additional questions that seem relevant to you as you address the difficult and important dilemmas that families will face in the next century.

The Major Social Forces

What are the major social forces that will affect families and gender in the future? To simplify and summarize, I group them into the categories of economic, social, demographic, and political trends. (For a more detailed discussion of these and other trends, see Coltrane, 1996.) After presenting the trends, I raise some questions about their potential impact on family life and gender meanings.

Economic Trends

As we saw from discussions on the historical development of separate spheres in earlier chapters, changes in the labor market tend to be the driving force behind many changes in family life and gender ideals. This is as true in the modern era as it was when people were making the initial transition from a rural agricultural society to an urban industrial one. The shifts in labor force participation for husbands and wives have been especially profound. In the 1940s and 1950s, so-called traditional families (husband breadwinners and wife homemakers) out-numbered other types of families by at least two to one. By the late 1970s, there were as many two-earner families as traditional families, with other families (including single mothers, single fathers, and others) following close behind. Today, there are twice as many two-earner families as traditional families, and almost as many "other" families as dual-earner ones (Ahlburg & DeVita, 1992; Hayge, 1990; U.S. Bureau of the Census, 1995a). By the year 2010, there will be even fewer traditional families and a preponderance of others (see Figure 7.1).

When young women are employed, their position on the marriage market and in the home changes. As I discussed in Chapters 2 and 6, the marriage bargain has not given women much leverage in the past, so recent employment gains have allowed them to be a little more wary of the deal they are striking if they get married. This is a large part of why women are waiting longer to marry, deciding not to get married at all, or divorcing when the marriage does not work out. When women and mothers are employed, it also begins to change how work is divided in the home, with married couples sharing more of it and single mothers relying on kin, children, and others for paid and unpaid help.

As we saw in Chapters 3 and 4, the changes in household labor are smaller than one would expect if families divided jobs in the most efficient or democratic way, primarily because of the lasting impact of the ideal of separate spheres. Nevertheless, as women earn more money and spend more time on the job, their bargaining power increases. If they are married, they can bargain for more help with child care and housework from husbands. If they are unmarried or divorced but have well-paying jobs, they can pay for services such as child care, restaurant meals, and a housekeeper. But this hired help is primarily the low-paid labor of other women. For many working-class women and women of color, labor market participation barely gains them enough to live on. If they are married, their low-paying jobs may enable them to ask a little more of their husbands. But marriages are more fragile for those living near the poverty line, and increasing numbers of women will stay single or separate from their partners, even if they

FIGURE 7.1

The Decline of "Traditional" Families From 1940 to 2010
SOURCE: Ahlburg & DeVita, 1992, p. 25; Hayge, 1990, p. 16.
NOTES: "Traditional" families = husband breadwinner/wife homemaker.
Dual-earner families = husband and wife workers.
Other families = single-parent families, couples with only wife worker, no workers, and other related people living together.
Projections shown for 1997 through 2010 are my estimates.

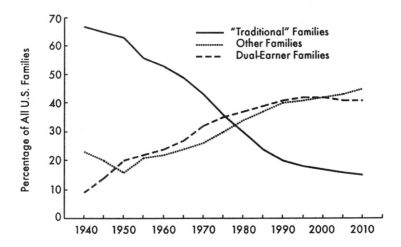

have children. The double duty of a low-paying service job, or other people's domestic work, will be added to their own housework, leaving little time for leisure or money for recreation.

Not only have women been entering the labor market in record numbers, but the pattern of their labor force participation is coming to resemble that of men. The most dramatic changes have occurred for married women with children. As discussed in Chapter 4, pregnant women are less likely to quit their jobs and more likely to return to work shortly after giving birth than ever before (U.S. Bureau of the Census, 1990). In 1960, less than 20% of married women with preschool-age children were in the paid labor force, but today more than 60% are. The increase for women with school-age children is even more profound. In 1960, less than 40% were employed, whereas more than 75% are employed today (U.S. Bureau of the Census, 1995b; see Figure 3.3). Mothers with younger children are more likely to work part-time than those with older children, but the trend is toward mothers working more hours because of financial necessity.

What will happen with women's labor force participation in the future? That will depend on developments in the larger economy, but indications are strong that things will continue in the direction they are heading. Additional information to address this question comes from young people's plans for the future. Considerable evidence suggests that the educational and career expectations of young American women and men have converged and that they will continue to do so.

The overall gender segregation of college majors in the past three decades has steadily declined, and women now outnumber men in colleges across the country (U.S. Bureau of the Census, 1995b). In the 1960s, boys had higher educational and occupational aspirations than did girls (Marini & Greenberger, 1988). By the 1980s, however, there were few if any gender differences in youth aspirations, and some surveys found that girls had higher occupational aspirations than did boys (Farmer, 1983). More than 90% of adolescent girls now expect to be employed after they marry, and virtually all those expect to be working after they become mothers (most after taking some time off following the birth). Most adolescent boys similarly expect their future wives to hold paid jobs, although many express uncertainty about whether their wives will continue to hold jobs after having children (Dennehy & Mortimer, 1992; Tittle, 1981). That teenage girls have expectations for more continuous labor force participation than teenage boys have for them could portend future trouble (Machung, 1989). If young women's attitudes are changing faster than young men's, marital conflicts over jobs and family work are likely to ensue.

Young people's expectations about the future have a way of shifting to correspond to the practical choices they face in life. Most of those choices will be shaped by developments in the larger economy. Analysis of recent changes in the economy are many and varied, but there is a broad consensus on some of the most essential points. Analysts agree that there has been a global transformation of finance, business, and industry, with capital becoming more internationalized and competitive markets around the world becoming more closely linked. Employers in the United States and throughout the world have attempted to maximize profits and increase efficiency through restructuring, technological innovation, and reduction of labor costs. They have often moved production from factory and office to private homes, from older urban areas to less expensive rural areas, and from industrialized countries to less developed countries (Acker, 1992). These changes in the global division of labor have occurred as the general economy has shifted away from large-scale manufacturing, particularly in the male-dominated smokestack industries. The movement of capital and employment has been toward service industries that are the bedrock of the information economy (Ciancanelli & Berch, 1987; Porter, 1990; Wood, 1989).

Because of continued global restructuring and growth in the service sector, the demand for lower-wage jobs is projected to increase. Most of the new jobs will be filled by women (Acker, 1992). Women are a majority of workers in the three occupational categories that are projected to have the most job openings in the last part of the 1990s and into the next decade: service, administrative support, and professional specialty. Health and personal service occupations, both composed primarily of women, are also projected to have extremely high growth rates in the coming decades (Silvestri & Lukasiewicz, 1991). By the year 2005, women will constitute nearly half the total labor force (Kutscher, 1991).

In fields in which women are already significantly represented, female representation in higher-paying jobs (e.g., professional specialties and executive, administrative, and managerial jobs) will likely increase (Silvestri & Lukasiewicz, 1991). Others predict that gains for women in management will level off as restructuring eliminates significant numbers of middle-level management positions and favors the incumbency of men (Acker, 1992). Part-time positions (about 20% of all workers) are also projected to increase substantially. Part-time and flexible work situations typically allow for integrating family work and paid work, but such positions also tend to lack benefits (health insurance, vacation pay, parental leave, etc.), and few offer opportunities for career advancement. Women hold almost two thirds of current part-time jobs, and growth in this area will mean employment for many more women in the near future. Nevertheless, because of financial necessity, job availability, and personal preference, most employed women will continue to work full-time (Acker, 1992).

Even if the economy falters or overheats, more women can be expected in the labor force in the next decades. Some women will continue to enter higher-paying management and professional positions, but the majority will occupy lower-paying, second-tier positions. Aggregate projections for minority women and men are relatively pessimistic, with continued overall decreases expected in their earning power (Kutscher, 1991). As manufacturing jobs decline, however, the relative positions of men and women will continue to converge. Men's real wages (adjusted for inflation) are likely to continue their downward slide, and in the more bleak projections, unemployment for men is expected to increase significantly. The major economic dividing line between families will become the number of earners in the household, with two-job couples faring better, on average, than single-breadwinner families or single-parent families. For subgroups with high rates of male unemployment or underemployment and/or increasing female earnings (i.e., African Americans and Latinos), there will be less incentive for women to stay married or to marry in the first place. Single mothers and their children, especially in minority communities, will continue to struggle economically, and most will be at risk for living in poverty.

Equality of employment is definitely not just around the corner, but according to the economic forces outlined above, the gap between men's and women's labor force participation rates and pay scales will continue to narrow. This should lead to more parity in men's and women's bargaining position on the marriage market and within the home. Nevertheless, increasing equality between men and women will occur in the context of increasing income inequality in the population at large. Real wages have been falling since the 1970s, and the gap between rich and poor has been widening. Particularly for those with little education, wages have remained low and are expected to continue at low levels. The U.S. Bureau of the Census began studying the distribution of income in the late 1940s. Between 1947 and 1968, income inequality decreased (as measured by the Gini index). After 1968, income inequality began to rise. In the 1980s, it surpassed the 1947 level and today sits at an all-time high (Weinberg, 1996).

An alternative way of looking at income inequality is to divide U.S. households into five equal groups and assess how much of the nation's income is earned by each. Figure 7.2 shows that the bottom fifth (lowest 20% of the population) gets under 4% of the income. The proportion of income earned by the bottom fifth has fallen 16% since 1974. The middle three fifths (60% of the population) earn about half the income, with their share falling from 52% in 1974 to 47% in 1994. The top

FIGURE 7.2

The Rich Get Richer, the Poor Get Poorer: Distribution of Aggregate Household Income, 1974 to 1994
SOURCE: DeVita, 1996, Figure 16; U.S. Bureau of the Census, 1996a, Figure 2.

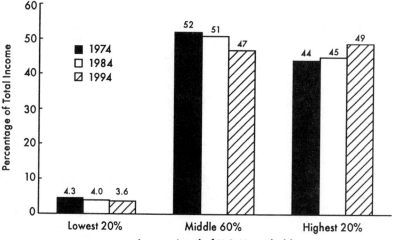

fifth (highest 20% of the population), in contrast, has seen its share of the income increase from 44% in 1974 to 49% in 1994 (DeVita, 1996, p. 40; see Figure 7.2). The top 5% of the population (not shown separately on Figure 7.2) controls more than 20% of all the income and an even greater share of the total wealth (e.g., stocks, bonds, securities, real estate, and other assets).

We can thus see an alarming trend: The disparity between the rich and the poor accelerated rapidly during the 1980s and continues upward. Despite the positive evaluation of the U.S. economy from most observers, and increasing dividends for corporations and wealthy individuals, restructuring and downsizing have not benefited most American workers. The income of the middle class is declining, and the middle class itself appears to be shrinking. The ranks of the poor are swelling, with people of color and single-mother households most likely to be mired in poverty (O'Hare, 1996).

If income inequality in the overall population continues in the direction it is heading, there will be increasing pressure on both spouses in married couples to become and stay employed. Two-job families will be able to stay in the middle-class, whereas one-earner families will have to fight to stay out of poverty. Workers at the bottom of the income pyramid, such as undereducated Latinos, will tend to live in poverty-level households, even if they are married. Because income inequality is increasing, we should guard against thinking that women's increasing labor force participation is simply a movement toward equity for women. Recent developments represent significant new pressures to work at undesirable jobs for both men and women and to spend more hours in paid employment per family member than at any time in the past four decades.

Social Trends

Along with economic factors, social attitudes will continue to influence family lives and gender relations. As outlined in previous chapters, individualism has been increasingly emphasized and accepted in the United States and other industrialized nations during this century. The ideal of mutual love and sex within marriage paralleled the rise of the individual marital market. When people began negotiating their own marriage matches, instead of serving as pawns in a system of patriarchal kinship networks and property exchanges, more emphasis was placed on romantic love. As people increasingly engaged in open competition for sexual partners through face-to-face interaction, a cult of individualism developed, with the self becoming the sacred object (Goffman, 1967). As shown in Chapter 2, in modern courtship rituals, the lovers tend to idealize each other, and the sex and love that they share come to symbolize the relationship (Collins, 1988). In the past, formal marriage has legitimated this exclusive emotional and sexual relationship, but as mate selection has become more individualized, so has the institution of marriage. For example, growing individualism is reflected in increasing levels of cohabitation and divorce.

As we saw in Chapter 3, the increasing emphasis on individualism also affected parents' attitudes toward children. Surveys of child-rearing values from the 1920s to the 1970s show American parents placing decreasing emphasis on obedience, loyalty to church, and conformity, while placing increasing emphasis on autonomy, tolerance, and thinking for one's self (Alwin, 1988). The gradual increases in tolerance and independence go hand in hand with the loosening of normative prescriptions about family life and sexual activity. Between the 1960s and late 1970s, Americans became less likely to agree that everyone should marry and have children and less likely to disapprove of cohabitation, extramarital affairs, and divorce (Thornton, 1989). Living together without being married was considered new and radical in the 1960s, but it was much more acceptable by the late 1970s and was even considered as a form of tentative marriage by most Americans. The attitude changes can be summarized by saying that the cultural imperative to marry, remain married, have children, restrict intimate relations to marriage, and maintain separate roles for men and women weakened considerably in the 1970s and early 1980s (Thornton, 1989). At the same time, however, the vast majority of Americans continued to say that they valued marriage, parenthood, and family life.

In the 1980s and into the 1990s, public opinion shifted somewhat, and the acceptance of different types of family arrangements leveled off. In only one area did attitudes continue to change as fast, or faster, than they did in the 1970s: gender ideals. Attitudes toward gender were already relatively liberal by the end of the 1970s, but they became even more so in the following decades. In answer to questions about who should make family decisions, who should hold a job, who should take care of children, and who should be involved in politics or other extrafamilial activities, Americans continued to become more accepting of women's increasing independence and opportunities (Grigsby, 1992). This was especially so for younger people, as indicated by surveys of high school students

(Thornton, 1989). In addition, Americans became less worried about the negative impacts of maternal employment and day care on children, an attitude change that paralleled the dramatic increase in both these activities during the same period. In sum, during the past three decades, there has been a definite increase in individualism and a decline in the cultural ideal of separate spheres (at least as measured by responses to national opinion polls).

Most attitude surveys focused on changing attitudes about women, but there is some indication that attitudes about men are also changing. For example, national surveys of young people show an upward trend from the 1970s into the 1990s, with more than three quarters of female high school students and more than two thirds of male high school students agreeing that husbands should take on more of the housework and child care when their wives are employed (Grigsby, 1992; Thornton, 1989). In addition, these percentages tend to go up once the young people move out on their own (Thornton, 1989) and tend to hold even for youth who identify as traditional in other ways (Machung, 1989). As noted in Chapter 4, a large number of studies also show that men in the United States and in many other industrialized countries rank fatherhood as more important than paid work (although they may spend most of their time on the job; J. Pleck, 1983; Wilkie, 1993).

Most Americans, especially if they are younger, already say they subscribe to the ideal of equality of opportunity for men and women. It is likely that even more Americans will endorse such concepts in the future. As the labor force participation of men and women becomes more similar, and if men's and women's wages continue to converge, we can expect more emphasis on individual well-being and a further weakening of the separate spheres ideal. In general, these shifts in attitude signal that courtship and marriage will become more balanced and individualized. Women will be more assertive in mate selection, and men will be less able to use employment as an excuse to escape domestic responsibilities. The continuing tendency for Americans to value personal well-being and individual achievement also means that women and men will not be likely to stay in relationships that are considered harmful or incompatible.

Within marriages, the expectations, bargaining strategies, and fairness perceptions of both spouses will undergo change as gender attitudes become less rigid. Men and women will define fewer activities as solely the province of one spouse or the other. This does not mean that changes in attitudes (or behaviors) will be swift or uniform. Men's attitudes about gender are almost certain to remain more conservative than those of women, and many will continue to maintain their privileged position by not noticing when household tasks need doing, acting incompetent, or remaining emotionally unavailable (see Goode, 1992; Segal, 1990). But because Americans are more likely than ever to agree that children need frequent contact with their fathers, there will be continuing ideological support for fathers to be involved with their children.

Demographic Trends

Changing attitudes toward gender and family are tied to changing economic circumstances, as mentioned above. Changing attitudes and economic conditions also contribute to changes in marriage rates and other demographic trends, as noted in the discussion of individualism. In the future, employment trends and a continuing emphasis on individual self-fulfillment are likely to sustain high levels of geographic mobility, educational attainment, cohabitation, delayed marriage, single parenthood, divorce, and remarriage.

In a relatively short time, cohabitation went from being a deviant and rare activity to being a normal step to getting married. In 1970, there were only about half a million cohabiting couples in the United States, but by the early 1990s, there were about 3 million (Ahlburg & DeVita, 1992). This is still a relatively small proportion of all couples, however. More than 56 million American households are composed of married couples. Cohabiting couples act much the same as married couples, and a large proportion of these relationships end in a formal marriage (about 40%; Laumann et al., 1994). About one third of all cohabiting male-female couples have children, not remarkably different from the one half of all married couples with children. Cohabiting couples and married couples have more similar patterns of sexual possessiveness and mutual economic support than couples who do not live together. Relatively few differences are found between cohabitors and married couples (Blumstein & Schwartz, 1983), but cohabitors have more sexual partners than married couples (although fewer than noncohabitors; Laumann et al., 1994). This suggests that cohabitation is a sort of halfway point between being single and being married and is likely to be a normal transition to marriage in the future. As noted in Chapter 6, cohabitation, although easier to break up than marriage, is sometimes treated as a form of marriage, insofar as separating individuals increasingly rely on the courts to sort out their property and child support obligations after they break up. A strong motivation for cohabitors to marry is to take advantage of employment benefits such as medical care, dental care, insurance coverage, and retirement plans that are confined to spouses. This is one of the reasons that gays and lesbians have mobilized for the legalization of same-sex marriages (Stacey, 1996).

Although cohabitation is increasing, the high value placed on romantic and family relationships, coupled with increasing dependence on two incomes, will keep U.S. marriage and remarriage rates relatively high. Contrary to the political rhetoric about the disappearance of marriage, the number of married people in the United States is rising. There will be differential rates for various subgroups, with a tendency for existing cultural patterns to continue. Thus, single-female households, long common among African Americans, will continue at their current high levels. Asian American and Latino marriage rates will continue to be higher than for African Americans, but they will be strongly influenced by economic opportunity. If job prospects improve for these groups (especially for the men), then marriage rates will stay at current levels. If there is increasing income inequality, then all minority marriage rates will go down. Among whites, marriage rates will continue to fall, but only slightly. The relative proportion of all adults who are married will decline slightly, but more than 90% of Americans will marry in the future (U.S. Bureau of the Census, 1992b). People will wait longer to marry, with the average age at marriage moving into the later 20s (U.S. Bureau of the Census, 1992a). Teenage pregnancy will continue to be higher among disadvantaged groups. The age gap in marriage, with men being older than the women they marry, is also likely to decline somewhat, especially in remarriages. There will also be more remarried couples in the future, with their more complicated forms of parenting and family labor sharing, especially among the middle class of all races and ethnicities.

Individualism and career commitments will cause more people to postpone marriage and childbearing, but the increasing emotional value of children will ensure that most couples will eventually have children. Forecasts suggest that fewer than 15% of women born during the 1950s will ultimately remain childless and that the statistically average woman will have two children (U.S. Bureau of the Census, 1991b). Birthrates among women of childbearing age have recently increased (U.S. Bureau of the Census, 1995b). Although teenage births have been falling slightly, they are likely to remain at relatively high levels unless more aggressive birth control policies are adopted. Teenage birthrates among African American women are much higher than for other groups and will likely remain so unless living conditions and job opportunities in urban areas improve appreciably. Delaying childbirth until the mid- or late 20s has been, and will continue to be, more common, especially for white women. In the aggregate, births to women over 30 have climbed faster than any other age group and now constitute about one third of all U.S. births (U.S. Bureau of the Census, 1991a; U.S. Department of Health and Human Services, 1996). Delayed birth is linked to higher levels of employment for women. Demographers predict that recent trends toward delaying parenthood will continue, or perhaps increase, in the coming decades (Rindfuss, Morgan, & Swicegood, 1984), although the rates will continue to vary by race, ethnicity, and social class.

What difference does it make that women are waiting longer to have children? Not surprisingly, this trend is linked to the economic and attitude shifts noted above. Women who delay having children will spend more of their early adult years in college and in better-paying jobs or careers. They are also less likely to give up their jobs when they become mothers and will take less time off from work leading up to and following the births of their children (U.S. Bureau of the Census, 1990). Delayed marriage and birth, along with having fewer children, will also be associated with more equal marriage bargains and more sharing of family work among couples (Coltrane, 1996).

Although most U.S. women still have children after they are married, another significant recent change is that marriage and parenting are not as automatically linked as they were earlier in the century. As noted in Chapter 4, the number of births to unmarried women has increased dramatically in the past few decades, with the highest percentages for black women, who are now much more likely to give birth outside marriage than in it (see Figure 4.2). Contrary to popular opinion, the *rate* of increase in nonmarital births has been even greater for whites than for blacks in recent years (although it started at a much lower rate; U.S. Bureau of the Census, 1989; U.S. Department of Health and Human Services, 1990, 1996). Also contrary to a common assumption, most of the increase in nonmarital birth is the result of women over the age of 20 having babies, not an increase in the rate of teenage pregnancies (Ahlburg & DeVita, 1992). Almost a third of all births will occur outside marriage during the 1990s. Although many observers are alarmed by this percentage, as noted in Chapter 4, trends in the United States are roughly similar to those of many modern industrial societies.

As a result of increases in nonmarital birth and divorce, the number of single-parent households in the United States has more than doubled since the 1970s. About 86% of single-parent households are headed by mothers, but the rate of growth for single-father households has been even higher than for single-mother households (U.S. Bureau of the Census, 1989, 1995b). About half of all recently born children can expect to spend some time in a single-parent family before they reach the age of 18 (Bumpass, 1990). Although many single parents do not remarry (or marry for the first time), the majority still do, especially if they are white. As a result, a third of all American children born in the 1980s are expected to spend some time in a stepparent household, and rates are expected to be similar for those born in the 1990s. These aggregate rates, however, represent the experience of the hypothetical average child, and one of the most dramatic trends of the past few decades has been the declining well-being of minority children (Hernandez, 1993; Starrels et al., 1994).

Another dramatic demographic shift has to do with the relative longevity of women and men (how long they live). Women used to outlive men by only one year on average; now they tend to outlive them by about eight years (U. S. Bureau of the Census, 1995b). This means that women are much more likely than men to be widowed, and the difference in longevity makes the aging population overwhelmingly female. Among those over age 65, there are about three females for every two males, with about 80% of the men, but just 40% of the women, married. The imbalances are even larger as people get older. The differences in mortality patterns mean that many more elderly women than men are living alone. In contrast, there are slightly more men than women under 45 living alone (see Figure 7.3).

There are undoubtedly interesting causes and consequences related to gender in the increasing mortality rate differences between men and women, but social scientists have yet to figure them out. The causes are probably not biological because they only appeared during the latter part of this century. Some have assumed that the stresses and strains associated with jobs have caused men to die earlier, but this reason is suspect because the mortality age gap has widened at the same time that women have entered the labor force in record numbers. The reason for men's earlier death is probably related to socially constructed gender differences, insofar as men are encouraged to take more physical risks, pay less attention to nutrition, bottle up their emotions, be self-reliant, and ignore pain. Research remains to be done in this area.

One of the consequences of the differential mortality rates is in caregiving patterns for persons who are frail. Women are likely to care for their husbands when they grow old and if they become infirm. Husbands are typically a couple of years older than wives to begin with, and then wives outlive them by eight years, so the average married woman is around for a decade longer than her spouse. As noted in Chapter 4, most of the care given to older women when they become frail is provided by their daughters or other female relatives. Some slight

FIGURE 7.3

Older Women Are Most Likely to Live Alone: Percentage of Adults Living Alone, by Age and Sex, 1970 and 1994
SOURCE: U.S. Bureau of the Census, 1994c.

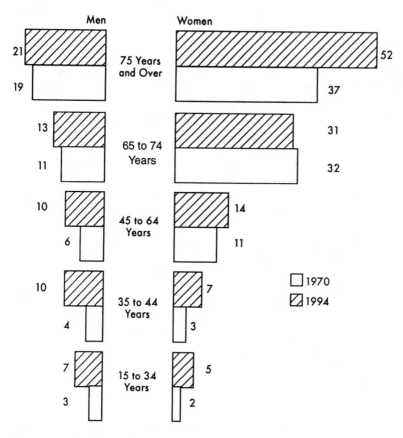

changes in this division of caring labor are occurring, but these changes are even smaller than are those for tending young children.

Political Trends

In addition to the economic, social, and demographic trends discussed above, a number of institutional and political trends will undoubtedly affect family life and gender relations in the coming decades. As shown in Chapter 6, legal reforms have been mostly in the direction of making marriage a more equal institution and toward making most new laws gender neutral. Because more women will become attorneys, administrators, and elected officials in the future, I expect this trend toward gender neutrality in the law to continue. Although support for affirmative action programs to promote gender equity (or racial equity) in hiring and college admissions may decline in the late 1990s, popular support for women's extra-familial rights remains strong. In general, women will maintain rights to exercise self-control, and the vestiges of a patriarchal justice system will continue to be dismantled.

Men who have been denied child custody or visitation following divorce will continue to press for legal reforms that make custody and support determinations gender neutral. As custody awards become standardized and as child support enforcement through automatic wage withholding becomes more efficient, more children will receive payments. This will lift a small portion of children above the poverty level, but fathers with few job prospects will still be reluctant to marry initially and will be unable to make child support payments on a continuing basis. More vigorous child support enforcement and paternity establishment efforts will encourage more visitation between some noncustodial fathers and their children but more animosity toward ex-wives among others. This will sustain political pressure on legislators to grant joint custody or liberal visitation to fathers.

What will happen to government support for families? In the face of a restructuring economy, a large federal deficit, and an aging population, government support to families is likely to be cut back or remain limited. For instance, the size of direct welfare payments to families (AFDC) is likely to decrease, even as the need for this type of support is expanding. Future reforms are expected to tighten qualification guidelines, limit participation to a short time, and require that single mothers take minimum wage jobs. Reforms in federal child support policies that began to transform AFDC from an income support scheme to a workfare and debt collection program are likely to continue in the near term. Similarly, funding for other programs to help poor families, such as education, job training, child care, nutritional assistance, and medical care, is likely to stay the same or decline in the near term, even though the need for such programs is increasing. As the overall population ages, demands to fund the already much larger social insurance programs such as social security will expand (see Figure 6.1). As bleak as this scenario sounds, things could change, especially if child advocates could sustain a strong social movement.

As noted in the last chapter, other modern industrial democracies are much more likely than the United States to fund child-centered and (parent-centered) programs (such as paid parental leave, child care centers, and universal health insurance). These nations promote optimal child development by subsidizing programs that serve children directly. The United States, in contrast, assumes that private families are individually responsible for the health and well-being of their children. Because many poor mothers and fathers have limited access to jobs or insurance, large numbers of children (and a disproportionate share of ethnic minority children) are at risk. The assumption that individual parents are the only ones responsible for their children also puts pressure on families (mostly mothers) to work out their own child care and health care arrangements. If, on the other hand, we in the United States began to recognize the links between child poverty and other social problems, and if we reoriented our thinking to be more community minded, then we might move away from scapegoating single welfare mothers and their children. We could then move our social policies toward collective responsibility for all children and develop safety net programs such as those that exist in most other industrialized countries (see Table 6.1).

What changes in child care practices can we expect in the future? Child care by relatives has been the most common form of care for preschool children in the past, especially among families who are poor. Today, about half of all preschoolers with employed mothers are cared for by family or relatives (including fathers, grandparents, siblings, and other family members; see Figure 4.3). Patterns vary by part-time versus full-time employment of the mother, but fathers and grandparents will continue to provide substantial amounts of care. Among the middle and upper classes, in-home sitters, nannies, and housekeepers are still common, and will continue to be, especially if the income inequality trends discussed previously continue. The use of family day care homes, recently on a downward trend, will continue to be important in the future, especially in working-class neighborhoods with few other alternatives (U.S. Bureau of the Census, 1996b).

As discussed in Chapter 4, care in organized facilities has increased rapidly. Between the 1960s and the late 1980s, the proportion of preschoolers cared for in day care centers rose more than 400% (Phillips, 1989). Of preschool children with working mothers, 30% are now served by organized child care facilities (U.S. Bureau of the Census, 1996b). When children reach school age, care arrangements often change, with father care, sibling care, and self-care increasing in frequency. Fathers and siblings are now the most common after-school caregivers, especially when mothers work part-time or have a nonday shift. To stay employed on a continuous basis, most American parents rely on multiple forms of child care and adjust them if one fails, if parents gain flexibility at their workplace, or if family income goes up or down (Spitze, 1988).

Although care in organized facilities is increasing, the combined capacity of private and public day care centers in the United States represents only a fraction of the demand (Phillips, 1989). The child care shortage is not likely to improve much in the coming years because more mothers will be working, child care centers are not usually profitable, and substantial child care subsidies from the government are unlikely. Another demographic factor is compounding the problem—the large size of the baby boom cohort. Baby boomers are not having as many children as previous generations, and they are waiting longer to have them. Because there are so many of them, the number of preschool children has been rising. This has strained the capacity of day care centers and schools, but an even bigger problem for most working parents has been the affordability of good day care.

Because maternal employment is not just a passing fad, and because of increasing numbers of children, pressure will mount on businesses to provide job leaves, flexible scheduling, and on-site child care. Pressure will also increase on governments to fund community day care facilities, to regulate private and nonprofit care centers, and to provide recreation facilities for school-age children. In the face of economic restructuring and limited government revenues, however, it is unlikely that a European-style commitment to child care will emerge in the United States without a significant social movement supporting it.

As we saw in Chapter 4, most people continue to assume that women should do the child care, whether they are mothers or child care workers. This has allowed for extreme pay disparities between care providers (mostly women) and workers in production industries (mostly men) for jobs that require comparable amounts of education, training, skill, experience, and effort (Reskin & Roos, 1990). Of U.S. child care workers, 98% are women, and they are in the lowest 10th of all wage earners. Of child care providers who work in private homes, 9 of 10 earn below poverty-level wages, and even those who work in organized day care centers earn a median income of less than $10,000 per year (Phillips, 1989). Despite low pay and few benefits, child care workers are expected to create familylike environments and work wonders with children.

Because the economics of the marketplace will provide neither adequate wages to child care workers nor affordable child care for parents, it is appropriate for the government to step in. This is what has happened in virtually all other modern industrialized democracies. For the reasons noted above and in Chapter 6, it is unlikely that most politicians will wholeheartedly embrace feminist proposals for legislation to establish equal pay scales for "women's" jobs. Comparable worth and pay equity programs are costly and require significant government involvement to be effective. Therefore, it will take a strong political showing for the government to reorder its labor market regulatory policies. Because women's equal labor force participation is the engine driving most of the other changes I have reviewed, the standardization of wage rates and the equalization of opportunity structures in the job market would do more for child care and family gender equity than any other policy initiative.

Short of aggressive affirmative action and massive pay equity programs, elevating the status of child care workers is likely to be dependent on changing the cultural definition of caring. As fathers take on more responsibility for children and as more men enter into caring occupations (nursing, counseling, teaching, child care, etc.), caring is likely to become less exclusively associated with women. This has the potential to cause a gradual shift toward less gender differentiation and more gender equality. If the society valued children more, ensured that all children received adequate day care and health care, and paid its child care workers better wages, we would likely see some movement toward more balanced gender relations.

But countervailing forces are also at work. Compared with men, women more often hold part-time jobs, often in caring and service industries, and earn significantly lower wages. This makes women dependent on men or on networks of other women and encourages them to be the child care and housework experts in their own homes. Women's family obligations, in turn, are used by many employers as an excuse for paying them less on the job. This separate spheres approach to home labor and productive labor, as this book has shown, tends to be self-perpetuating. Nevertheless, significant changes are under way, particularly among younger men and women, who have more similar patterns of education, labor force participation, wages, and career aspirations than previous generations.

Putting It All Together

What are the implications of these trends for families and gender? Economic changes will continue to be the main driving force behind changes in both family life and gender relations. As more women are employed, and as their wages and work hours approach those of men, we will see significantly more sharing of family work by men. The ideology of separate spheres will continue to weaken. Marriage will be even more individualized in the future, with continuing high levels of cohabitation and divorce. Marriage and remarriage rates will continue a slow decline but will remain the norm for middle-class whites. Most people will marry late and have few children (relative to past decades). As marriage becomes a more equal institution, it will also become more optional. Patterns of courtship and mate selection will also shift, so that women will be more likely to consider men's caregiving abilities, and men will be more likely to consider women's breadwinning abilities.

More women will remain attached to their jobs throughout their adulthood, taking only limited time off to have babies. In heterosexual couples, if wives earn more money or work longer hours than husbands, the men will do more in the home. As women become less dependent on men's earnings, more of them will choose to remain single or to have children without husbands. Among the middle class, the majority of babies will be born to married couples, and most children will continue to live in two-parent homes (although a larger percentage of them will be stepfamilies). Most families will need two earners to maintain a middle-class standard of living, providing a counterbalancing influence to the increasingly contingent and individualized nature of marriage. Those with better job prospects will fare better in the marriage (and remarriage) market. The marital relationship, in turn, will become the most crucial element affecting one's social class position.

Will family life look much different as a result of these changes? Yes and no. Families will be slightly smaller and shift around a little more, but they will be, for the most part, similar to today's families. There will be an even wider range of family types and individual choices to make. With continued emphasis on individual needs and emotional fulfillment, people will still focus on romantic relationships with partners, although there will be less pressure to marry. The emphasis on individualism and dual careers will encourage more couples to remain childless. For those at the bottom of the income pyramid, having children will remain much more fulfilling than any role they would play in the economy. The emphasis on the emotional side of child rearing will thus continue to motivate couples and single women to have children and invest heavily in them. The forces for ritualizing and idealizing relationships with children will continue to grow, in part because they will spend even more time in the care of others. Fathers' contributions to child care will increase for both sentimental and practical reasons.

In a majority of married couples, women will continue to be seen as primary parents and main homemakers, and men will continue to be seen as primary breadwinners. But women will increasingly be seen as providing economically, and men will increasingly be seen as contributing practically and emotionally to the running of the household. There will likely be more negotiation, and perhaps more conflict, as new patterns emerge to balance various family tasks. New rituals and everyday practices will develop to solidify and symbolize the shifting of family responsibilities. New ideals of shared spheres will begin to develop, at first in just a few areas (such as child care and grocery shopping), but will spread to other tasks (such as cooking and cleaning) if men's and women's job experiences continue to converge. Because marriage will be more contingent, there will be plenty of breakups, but because people will still desire continuing love and companionship, and because two incomes will be even more important, there will be plenty of remarriages.

In the future, ritual celebrations such as Thanksgiving may look a little different. In some households, strong breadwinner fathers will still get to carve the turkey. In other households, the men and women will not be so separated. The men won't get to "kick back" as much and the women and older girls won't be the only ones to prepare the food and clean up afterward. Other households may not even have any men around at all. In many homes, a unique blending of kin and non-kin will make up new families.

The one-sided courtship rituals described in the love advice columns and want ads will become a little more balanced as men's and women's bargaining positions become more equal. Plenty of bargaining and matching will still go on in both same-sex and cross-sex relationships. I predict that most people will be less quick to assign housework on the basis of genitals. There will be fewer assumptions that only certain family members can fulfill certain roles. The links between family and gender, however, will not fade away completely.

As families move slowly in the direction of parental equality, they will also put in motion some processes that could have long-lasting effects on future generations. The patterns of gender socialization described in Chapter 5 will shift toward a more balanced and equal treatment of boys and girls. If more men get involved in child care and if adults treat boys and girls similarly, then children's emotional dispositions and cognitive frameworks will become more similar. This will prepare the next generation for a world that is less gender polarized than that of previous generations. It may also produce a generation of Americans who are more committed to meeting the needs of children. But this will not happen automatically.

If more people become aware of the practice and ideology of separate spheres and want to change them, then they can. If they tend to their own relationships first, and then work outward to advocate additional social and economic changes, then gender will become less automatically associated with specific family activities. Family roles will not be totally transformed, even if most people begin to question the rigid division of family activities based on gender. Men and women will not become interchangeable. Nevertheless, there is likely to be more room for more individual choice about what to do in the family and how to relate to other family members. New family rituals and practices will undoubtedly emerge. My hunch is that men and women will slowly move toward more similarity in the things that they can do both inside and outside families. But it is also likely that new family practices will emerge that tend to promote old patterns of race, class, and gender inequality.

Social constructionist theories remind us that society is the product of human interaction. Along with other people, you create the world in which you live. This is a liberating insight, but it also means you must assume ethical responsibility for your future and the future of society. Despite a substantial number of economic and cultural barriers to change, you are not locked into a predetermined course of action. In everything that you do, you make a choice. It is up to each one of us, personally and collectively, to choose the right path. The future of gender and family relationships is in your hands.

REFERENCES

Abel, E. K. (1990). Family care of the frail elderly. In E. Abel & M. Nelson (Eds.), *Circles of care: Work and identity in women's lives* (pp. 65-91). Albany, NY: State University of New York Press.

Abel, E. K., & Nelson, M. K. (Eds.). (1990). *Circles of care: Work and identity in women's lives*. Albany, NY: State University of New York Press.

Acker, J. (1992). The future of women and work. *Sociological Perspectives, 35*, 53-68.

Agger, B., & Shelton, B. A. (1993). Shotgun wedding, unhappy marriage, no-fault divorce? Rethinking the feminism-Marxism relationship. In P. England (Ed.), *Theory on gender, feminism on theory* (pp. 25-42). New York: Aldine de Gruyter.

Ahlburg, D. A., & DeVita, C. J. (1992). *New realities of the American family* (Population Bulletin, Vol. 47, No. 2). Washington, DC: Population Reference Bureau.

Albert, A. A., & Porter, J. R. (1988). Children's gender-role stereotypes: A sociological investigation of psychological models. *Sociological Forum, 3*, 184-210.

Aldous, J. (1982). *Two paychecks*. Beverly Hills, CA: Sage.

Aldous, J., & Dumon, W. (1990). Family policy in the 1980s: Controversy and consensus. *Journal of Marriage and the Family, 52*, 1136-1152.

Allgeier, E. R., & Wiederman, M. W. (1991). Love and mate selection in the 1990s. *Free Inquiry, 11*, 25-27.

Alwin, D. F. (1988). From obedience to autonomy: Changes in traits desired in children, 1924-1978. *Public Opinion Quarterly, 52*, 33-52.

Amato, P. R. (1993). Children's adjustment to divorce: Theories, hypotheses and empirical support. *Journal of Marriage and the Family, 55*, 23-38.

Amott, T. L., & Matthaei, J. A. (1991). *Race, gender and work: A multicultural economic history of women in the United States*. Boston: South End.

Andelin, H. B. (1963). *Fascinating womanhood: A guide to happy marriage*. Santa Barbara, CA: Pacific Press.

Anderson, M. (1994). What is new about the modern family? In M. Drake (Ed.), *Time, family and community: Perspectives on family and community history* (pp. 67-90). Oxford, UK: Open University/Blackwell.

Anderson, M. L., & Collins, P. H. (Eds.). (1995). *Race, class and gender: An anthology* (2nd ed.). Belmont, CA: Wadsworth.

Archer, W. G. (1957). *The loves of Krishna in Indian painting and poetry.* London: Allen & Unwin.

Arendell, T. (1986). *Mothers and divorce.* Berkeley: University of California Press.

Ariès, P. (1962). *Centuries of childhood: A social history of family life* (R. Baldick, Trans.). New York: Random House.

Associated Press. (1996, February 3). Killer dad, gay mom wage custody battle. *San Diego Union-Tribune.*

Baehr v. Lewin, 74 Haw. 530, 1993.

Baehr v. Miike, Haw. 91-1394, 1996.

Bailey, B. L. (1988). *From front porch to back seat: Courtship in twentieth century America.* Baltimore: Johns Hopkins University Press.

Balbus, I. (1983). *Marxism and domination.* Princeton, NJ: Princeton University Press.

Bane, M. J., & Jargowsky, P. (1989). The links between government policy and family structure: What matters and what doesn't. In A. J. Cherlin (Ed.), *The changing American family and public policy* (pp. 219-262). Washington, DC: Urban Institute.

Baran, S. J., Mok, J. J., Land, M., & Kang, T. Y. (1989). You are what you buy: Mass-mediated judgements of people's worth. *Journal of Communication, 39,* 46-54.

Bardewell, J. R., Cochran, S. W., & Walker, S. (1986). Relationship of parental education, race, and gender to sex role stereotyping in 5-year-old kindergarteners. *Sex Roles, 15,* 275-281.

Bardwell v. Illinois, 83 U.S. 442 (1973).

Baron, A. (1981). Protective labor legislation and the cult of domesticity. *Journal of Family Issues, 2,* 25-38.

Baron, A. (1987). Feminist legal strategies: The powers of difference. In B. Hess & M. M. Ferree, *Analyzing gender: A handbook of social science research* (pp. 474-503). Newbury Park, CA: Sage.

Barthel, D. (1988). *Putting on appearances.* Philadelphia: Temple University Press.

Baruch, G. K., & Barnett, R. C. (1986a). Consequences of fathers' participation in family work. *Journal of Personality and Social Psychology, 51,* 983-992.

Baruch, G. K., & Barnett, R. C. (1986b). Role quality, multiple role involvement, and psychological well-being in mid-life women. *Journal of Personality and Social Psychology, 51,* 578-585.

Basch, N. (1982). *In the eyes of the law: Women, marriage, and property in nineteenth century New York.* Ithaca, NY: Cornell University Press.

Baxter, J. (1993). *Work at home: The domestic division of labor.* St. Lucia, Australia: Queensland Unversity Press.

Becker, G. (1981). *A treatise on the family.* Cambridge, MA: Harvard University Press.

Bem, S. L. (1983). Gender schema theory and its implications for child development: Raising gender-aschematic children in a gender-schematic society. *Signs, 8,* 598-616.

Bem, S. L. (1989). Genital knowledge and constancy in preschool children. *Child Development, 60,* 649-662.

Bem, S. L. (1993). *The lenses of gender.* New Haven, CT: Yale University Press.

Benería, L., & Stimpson, C. (Eds.). (1987). *Women, households, and the economy.* New Brunswick, NJ: Rutgers University Press.

Benjamin, J. (1988). *The bonds of love: Psychoanalysis, feminism, and the problem of domination.* New York: Pantheon.

Berger, P. (1963). *Invitation to sociology: A humanistic perspective.* New York: Doubleday.

Berger, P., & Kellner, H. (1964). Marriage and the construction of reality. *Diogenes, 46,* 1-23.

Berger, P., & Luckmann, T. (1966). *The social construction of reality: A treatise on the sociology of knowledge.* Garden City, NY: Doubleday.

Bernard, J. (1978). *Self-portrait of a family: Letters by Jessie, Dorothy Lee, Claude, and David Bernard.* Boston: Beacon.

Bernard, J. (1981). The good-provider role: Its rise and fall. *American Psychologist, 36,* 1-12.

Berscheid, E. (1985). Interpersonal attraction. In G. Lindzey & E. Aronson (Eds.), *The handbook of social psychology.* New York: Random House.

Bianchi, S. M., & Spain, D. (1986). *American women in transition.* New York: Russell Sage.

Bielby, D. D. (1992). Commitment to work and family. *Annual Review of Sociology, 18,* 281-302.

Bielby, D. D., & Bielby, W. (1988). She works hard for the money. *American Journal of Sociology, 93,* 1031-1059.

Biller, H. B. (1993). *Fathers and families: Paternal factors in child development.* Westport, CT: Auburn House.

Blackstone, W. (1832). *Commentaries on the laws of England* (Vol. 1). New York: Collins & Hannay. (Original work published 1765)

Blankenhorn, D. (1995). *Fatherless America: Confronting our most urgent social problem.* New York: Basic Books.

Bleier, R. (1984). *Science and gender.* New York: Pergamon.

Blumberg, R. L. (1984). A general theory of gender stratification. In R. Collins (Ed.), *Sociological theory 1984.* San Francisco: Jossey-Bass.

Blumberg, R. L. (Ed.). (1991). *Gender, family and economy: The triple overlap.* Newbury Park, CA: Sage.

Blumberg, R. L., & Coleman, M. T. (1989). A theoretical look at the gender balance of power in the American couple. *Journal of Family Issues, 10,* 225-250.

Blumer, H. (1969). *Symbolic interactionism: Perspective and method.* Berkeley: University of California Press.

Blumstein, P., & Schwartz, P. (1983). *American couples: Money, work, sex.* New York: William Morrow.

Booth, A., Johnson, D., & White, L. (1984). Women, outside employment, and marital instability. *American Journal of Sociology, 90,* 76-83.

Bose, C. E. (1987). Dual spheres. In B. Hess & M. Ferree (Eds.), *Analyzing gender* (pp. 267-285). Newbury Park, CA: Sage.

Boulding, E. (1976). *The underside of history.* Boulder, CO: Westview.

Boydston, J. (1990). *Home and work: Housework, wages, and the ideology of labor in the early republic.* New York: Oxford University Press.

Bradbard, M. R. (1985). Sex differences in adults' gifts and children's toy requests at Christmas. *Psychological Reports, 56,* 969-970.

Brehm, S. S. (1992). *Intimate relationships* (2nd ed.). New York: McGraw-Hill.

Briesemeister, L. H., & Haines, B. A. (1988). The interactions of fathers and newborns. In K. L. Michaelson (Ed.), *Childbirth in America: Anthropological perspectives* (pp. 228-251). South Hadley, MA: Bergin & Garvey.

Broverman, I., Broverman, D., Clarkson, F., Rosenkrantz, P., & Vogel, S. (1970). Sex-role stereotypes and clinical judgements of mental health. *Journal of Consulting and Clinical Psychology, 34,* 1-7.

Bumpass, L. L. (1990). What's happening to the family? *Demography, 27,* 483-498.

Burgess, N. J. (1995). Female-headed households in sociohistorical context. In B. J. Dikerson (Ed.), *African American single mothers: Understanding their lives and families.* Thousand Oaks, CA: Sage.

Buss, D. M. (1989). Sex differences in human mate preference: Evolutionary hypothesis tested in 37 cultures. *Behavioral and Brain Sciences, 12,* 1-49.

Butler, J. (1990). *Gender trouble: Feminism and the subversion of identity.* New York: Routledge.

Byars, J. (1991). *All that Hollywood allows: Re-reading gender in 1950s melodrama.* Chapel Hill: University of North Carolina Press.

Byng-Hall, J. (1988). Scripts and legends in families and family therapy. *Family Process, 27,* 167-179.

Cahill, S. E. (1986). Childhood socialization as a recruitment process: Some lessons from the study of gender development. *Sociological Studies of Child Development, 1,* 163-186.

Caldera, Y. M., Huston, A. C., & O'Brien, M. (1989). Social interactions and play patterns of parents and toddlers with feminine, masculine, and neutral toys. *Child Development, 60,* 70-76.

Callan, V. J. (1987). The personal and marital adjustment of mothers and involuntarily childless wives. *Journal of Marriage and the Family, 49,* 847-856.

Campbell, E. (1985). *The childless marriage: An exploratory study of couples who do not want children.* London: Tavistock.

Cancian, F. (1987). *Love in America.* New York: Cambridge University Press.

Cancian, F. (1994). Marital conflict over intimacy. In G. Handel & G. Whitchurch (Eds.), *The psychosocial interior of the family* (pp. 401-417). New York: Aldine de Gruyter.

Cancian, F., & Oliker, S. (forthcoming). *A gendered view of care.* Thousand Oaks, CA: Pine Forge.

Cantor, M. (1990). Prime-time fathers: A study in continuity and change. *Critical Studies in Mass Communication, 7,* 275-285.

Cantor, M. G., & Cantor, J. M. (1992). *Prime-time television: Content and control* (2nd ed.). Newbury Park, CA: Sage.

Carnes, M., & Griffen, C. (1990). *Meanings for manhood: Constructions of masculinity in Victorian America.* Chicago: University of Chicago Press.

Cavell, S. (1981). *Pursuits of happiness: The Hollywood comedy of remarriage.* Cambridge, MA: Harvard University Press.

Chafetz, J. S. (1988). *Feminist sociology: An overview of contemporary theories.* Itasca, IL: F. E. Peacock.

Chafetz, J. S. (1990). *Gender equity: An integrated theory of stability and change.* Newbury Park, CA: Sage.

Cherlin, A. J. (1992). *Marriage, divorce, remarriage* (2nd ed.). Cambridge, MA: Harvard University Press.

Cherlin, A. J., & Furstenberg, F. F. (1994). Stepfamilies in the United States: A reconsideration. *Annual Review of Sociology, 20,* 359-381.

Cherry, L., & Lewis, M. (1976). Mothers and two-year-olds: A study of sex-differentiated aspects of verbal interaction. *Developmental Psychology, 12,* 278-282.

Chesler, P. (1986). *Mothers on trial: The battle for children and custody.* Seattle, WA: Seal Press.

Chodorow, N. (1976). Oedipal asymmetries and heterosexual knots. *Social Problems, 23,* 454-467.

Chodorow, N. (1978). *The reproduction of mothering: Psychoanalysis and the sociology of gender.* Berkeley: University of California Press.

Chodorow, N. (1985). Beyond drive theory: Object relations and the limits of radical individualism. *Theory & Society, 14,* 271-319.

Chodorow, N., & Contratto, S. (1992). The fantasy of the perfect mother. In B. Thorne (with M. Yalom, Eds.), *Rethinking the family: Some feminist questions* (2nd ed., pp. 191-214). Boston: Northeastern University Press.

Chow, E. N.-L. (1987). The development of feminist consciousness among Asian American women. *Gender & Society, 1,* 284-299.

Chow, E. N.-L. (1994). Asian American women at work. In M. Baca Zinn & B. T. Dill (Eds.), *Women of color in U.S. society* (pp. 203-227). Philadelphia: Temple University Press.

Chow, E. N.-L. (1996). Family, economy, and the state: A legacy of struggle for Chinese American women. In S. Pedraza & R. G. Rumbaut (Eds.), *Origins and destinies: Immigration, race, and ethnicity in America* (pp. 110-124). Belmont, CA: Wadsworth.

Ciancanelli, P., & Berch, B. (1987). Gender and the GNP. In B. Hess & M. M. Ferree (Eds.), *Analyzing gender.* Newbury Park, CA: Sage.

Clark, E. B. (1993). Slavery and divorce in nineteenth-century America. In L. Tepperman & S. J. Wilson (Eds.), *Next of kin* (pp. 285-290). Englewood Cliffs, NJ: Prentice Hall.

Cochran, S. D., & Peplau, L. A. (1985). Value orientations in heterosexual relationships. *Psychology of Women Quarterly, 9,* 477-488.

Collins, P. H. (1990). *Black feminist thought.* New York: Routledge.

Collins, R. (1971). A conflict theory of sexual stratification. *Social Problems, 19,* 3-21.

Collins, R. (1975). *Conflict sociology: Toward an explanatory science.* New York: Academic Press.

Collins, R. (1986). Courtly politics and the status of women. In R. Collins, *Weberian sociological theory.* New York: Cambridge University Press.

Collins, R. (1988). *Theoretical sociology.* San Diego, CA: Harcourt Brace Jovanovich.

Collins, R., Chafetz, J., Blumberg, R., Coltrane, S., & Turner, J. (1993). Toward an integrated theory of gender stratification. *Sociological Perspectives, 36,* 185-216.

Collins, R., & Coltrane, S. (1995). *Sociology of marriage and the family* (4th ed.). Chicago: Nelson-Hall.

Coltrane, S. (1988). Father-child relationships and the status of women. *American Journal of Sociology, 93,* 1060-1095.

Coltrane, S. (1989). Household labor and the routine production of gender. *Social Problems, 36,* 473-490.

Coltrane, S. (1992). The micropolitics of gender in nonindustrial societies. *Gender & Society, 6,* 86-107.

Coltrane, S. (1996). *Family man: Fatherhood, housework, and gender equity.* New York: Oxford University Press.

Coltrane, S., & Adams, M. (forthcoming). Children and gender. In T. Arendell (Ed.), *Parenting: Contemporary issues and challenges.* Thousand Oaks, CA: Sage.

Coltrane, S., & Allan, K. (1994). New fathers and old stereotypes: Representations of masculinity in 1980s television advertising. *Masculinities, 2,* 43-66.

Coltrane, S., & Hickman, N. (1992). The rhetoric of rights and needs: Moral discourse in the reform of child custody and child support laws. *Social Problems, 39,* 400-420.

Coltrane, S., & Valdez, E. (1993). Reluctant compliance: Work-family role allocation in dual-earner Chicano families. In J. Hood (Ed.), *Men, work, and family* (pp. 151-174). Newbury Park, CA: Sage.

Connell, R. W. (1987). *Gender and power: Society, the person and sexual politics.* Stanford, CA: Stanford University Press.

Connell, R. W. (1993). The big picture: Masculinities in recent world history. *Theory & Society, 22,* 597-624.

Connell, R. W. (1995). *Masculinities.* Berkeley: University of California Press.

Coontz, S. (1992). *The way we never were.* New York: Basic Books.

Coontz, S., & Henderson, P. (1986). *Women's work, men's property: The origins of gender and class.* London: Verso.

Coser, R. L. (1964). Authority and structural ambivalence in the middle-class family. In R. Coser (Ed.), *The family: Its structure and functions* (pp. 370-383). New York: St. Martin's.

Cott, N. F. (1977). *The bonds of womanhood.* New Haven, CT: Yale University Press.

Cott, N. F. (1978). Passionlessness: An interpretation of Victorian sexual ideology, 1790-1850. *Signs, 4,* 219-236.

Cowan, C. P., & Cowan, P. A. (1992). *When partners become parents.* New York: Basic Books.

Cowan, G., & Hoffman, C. (1986). Gender stereotyping in young children: Evidence to support a concept-learning model. *Sex Roles, 14,* 211-224.

Croll, E., Davin, D., & Kane, P. (Eds.). (1985). *China's one-child family policy.* New York: St. Martin's.

Crouter, A. C., McHale, S. M., & Bartko, W. T. (1993). Gender as an organizing feature in parent-child relationships. *Journal of Social Issues, 49,* 161-174.

Daniels, A. K. (1988). *Invisible careers.* Chicago: University of Chicago Press.

Dateline [Personal ads]. (1996, September 15). *Los Angeles Times,* pp. E5-E6.

Davidoff, L., & Hall, C. (1987). *Family fortunes.* London: Hutchinson.

Davis, S. (1990). Men as success objects and women as sex objects: A study of personal advertisements. *Sex Roles, 23,* 43-50.

Deaux, K. (1984). From individual differences to social categories: Analysis of a decade's research on gender. *American Psychologist, 39,* 105-116.

Degler, C. (1980). *At odds: Women and the family in America from the revolution to the present.* New York: Oxford University Press.

Delphy, C. (1984). *Close to home: A materialist analysis of women's oppression* (D. Leonard, Trans.). London: Hutchison.

Demos, J. (1982). The changing faces of fatherhood. In S. Cath, A. Gurwitt, & J. Ross (Eds.), *Father and child: Developmental and clinical perspectives.* Boston: Little, Brown.

Demos, J. (1986). *Past, present, and personal: The family and the life course in American history.* New York: Oxford University Press.

Dennehy, K., & Mortimer, J. (1992, August). *Work and family orientations of contemporary adolescent boys and girls in a context of social change.* Paper presented at the 87th meeting of the American Sociological Association, Pittsburgh, PA.

Dennis, W. (1992). *Hot and bothered: Sex and love in the nineties.* New York: Viking/Penguin.

de Rougemont, D. (1956). *Love in the western world.* New York: Pantheon.

Deutsch, H. (1944). *The psychology of women: A psychoanalytic interpretation* (Vol. 1). New York: Bantam.

DeVault, M. (1991). *Feeding the family: The social construction of caring as gendered work.* Chicago: University of Chicago Press.

DeVita, C. (1996). *The United States at mid-decade* (Population Bulletin, Vol. 50, No. 4). Washington, DC: Population Reference Bureau.

Dickens, A. G. (1977). *The courts of Europe, politics, patronage and royalty, 1400-1800.* New York: McGraw-Hill.

diLeonardo, M. (1987). The female world of cards and holidays: Women, families, and the work of kinship. *Signs, 12,* 440-453.

Dill, B. T. (1988). Our mother's grief: Racial ethnic women and the maintenance of families. *Journal of Family History, 13,* 415-431.

Dill, B. T. (1994). *Across the boundaries of race and class.* New York: Garland.

Dinnerstein, D. (1976). *The mermaid and the minotaur: Sexual arrangements and sexual malaise.* New York: Harper & Row.

Dix, D. [Gilmer, E. M.]. (1974). *How to win and hold a husband.* New York: Arno. (Original work published 1939)

Dobash, R. E., & Dobash, R. (1979). *Violence against wives: A case against the patriarchy.* New York: Free Press.

Dover, K. J. (1978). *Greek homosexuality.* Cambridge, MA: Harvard University Press.

Duncan, G. J., & Hoffman, S. D. (1985). A reconsideration of the economic consequences of divorce. *Demography, 22,* 485-497.

Durkheim, E. (1957). *The elementary forms of the religious life.* New York: Free Press. (Original work published 1915)

Easlea, B. (1981). *Science and sexual oppression.* London: Weidenfeld & Nicolson.

Eccles, J. S., Jacobs, J. E., & Harold, R. D. (1990). Gender role stereotypes, expectancy effects, and parents' socialization of gender differences. *Journal of Social Issues, 46,* 183-201.

Edelman, M. W. (1987). *Families in peril: An agenda for social change.* Cambridge, MA: Harvard University Press.

Edelman, M. W. (1989). Black children in America. In J. Dewart (Ed.), *The state of black America: 1989* (pp. 63-76). New York: National Urban League.

Edwards, R. R., & Spector, S. (1991). *The old daunce: Love, friendship, sex, and marriage in the medieval world.* Albany: State University of New York Press.

Edwards, S. (1985). *Gender, sex, and the law.* London: Croom Helm.

Ehrensaft, D. (1987). *Parenting together.* New York: Free Press.

Eisenstein, Z. H. (1984). *Feminism and sexual equality: Crisis in liberal America.* New York: Monthly Review Press.

Elder, G. H., Jr. (1974). *Children of the Great Depression.* Chicago: University of Chicago Press.

Elder, G. H., Jr., Modell, J., & Parke, R. D. (1993). *Children in time and place: Developmental and historical insights.* New York: Cambridge University Press.

Ellwood, D. T. (1987). *Divide and conquer: Responsible security for America's poor.* New York: Ford Foundation.

England, P., & Browne, I. (1992). Trends in women's economic status. *Sociological Perspectives, 35,* 17-51.

Entman, R. M. (1993). Framing: Toward clarification of a fractured paradigm. *Journal of Communication, 43,* 51-58.

Epstein, C. F. (1988). *Deceptive distinctions: Sex, gender, and the social order.* New Haven, CT: Yale University Press.

Erikson, E. H. (1950). *Childhood and society.* New York: Norton.

Erikson, E. H. (1958). *Young man Luther: A study in psychoanalysis and history.* New York: Norton.

Espiritu, Y. L. (1997). *Asian American women and men: Labor, laws, and love.* Thousand Oaks, CA: Pine Forge.

Etaugh, C., & Liss, M. (1992). Home, school, and playroom: Training grounds for adult gender roles. *Sex Roles, 26,* 129-147.

Etzioni, A. (1993). Children of the universe. *Utne Reader, 57,* 52-61.

Fagot, B. I. (1974). Sex differences in toddlers' behavior and parental reaction. *Developmental Psychology, 10,* 554-558.

Fagot, B. I. (1978). The influence of sex of child on parental reactions to toddler children. *Child Development, 49,* 459-465.

Fagot, B. I. (1985). Changes in thinking about early gender-role development. *Developmental Review, 5,* 83-96.

Fagot, B. I., & Leinbach, M. D. (1993). Gender-role development in young children: From discrimination to labeling. *Developmental Review, 13,* 205-224.

Fagot, B. I., Leinbach, M. D., & O'Boyle, C. (1992). Gender labeling, gender stereotyping, and parenting behaviors. *Developmental Psychology, 28,* 225-230.

Faludi, S. (1991). *Backlash: The undeclared war against American women.* New York: Crown.

Farmer, H. S. (1983). Career and homemaking plans for high school youth. *Journal of Counseling Psychology, 30,* 40-45.

Fein, R. A. (1978). Research on fathering: Social policy and an emergent perspective. *Journal of Social Issues, 34,* 122-135.

Fenstermaker-Berk, S. (1985). *The gender factory.* New York: Plenum.

Ferree, M. (1987). She works hard for a living. In B. Hess & M. Ferree (Eds.), *Analyzing gender* (pp. 322-347). Newbury Park, CA: Sage.

Ferree, M. (1990). Beyond separate spheres: Feminism and family research. *Journal of Marriage and the Family, 52,* 866-884.

Ferree, M. (1991). The gender division of labor in two-earner marriages: Dimensions of variability and change. *Journal of Family Issues, 12,* 158-180.

Ferreiro, B. W. (1990). Presumption of joint custody. *Family Relations, 39,* 420-426.

Finch, J., & Groves, D. (Eds.). (1983). *A labour of love: Women, work, and caring.* London: Routledge & Kegan Paul.

Fineman, M., & Opie, A. (1987). The uses of social science data in legal policymaking: Custody determinations at divorce. *Wisconsin Law Review, 107,* 107-158.

Finkelhor, D., Gelles, R. J., Hotaling, G. T., & Straus, M. A. (Eds.). (1983). *The dark side of families.* Beverly Hills, CA: Sage.

Fischer, L. (1950). *The life of Mahatma Gandhi.* New York: Harper.

Flandrin, J. L. (1979). *Families in former times: Kinship, household and sexuality.* Cambridge, UK: Cambridge University Press.

Folberg, J. (1984). *Joint custody and shared parenting.* Washington, DC: Bureau of National Affairs.

Frazier, P. A., & Esterly, E. (1990). Correlates of relationship beliefs: Gender, relationship experience and relationship satisfaction. *Journal of Social and Personal Relationships, 7,* 331-352.

Freed, D. J., & Walker, T. B. (1988). Family law in the fifty states: An overview. *Family Law Quarterly, 4,* 417-570.

Freud, S. (1924). *A general introduction to psychoanalysis.* New York: Boni & Liveright.

Freud, S. (1938). Three contributions to the theory of sex. In A. A. Brill (Ed.), *The basic writings of Sigmund Freud*. New York: Random House. (Original work published 1905)

Furstenberg, F. F. (1988). Good dads—bad dads: Two faces of fatherhood. In A. Cherlin (Ed.), *The changing American family and public policy* (pp. 193-218). Washington, DC: Urban Institute.

Furstenberg, F. F., & Nord, C. W. (1985). Parenting apart: Patterns of childrearing after marital disruption. *Journal of Marriage and the Family, 47,* 893-904.

Furstenberg, F. F., Sherwood, K. E., & Sullivan, M. L. (1992). *Caring and paying: What fathers and mothers say about child support.* New York: Manpower Demonstration.

Gallagher, S. K., & Gerstel, N. (1993). Kinkeeping and friend keeping among older women: The effect of marriage. *Gerontologist, 33,* 675-681.

Gamson, W., Croteau, D., Hoynes, W., & Sasson, T. (1992). Media images and the social construction of reality. *Annual Review of Sociology, 18,* 373-393.

Gandhi, M. K. (1963). *The collected works of Mahatma Gandhi* (Vol. 9, September 1908-November 1909). Delhi: Government of India, Ministry of Information and Broadcasting, Publications Division.

Garfinkel, H. (1967). *Studies in ethnomethodology.* Englewood Cliffs, NJ: Prentice Hall.

Geertz, C. (1973). *The interpretation of cultures.* New York: Basic Books.

Gelber, M. (1986). *Gender and society in the New Guinea highlands.* Boulder, CO: Westview.

Gélis, J. (1991). *History of childbirth: Fertility, pregnancy and birth in early modern Europe.* Cambridge, MA: Polity.

Gershuny, J., & Robinson, J. (1988). Historical changes in the household division of labor. *Demography, 25,* 537-552.

Gerson, K. (1985). *Hard choices: How women decide about work, career and motherhood.* Berkeley: University of California Press.

Gerson, K. (1993). *No man's land: Men's changing commitment to family and work.* New York: Basic Books.

Gerstel, N., & Gallagher, S. (1994). Caring for kith and kin: Gender, employment, and the privatization of care. *Social Problems, 41,* 519-539.

Gilder, G. (1973). *Sexual suicide.* New York: Quadrangle.

Gilligan, C. (1982). *In a different voice.* Cambridge, MA: Harvard University Press.

Girdner, L. K. (1986). Child custody determination. In E. Seidman & J. Rappaport (Eds.), *Redefining social problems* (pp. 165-183). New York: Plenum.

Glendon, M. A. (1989). *The transformation of family law: State, law, and family in the United States and Western Europe.* Chicago: University of Chicago Press.

Glenn, E. N. (1992). From servitude to service work: Historical continuities in the racial division of women's work. *Signs, 18,* 1-43.

Glenn, E. N. (1994). Social constructions of mothering. In E. N. Glenn, G. Chang, & L. R. Forcey (Eds.), *Mothering: Ideology, experience, and agency* (pp. 1-29). New York: Routledge.

Glenn, E. N., Chang, G., & Forcey, L. R. (Eds.). (1994). *Mothering: Ideology, experience, and agency.* New York: Routledge.

Glenn, N. (1991). Quantitative research on marital quality in the 1980s. In A. Booth (Ed.), *Contemporary families* (pp. 28-41). Minneapolis, MN: National Council on Family Relations.

Goffman, E. (1967). *Interaction ritual.* New York: Doubleday.

Goldscheider, F. K., & Waite, L. J. (1991). *New families, no families? The transformation of the American home.* Berkeley: University of California Press.

Goode, W. J. (1963). *World revolution and family patterns.* New York: Free Press.

Goode, W. J. (1992). Why men resist. In B. Thorne (with M. Yalom, Eds.), *Rethinking the family* (pp. 287-310). Boston: Northeastern University Press.

Goodman, N. (1985). Socialization I: A sociological overview. In H. A. Farberman & R. S. Perinbanayagam (Eds.), *Foundations of interpretive sociology: Studies in symbolic interaction* (pp. 73-94). Greenwich, CT: JAI.

Goodnow, J. (1988). Children's housework: Its nature and functions. *Psychological Bulletin, 103,* 5-26.

Goody, J. (1983). *The development of the family and marriage in Europe.* Cambridge, UK: Cambridge University Press.

Gordon, L. (1989). *Heroes of their own lives: The politics and history of family violence, Boston, 1889-1960.* New York: Penguin.

Gottfried, A. E., & Gottfried, A. W. (Eds.). (1994). *Redefining families: Implications for children's development.* New York: Plenum.

Gray, J. (1992). *Men are from Mars, women are from Venus: A practical guide for improving communication and getting what you want in your relationships.* New York: HarperCollins.

Greven, P. J., Jr. (1970). *Four generations: Population, land and family in colonial Andover, Massachusetts.* Ithaca, NY: Cornell University Press.

Grigsby, J. (1992). Women change places. *American Demographics, 14,* 46-50.

Griswold, R. (1993). *Fatherhood in America: A history.* New York: Basic Books.

Griswold del Castillo, R. (1984). *La familia* [The family]. Notre Dame, IN: University of Notre Dame Press.

Gubrium, J., & Holstein, J. (1990). *What is family?* Mountain View, CA: Mayfield.

Gutman, H. G. (1976). *The black family in slavery and freedom, 1750-1925.* New York: Pantheon.

Haas, L. (1986). Wives' orientation to breadwinning: Sweden and the United States. *Journal of Family Issues, 7,* 358-381.

Haas, L. (1992). *Equal parenthood and social policy.* Albany: State University of New York Press.

Haas, L. (1995, November). *The politics of selfishness and shortsightedness: Studying family policy in the 1990s.* Paper presented at the annual meeting of the National Council on Family Relations, Portland, OR.

Hadas, M. (1950). *A history of Greek literature.* New York: Columbia University Press.

Hale-Benson, J. E. (1986). *Black children: Their roots, culture, and learning styles.* Provo, UT: Brigham Young University Press.

Haller, J. S. (1972). From maidenhood to menopause: Sex education for women in Victorian America. *Journal of Popular Culture, 6,* 46-69.

Hamamotto, D. Y. (1992). Kindred spirits: The contemporary Asian American family on television. *Amerasia Journal, 18,* 35-53.

Handel, G. (Ed.). (1985). *The psychosocial interior of the family.* New York: Aldine.

Hantover, J. P. (1995). The boy scouts and the validation of masculinity. In M. Kimmel & M. Messner (Eds.), *Men's lives* (pp. 74-81). Boston: Allyn & Bacon.

Hardesty, C., Wenk, D., & Morgan, C. S. (1995). Paternal involvement and the development of gender expectations in sons and daughters. *Youth & Society, 26,* 283-297.

Hareven, T. K. (1982). *Family time and industrial time: The relationship between the family and work in a New England industrial town.* Cambridge, UK: Cambridge University Press.

Hartmann, H. (1981). The family as the locus of gender, class, and political struggle: The example of housework. *Signs, 6,* 366-394.

Hartsock, N. (1983). *Money, sex, and power.* New York: Longman.

Hauserman, N. (1983). Sexual equality: An essay on the importance of recognizing difference. *Legal Studies Forum, 2*(2-3), 251-269.

Hayghe, H. (1990). Family members in the workforce. *Monthly Labor Review, 113*(3), 14-19.

Hendrick, C., & Hendrick, S. (1989). Research on love: Does it measure up? *Journal of Personality and Social Psychology, 56,* 784-794.

Hendrick, C., & Hendrick, S. (1996). Gender and the experience of heterosexual love. In J. T. Wood (Ed.), *Gendered relationships* (pp. 131-148). Mountain View, CA: Mayfield.

Henley, N. M. (1977). *Body politics: Power, sex, and nonverbal communication.* Englewood Cliffs, NJ: Prentice Hall.

Herdt, G. (1981). *Guardians of the flutes: Idioms of masculinity.* New York: McGraw-Hill.

Hernandez, D. J. (1993). *America's children: Resources from family, government, and the economy.* New York: Russell Sage.

Hertz, R. (1986). *More equal than others: Women and men in dual-career marriages.* Berkeley: University of California Press.

Higginbotham, E., & Weber, L. (1992). Moving up with kin and community: Upward social mobility for black and white women. *Gender & Society, 6,* 416-440.

Hill, B. (1989). *Women, work and sexual politics in eighteenth-century England.* Oxford, UK: Basil Blackwell.

Hobsbawm, E. (Ed.). (1982). *The history of Marxism.* Brighton, UK: Harvester.

Hochschild, A. (1983). *The managed heart.* Berkeley: University of California Press.

Hochschild, A. (with Manning, A.). (1989). *The second shift.* New York: Viking.

Hoffman, L. W. (1989). Effects of maternal employment in the two-parent family. *American Psychologist, 44,* 283-292.

Hondagneu-Sotelo, P., & Messner, M. (1994). Gender displays and men's power: The "new man" and the Mexican immigrant man. In H. Brod & M. Kaufman (Eds.), *Theorizing masculinities* (pp. 200-218). Thousand Oaks, CA: Sage.

Hood, J. A. (1983). *Becoming a two-job family.* New York: Praeger.

Hood, J. A. (1986). The provider role: Its meaning and measurement. *Journal of Marriage and the Family, 48,* 349-359.

hooks, b. (1984). *Feminist theory: From margin to center.* Boston: South End.

Horney, K. (1967). *Feminine psychology.* New York: Norton.

Houseknecht, S. K. (1987). Voluntary childlessness. In M. B. Sussman & S. K. Steinmetz (Eds.), *Handbook of marriage and the family.* New York: Plenum.

Howard, J., & Hollander, J. (1997). *Gendered situations, gendered selves: A gender lens on social psychology.* Thousand Oaks, CA: Sage.

Huston, A. H. (1983). Sex-typing. In E. M. Hetherington & P. H. Mussen (Eds.), *Handbook of child psychology* (Vol. 4). New York: John Wiley.

Ibarra, P., & Kitsuse, J. (1993). Vernacular constituents of moral discourse: An interactionist proposal for the study of social problems. In J. A. Holstein & G. Miller (Eds.), *Reconsidering social constructionism* (pp. 25-58). New York: Aldine de Gruyter.

Imber-Black, E., Roberts, J., & Whiting, R. (Eds.). (1988). *Rituals in families and family therapy.* New York: Norton.

Jacklin, C. N., DiPietro, J. A., & Maccoby, E. E. (1984). Sex-typing behavior and sex-typing pressure in child/parent interaction. *Archives of Sexual Behavior, 13,* 413-425.

Jacob, H. (1988). *Silent revolution: The transformation of divorce law in the United States.* Chicago: University of Chicago Press.

Jaynes, G. D., & Williams, R. M. (Eds). (1989). *A common destiny: Blacks and American society.* Washington, DC: National Academy Press.

Johnson, M. M. (1988). *Strong mothers, weak wives.* Berkeley: University of California Press.

Johnson, O. A., & Johnson, A. (1988). Oedipus in the political economy: Theme and variations in Amazonia. In R. Randolph, D. M. Schneider, & M. N. Diaz (Eds.), *Dialectics and gender* (pp. 38-56). Boulder, CO: Westview.

Johnson, R. A. (1980). *Religious assortative mating in the United States.* New York: Academic Press.

Jones, E. (1960). *The father: Letters to sons and daughters.* New York: Rinehart.

Joyner v. Joyner, 59 N.C. 322 (1862).

Kalmijn, M. (1991). Shifting boundaries: Trends in religious and educational homogamy. *American Sociological Review, 56,* 706-800.

Kamerman, S. (1989). Child care, women, work, and the family. In J. S. Lande, S. Starr, & N. Gunsenhauser (Eds.), *Caring for children* (pp. 105-107). Hillsdale, NJ: Lawrence Erlbaum.

Kamerman, S., & Kahn, A. J. (1988a). *Child support: From debt collection to social policy.* Newbury Park, CA: Sage.

Kamerman, S., & Kahn, A. J. (1988b). Social policy and children in the United States and Europe. In J. Palmer, T. Smeeding, & B. Torrey (Eds.), *The vulnerable* (pp. 351-380). Washington, DC: Urban Institute.

Kamerman, S., & Kahn, A. J. (1993). What Europe does for single-parent families. In L. Tepperman & S. J. Wilson (Eds.), *Next of kin* (pp. 226-230). Englewood Cliffs, NJ: Prentice Hall.

Kanter, R. (1977). *Work and family in the United States*. New York: Russell Sage.

Kaufman, M. (1993). *Cracking the armour: Power, pain, and the lives of men*. Toronto, Ontario, Canada: Viking.

Kephart, W. M. (1967). Some correlates of romantic love. *Journal of Marriage and the Family, 29*, 470-474.

Kessler, R., & McRae, J. (1982). The effects of wives' employment on the mental health of married men and women. *American Sociological Review, 47*, 216-227.

Kessler, S. J., & McKenna, W. (1985). *Gender: An ethnomethodological approach* (2nd ed.). Chicago: University of Chicago Press.

Kessler-Harris, A. (1982). *Out to work: A history of wage earning women in the United States*. New York: Oxford University Press.

Kimmel, M. (1987). The contemporary "crisis" of masculinity. In H. Brod (Ed.), *The making of masculinities*. Boston: Unwin Hyman.

Kimmel, M., & Messner, M. (1992). *Men's lives*. New York: Macmillan.

Kitano, H., & Daniels, R. (1988). *Asian Americans: Emerging minorities*. Englewood Cliffs, NJ: Prentice Hall.

Klinman, D. G., & Kohl, R. (1984). *Fatherhood U.S.A.* New York: Garland.

Kohlberg, L. (1966). A cognitive-developmental analysis of children's sex-role concepts and attitudes. In E. E. Maccoby (Ed.), *The development of sex differences* (pp. 82-173). Stanford, CA: Stanford University Press.

Kohn, M. (1977). *Class and conformity*. Chicago: University of Chicago Press.

Komter, A. (1989). Hidden power in marriage. *Gender & Society, 3*, 187-216.

Kraditor, A. (1968). *Up from the pedestal: Selected writings in the history of feminism*. Chicago: Quadrangle.

Kurz, D. (1995). *For richer, for poorer: Mothers confront divorce*. New York: Routledge.

Kutscher, R. E. (1991). New BLS projections. *Monthly Labor Review, 114*, 3-16.

Laing, R. D. (1971). *The politics of the family*. New York: Random House.

Lamb, M. (1981). *The role of the father in child development*. New York: John Wiley.

Lamphere, L., Zavella, P., & Gonzales, F. (1993). *Sunbelt working mothers: Reconciling family and factory*. Ithaca, NY: Cornell University Press.

Langer, W. L. (1972, February). Checks on population growth: 1750-1850. *Scientific American, 226*, 93-100.

LaRossa, R. (1988). Fatherhood and social change. *Family Relations, 37*, 451-457.

LaRossa, R., & LaRossa, M. (1981). *Transition to parenthood*. Beverly Hills, CA: Sage.

Lasch, C. (1977). *Haven in a heartless world*. New York: Basic Books.

Laslett, B., & Brenner, J. (1989). Gender and social reproduction: Historical perspectives. *Annual Review of Sociology, 15,* 381-404.

Laslett, P. (1971). *The world we have lost: England before the industrial age.* New York: Scribner.

Laslett, P. (1977). *Family life and illicit love in earlier generations.* Cambridge, UK: Cambridge University Press.

Laumann, E. O. (1973). *Bonds of pluralism: The form and substance of urban social networks.* New York: John Wiley.

Laumann, E. O., Gagnon, J. H., Michael, R. T., & Michaels, S. (1994). *The social organization of sexuality: Sexual practices in the United States.* Chicago: University of Chicago Press.

Leinbach, M. S., & Hort, B. (1989, April). *Bears are for boys: "Metaphorical" associations in the young child's gender schema.* Paper presented at the Biennial Conference of the Society for Research in Child Development, Kansas City, MO.

Lemon, N. (1981). Joint custody as a statutory presumption. *Golden Gate Law Review, 11,* 485-531.

Lerner, G. (1977). *The female experience.* Indianapolis, IN: Bobbs-Merrill.

Lester, B. Y. (1996). Part-time employment of married women in the U.S.A. *American Journal of Economics and Sociology, 55,* 61-72.

Levin, I., & Trost, J. (1992). Understanding the concept of family. *Family Relations, 41,* 348-351.

Lévi-Strauss, C. (1969). *The elementary structures of kinship.* Boston: Beacon.

Levy, G. D., & Fivush, R. (1993). Scripts and gender: A new approach for examining gender-role development. *Developmental Review, 13,* 126-146.

Lewis, J. (1980). *The politics of motherhood: Child and maternal welfare in England, 1900-1939.* London: Croom Helm.

Lichter, S. R., Lichter, L. S., & Rothman, S. (1994). *Prime time: How TV portrays American culture.* Washington, DC: Regnery.

Lisak, D. (1991). Sexual aggression, masculinity, and fathers. *Signs, 16,* 238-262.

Liss, L. (1987). Families and the law. In M. B. Sussman & S. K. Steinmetz (Eds.), *Handbook of marriage and the family* (pp. 767-793). New York: Plenum.

Little, M. A. (1991). *The impact of the custody plan on the family: A five year follow-up.* San Francisco: State of California, Administrative Office of the Courts, Family Court Services.

Lorber, J. (1994). *Paradoxes of gender.* New Haven, CT: Yale University Press.

Lorber, J., Coser, R. L., Rossi, A. S., & Chodorow, N. (1981). On the reproduction of mothering: A methodological debate. *Signs, 6,* 482-514.

Luxton, M. (1980). *More than a labor of love: Three generations of women's work in the home.* Toronto, Ontario, Canada: Women's Press.

Lynch, K. (1994, July 18-23). *Love, labour, equality and society.* Paper presented at the 30th World Congress of Sociology, International Sociological Association, Bielefeld, Germany.

Lynd, R. S., & Lynd, H. M. (1956). *Middletown: A study in American culture.* New York: Harcourt Brace Jovanovich. (Original work published 1929)

Lytton, H., & Romney, D. M. (1991). Parents' differential socialization of boys and girls: A meta-analysis. *Psychological Bulletin, 109,* 267-296.

Maccoby, E. E. (1992). The role of parents in the socialization of children: An historical overview. *Developmental Psychology, 28,* 1006-1017.

Maccoby, E. E., & Jacklin, C. N. (1974). *The psychology of sex differences.* Stanford, CA: Stanford University Press.

Macfarlane, A. (1979). *The origins of English individualism.* New York: Cambridge University Press.

Macfarlane, A. (1986). *Marriage and love in England: Modes of reproduction, 1300-1840.* Oxford, UK: Basil Blackwell.

Machung, A. (1989). Talking career, thinking job. *Feminist Studies, 15,* 35-58.

MacKinnon, C. A. (1989). *Toward a feminist theory of the state.* Cambridge, MA: Harvard University Press.

Majors, R. (1992). Cool pose: The proud signature of black survival. In M. Kimmel & M. Messner (Eds.), *Men's lives* (pp. 131-135). New York: Macmillan.

Marcuse, H. (1955). *Eros and civilization.* Boston: Beacon.

Mare, R. D. (1991). Five decades of educational assortative mating. *American Sociological Review, 56,* 15-32.

Marini, M. M., & Greenberger, E. (1988). Sex differences in occupational aspirations and expectations. *Sociology of Work and Occupations, 5,* 147-178.

Marsden, P. V. (1988). Homogeneity in confiding relationships. *Social Networks, 10,* 57-76.

Marsiglio, W. (1993). Contemporary scholarship on fatherhood: Culture, identity, and conduct. *Journal of Family Issues, 14,* 484-509.

Martin, C. L. (1993). New directions for investigating children's gender knowledge. *Developmental Review, 13,* 184-204.

Marvin v. Marvin, 18 Cal. 3d (1976).

Mason, P. L. (1996). *Joblessness and unemployment: A review of the literature* (Rep. No. LR-JU-96-03). Philadelphia: University of Pennsylvania, National Center on Fathers and Families.

Massey, D., & Denton, M. (1993). *American apartheid: Segregation and the making of the underclass.* Cambridge, MA: Harvard University Press.

McDaniel, A. (1990). The power of culture: A review of the idea of Africa's influence on family structure in antebellum America. *Journal of Family History, 15,* 225-238.

McDaniel, A. (1994). Historical racial differences in living arrangements of children. *Journal of Family History, 19,* 57-77.

McHale, S. M., Bartko, W. T., Crouter, A. C., & Perry-Jenkins, M. (1990). Children's housework and psychosocial functioning: The mediating effects of parents' sex-role behaviors and attitudes. *Child Development, 61,* 1413-1426.

McLanahan, S. (1985). The reproduction of poverty. *American Journal of Sociology, 90,* 873-901.

McLanahan, S., & Booth, K. (1991). Mother-only families: Problems, prospects, and politics. In A. Booth (Ed.), *Contemporary families: Looking forward, looking back* (pp. 405-428). Minneapolis, MN: National Council on Family Relations.

McLanahan, S., & Bumpass, L. (1988). Intergenerational consequences of family disruption. *American Journal of Sociology, 94,* 130-152.

McLanahan, S., & Sandefur, G. (1995). *Growing up with a single parent.* Cambridge, MA: Harvard University Press.

Mead, G. H. (1967). *Mind, self, and society.* Chicago: University of Chicago Press. (Original work published 1934)

Mead, M. (1949). *Male and female.* New York: William Morrow.

Mead, M. (1963). *Sex and temperament in three primitive societies.* New York: William Morrow. (Original work published 1935)

Menaghan, E., & Parcel, T. (1990). Parental employment and family life. *Journal of Marriage and the Family, 52,* 1079-1098.

Merton, R. K. (1948). The self-fulfilling prophecy. *Antioch Review, 8,* 193-210.

Messner, M. (1993). "Changing men" and feminist politics in the U.S. *Theory & Society, 22,* 723-737.

Miall, C. E. (1987). The stigma of involuntary childlessness. In A. Skolnick & J. Skolnick (Eds.), *Family in transition.* Glenview, IL: Scott, Foresman.

Michaelson, K. L. (1988). *Childbirth in America.* South Hadley, MA: Bergin & Garvey.

Miller, J., & Garrison, H. (1982). Sex roles: The division of labor at home and in the workplace. *Annual Review of Sociology, 8,* 237-262.

Miller-Loessi, K. (1992). Toward gender integration in the workplace. *Sociological Perspectives, 35,* 1-15.

Mindel, C. H., Habenstein, R. W., & Wright, R., Jr. (1988). Family lifestyles of America's ethnic minorities. In C. H. Mindel, R. W. Habenstein, & R. Wright, Jr. (Eds.), *Ethnic families in America* (3rd ed., pp. 1-16). New York: Elsevier.

Mintz, S. (1996, October). *From patriarchy to androgyny and other myths: Placing men's family roles in historical perspective.* Paper presented at the National Symposium on Men in Families, Pennsylvania State University, Philadelphia.

Mirowsky, J., & Ross, C. (1989). *Social causes of psychological distress.* New York: Aldine de Gruyter.

Mitchell, J. (1974). *Psychoanalysis and feminism: Freud, Reich, Laing and women.* New York: Random House.

Mnookin, R. H. (1975). Child custody adjudication: Judicial functions in the face of indeterminacy. *Law and Contemporary Problems, 39,* 226-293.

Mnookin, R. H., Maccoby, E., Depner, C., & Albiston, C. (1990). Private ordering revisited. In S. Sugarman & H. H. Kay (Eds.), *Divorce reform at the crossroads* (pp. 37-74). New Haven, CT: Yale University Press.

Moen, P. (1985). Continuities and discontinuities in women's labor force activity. In G. H. Elder, Jr. (Ed.), *Life course dynamics: Trajectories and transitions, 1968-1980* (pp. 113-155). Ithaca, NY: Cornell University Press.

Moen, P. (1992). *Women's two roles.* New York: Auburn House.

Moen, P., & Schorr, A. L. (1987). Families and social policy. In M. B. Sussman & S. K. Steinmetz (Eds.), *Handbook of marriage and the family* (pp. 795-813). New York: Plenum.

Moore, K., Spain, D., & Bianchi, S. M. (1984). The working wife and mothers. *Marriage and Family Review, 7*, 77-98.

Morgan, M. (1975). *The total woman.* New York: Pocket.

Morgan, S. P., McDaniel, A., Miller, A. T., & Preston, S. H. (1993). Racial differences in household and family structure at the turn of the century. *American Journal of Sociology, 98*, 798-828.

Muir, F., & Brett, S. (1980). *On children.* London: Heinemann.

Muller v. Oregon, 298 U.S. 412 (1908).

Murray, C. (1984). *Losing ground: American social policy, 1950-1980.* New York: Basic Books.

Murstein, B. (1974). *Love, sex, and marriage through the ages.* New York: Springer.

Navarro, M. (1996, August 31). Appeals court rebuffs lesbian in custody bid; child will stay with father who killed. *New York Times*, v. 145 7N, 7L, col 5.)

Nelson, K. (1986). *Event knowledge: Structure and function in development.* Hillsdale, NJ: Lawrence Erlbaum.

Oakley, A. (1974). *The sociology of housework.* New York: Pantheon.

O'Connell, M. (1993). *Where's papa: Fathers' role in child care.* (Population Trends and Public Policy, No. 20). Washington, DC: Population Reference Bureau.

O'Hare, W. P. (1992). *America's minorities: The demographics of diversity* (Population Bulletin, Vol. 47). Washington, DC: Population Reference Bureau.

O'Hare, W. P. (1996). *A new look at poverty in America* (Population Bulletin, Vol. 51, No. 2). Washington, DC: Population Reference Bureau.

O'Hare, W. P., & Felt, J. C. (1991). *Asian Americans: America's fastest growing minority group.* (Population Trends and Public Policy, No. 14). Washington, DC: Population Reference Bureau.

Osmond, M., & Thorne, B. (1991). Feminist theories: The social construction of gender in families and society. In P. Boss, W. Doherty, R. LaRossa, W. Schumm, & S. Steinmetz (Eds.), *Sourcebook of family theories and methods.* New York: Plenum.

Otten, L. A. (1993). *Women's rights and the law.* Westport, CT: Praeger.

Palmer, J. L., Smeeding, T., & Torrey, B. B. (1988). *The vulnerable.* Washington, DC: Urban Institute.

Pardo, M. (1990). Mexican American grassroots community activists: Mothers of East Los Angeles. *Frontiers, 11*, 1-7.

Pardo, M. (1995). Doing it for the kids: Mexican American community activists, border feminists? In M. M. Ferree & P. Y. Martin (Eds.), *Feminist organizations: Harvest of the new women's movement* (pp. 356-371). Philadelphia: Temple University Press.

Parke, R. D. (1981). *Fathers.* Cambridge, MA: Harvard University Press.

Parke, R. D. (1988). Families in life-span perspective: A multilevel developmental approach. In E. M. Hetherington, R. Lerner, & M. Perlmutter (Eds.), *Child development in life-span perspective* (pp. 151-190). Hillsdale, NJ: Lawrence Erlbaum.

Parke, R. D. (1996). *Fatherhood*. Cambridge, MA: Harvard University Press.

Parke, R. D., & Stearns, P. N. (1993). In G. H. Elder, J. Modell, & R. D. Parke (Eds.), *Children in time and place: Developmental and historical insights* (pp. 147-170). New York: Cambridge University Press.

Parke, R. D., & Tinsley, B. (1984). Fatherhood: Historical and contemporary perspectives. In K. A. McCloskey & H. W. Reese (Eds.), *Life-span developmental psychology: Historical and generational effects* (pp. 429-457). New York: Academic Press.

Patzer, G. (1985). *The physical attractiveness phenomena*. New York: Plenum.

Payne, K. (Ed.). (1983). *Between ourselves: Letters between mothers and daughters, 1750-1982*. Boston: Houghton Mifflin.

Pearson, J., West, R., & Turner, L. (1995). *Gender and communications*. Dubuque, IA: Brown & Benchmark.

Pérez, S. M., & Salazar, D. L. R. (1993). Economic, labor force, and social implications of Latino educational and population trends. *Hispanic Journal of Behavioral Sciences, 15*, 188-229.

Peterson, G. W., & Rollins, B. C. (1987). Parent-child socialization. In M. Sussman & S. Steinmetz (Eds.), *Handbook of marriage and the family* (pp. 471-507). New York: Plenum.

Phillips, D. (1989). Future directions and need for child care in the United States. In J. S. Lande, S. Starr, & N. Gunsenhauser (Eds.), *Caring for children*. Hillsdale, NJ: Lawrence Erlbaum.

Piaget, J. (1932). *The moral judgement of the child*. London: Kegan Paul.

Piotrkowski, C. (1978). *Work and the family system*. New York: Free Press.

Pleck, E. (1983). A mother's wages: Income earning among married Italian and black women, 1896-1911. In M. Gordon (Ed.), *The American family in socio-historical perspective*. New York: St. Martin's.

Pleck, J. (1983). Husbands' paid work and family roles. In H. Lopata & J. Pleck (Eds.), *Research in the interweave of social roles* (pp. 251-333). Greenwich, CT: JAI.

Pleck, J. (1984). The work-family role system. In P. Voydanoff (Ed.), *Work and family* (pp. 8-19). Palo Alto, CA: Mayfield. (Original work published 1977 in *Social Problems, 24*, 417-427)

Pleck, J. (1985). *Working wives/working husbands*. Beverly Hills, CA: Sage.

Pleck, J. (1987). American fathering in historical perspective. In M. Kimmel (Ed.), *Changing men* (pp. 83-97). Newbury Park, CA: Sage.

Pleck, J. (1993). Are "family-supportive" employer policies relevant to men? In J. C. Hood (Ed.), *Men, work, and family* (pp. 217-237). Newbury Park, CA: Sage.

Pogrebin, L. C. (1983). *Family politics*. New York: McGraw-Hill.

Pollock, L. (1983). *Forgotten children: Parent-child relations from 1500 to 1900*. Cambridge, UK: Cambridge University Press.

Pomerleau, A., Bolduc, D., Malcuit, G., & Cossette, L. (1990). Pink or blue: Environmental stereotypes in the first two years of life. *Sex Roles, 22*, 359-367.

Pomeroy, S. B. (1975). *Goddesses, whores, wives, and slaves: Women in classical antiquity*. New York: Schocken.

Popenoe, D. (1993). American family decline, 1960-1990. *Journal of Marriage and the Family, 55,* 527-544.

Popenoe, D. (1996). *Life without father.* New York: Martin Kessler/Free Press.

Porter, M. (1990). *The competitive advantage of nations.* New York: Free Press.

Power, E. (1975). *Medieval women.* Cambridge, UK: Cambridge University Press.

Presser, H. B. (1986). Shift work among American women and child care. *Journal of Marriage and the Family, 48,* 551-564.

Presser, H. B. (1988). Shift work and child care among dual-earner American parents. *Journal of Marriage and the Family, 50,* 133-148.

Presser, H. B. (1989). Can we make time for children? *Demography, 26,* 523-554.

Pruett, K. (1987). *The nurturing father.* New York: Warner.

Pyke, K., & Coltrane, S. (1996). Entitlement, gratitude, and obligation in family work. *Journal of Family Issues, 17,* 60-82.

Queen, S. A., & Habenstein, R. W. (1967). *The family in various cultures.* Philadelphia: Lippincott.

Radin, N. (1982). Primary caregiving and role-sharing fathers. In M. Lamb (Ed.), *Nontraditional families* (pp. 173-204). Hillsdale, NJ: Lawrence Erlbaum.

Radin, N. (1994). Primary caregiving fathers in intact families. In A. E. Gottfried & A. W. Gottfried (Eds.), *Redefining families: Implications for children's development* (pp. 11-54). New York: Plenum.

Rainwater, L., & Smeeding, T. M. (1995). *Doing poorly: The real income of American children in a comparative perspective* (Working Paper No. 127), Maxwell School of Citizenship and Public Affairs, Luxembourg Income Study. Syracuse, NY: Syracuse University.

Rapp, R. (1992). Family and class in contemporary America: Notes toward an understanding of ideology. In B. Thorne (Ed.), *Rethinking the family* (pp. 49-70). Boston: Northeastern University Press.

Rapping, E. (1994). *Mediations: Forays into the culture and gender wars.* Boston: South End.

The real Mother Goose (B. F. Wright, Illus.). (1916). Chicago: Rand McNally.

Reiss, I. L. (1971). *The family system in America.* New York: Holt.

Reskin, B. F., & Hartmann, H. (1986). *Women's work, men's work: Sex segregation on the job.* Washington, DC: National Academy Press.

Reskin, B. F., & Padavic, I. (1994). *Women and men at work.* Thousand Oaks, CA: Pine Forge.

Reskin, B. F., & Roos, P. A. (1990). *Job queues, gender queues.* Philadelphia: Temple University Press.

Rheingold, H. L., & Cook, K. V. (1975). The contents of boys' and girls' rooms as an index of parents' behavior. *Child Development, 46,* 459-463.

Rhode, D. L. (1989). *Justice and gender: Sex discrimination and the law.* Cambridge, MA: Harvard University Press.

Ridgeway, C. (Ed.). (1991). *Gender, interaction, and inequality.* New York: Springer-Verlag.

Riding Murphy Brown's coattails. (1992, September 21). *New York Times,* p. C1.

Rindfuss, R., Morgan, S. P., & Swicegood, C. G. (1984). *First births in America.* Berkeley: University of California Press.

Risman, B. (1986). Can men "mother"? Life as a single father. *Family Relations, 5,* 95-102.

Risman, B., & Schwartz, P. (Eds.). (1989). *Gender in intimate relationships.* Belmont, CA: Wadsworth.

Rivenburg, R. (1996, February 5). When the laws of God and man converge. *Los Angeles Times,* pp. E1, E3.

Robinson, C. C., & Morris, J. T. (1986). The gender-stereotyped nature of Christmas toys received by 36-, 48-, and 60-month-old children: A comparison between nonrequested vs. requested toys. *Sex Roles, 15,* 21-32.

Robinson, J. (1988). Who's doing the housework? *American Demographics, 10,* 24-28, 63.

Rohner, R. (1975). *They love me, they love me not.* New Haven, CT: HRAF.

Rolison, G. (1992). Black, single female headed family formation in large U.S. cities. *Sociological Quarterly, 33,* 473-481.

Rollins, J. (1985). *Between women: Domestics and their employers.* Philadelphia: Temple University Press.

Romero, M. (1992). *Maid in the USA.* New York: Routledge.

Rosaldo, M. (1980). The use and abuse of anthropology. *Signs, 5,* 389-417.

Rosen, E. (1987). *Bitter choices: Blue-collar women in and out of work.* Chicago: University of Chicago Press.

Rosenthal, R., & Jacobson, L. (1968). *Pygmalion in the classroom: Teacher expectations and pupils' intellectual development.* New York: Holt.

Ross, C. E., Mirowsky, J., & Huber, J. (1983). Dividing work, sharing work, and in-between: Marriage patterns and depression. *American Sociological Review, 48,* 809-823.

Rossi, A. S. (1977). A biosocial perspective on parenting. *Daedalus, 106,* 1-31.

Rotundo, A. (1993). *American manhood.* New York: Basic Books.

Rubin, G. (1975). The traffic in women: Notes on the political economy of sex. In R. Reiter (Ed.), *Toward an anthropology of women* (pp. 157-210). New York: Monthly Review Press.

Rubin, J., Provenzano, R., & Luria, Z. (1974). The eye of the beholder: Parents' views on sex of newborns. *American Journal of Orthopsychiatry, 44,* 512-519.

Rubin, L. (1976). *Worlds of pain: Life in the working class family.* New York: Basic Books.

Rubin, L. (1983). *Intimate strangers.* New York: Harper & Row.

Rubin, L. (1994). *Families on the fault line: America's working class speaks about the family, economy, and ethnicity.* New York: HarperCollins.

Rubin, Z., Peplau, L., & Hill, C. (1981). Loving and leaving: Sex differences in romantic attachments. *Sex Roles, 7,* 821-835.

Ruddick, S. (1989). *Maternal thinking: Toward a politics of peace.* Boston: Beacon.

Ruggles, S. (1994). The origins of African-American family structure. *American Sociological Review, 59,* 136-151.

Russell, G. (1983). *The changing role of fathers?* St. Lucia, Australia: University of Queensland Press.

Ryan, M. (1981). *The cradle of the middle class.* Cambridge, UK: Cambridge University Press.

Ryan, M. (1982). *The empire of the mother: American writing about domesticity, 1830-1860.* New York: Haworth.

Sachs, A. S., & Wilson, J. H. (1979). *Sexism and the law.* New York: Free Press.

Safilios-Rothschild, C. (1977). *Love, sex, and sex roles.* Englewood Cliffs, NJ: Prentice Hall.

Salmon, M. (1986). *Women and the law of property in early America.* Chapel Hill: University of North Carolina Press.

Sanday, P. (1981). *Female power and male dominance.* Cambridge, UK: Cambridge University Press.

Sattel, J. W. (1992). The inexpressive male. In M. S. Kimmel & M. A. Messner (Eds.), *Men's lives* (pp. 350-370). New York: Macmillan.

Schlafly, P. (1981). *The power of the Christian woman.* Cincinnati, OH: Stanford Publishing.

Schoen, R., & Weinick, R. M. (1993). Partner choice in marriages and cohabitations. *Journal of Marriage and the Family, 55,* 408-414.

Schur, E. (1984). *Labeling women deviant.* New York: Random House.

Schutz, A. (1970). *On phenomenology and social relations.* Chicago: University of Chicago Press.

Scott, J. W., & Tilly, L. A. (1975). Women's work and the family in nineteenth century Europe. *Comparative Studies in Society and History, 17,* 36-64.

Searle, E. (1988). *Predatory kinship and the creation of the Norman state, 840-1066.* Berkeley: University of California Press.

Segal, L. (1990). *Slow motion: Changing masculinities, changing men.* New Brunswick, NJ: Rutgers University Press.

Seidensticker, E. G. (1977). *Genji days.* New York: Kodansha International.

Seltzer, J. A. (1994). Consequences of marital dissolution for children. *Annual Review of Sociology, 20,* 235-266.

Settles, B. (1987). A perspective on tomorrow's families. In M. B. Sussman & S. K. Steinmetz (Eds.), *Handbook of marriage and the family* (pp. 157-180). New York: Plenum.

Shakin, M., Shakin, D., & Sternglanz, S. H. (1985). Infant clothing: Sex labeling for strangers. *Sex Roles, 12,* 955-963.

Shanley, M. L. (1989). *Feminism, marriage, and the law in Victorian England, 1850-1895.* Princeton, NJ: Princeton University Press.

Shelton, B. A. (1992). *Women, men, time.* New York: Greenwood.

Shikibu, M. (1976). *The tale of Genji* (E. Seidensticker, Trans.). New York: Knopf.

Shorter, E. (1975). *The making of the modern family.* New York: Basic Books.

Shweder, R. A., & Levine, R. A. (Eds.). (1984). *Culture theory: Essays on mind, self, and emotion.* Cambridge, UK: Cambridge University Press.

Sidel, R. (1990). *On her own: Growing up in the shadow of the American dream.* New York: Viking.

Signorella, M. L., Bigler, R. S., & Liben, L. S. (1993). Developmental differences in children's gender schemata about others: A meta-analytic review. *Developmental Review, 13,* 147-183.

Silvestri, G., & Lukasiewicz, J. (1991). Occupational employment projections. *Monthly Labor Review, 114,* 64-94.

Simpson, J. A., Campbell, B., & Bersheid, E. (1986). The association between romantic love and marriage: Kephart (1967) twice revisited. *Personality and Social Psychology Bulletin, 12,* 363-372.

Skocpol, T. (1979). *States and social revolution.* Cambridge, UK: Cambridge University Press.

Skolnick, A. (1987). *The intimate environment.* Boston: Little, Brown.

Skolnick, A. (1991). *Embattled paradise: The American family in an age of uncertainty.* New York: Basic Books.

Smart, C. (1984). *The ties that bind: Law, marriage and the reproduction of patriarchal relations.* London: Routledge & Kegan Paul.

Smith, J. E., Waldorf, V. A., & Trembath, D. L. (1990). Single white male looking for thin, very attractive . . . *Sex Roles, 23,* 675-685.

Sonestein, F. L., & Acs, G. (1996). *Welfare reform: An analysis of the issues: Teenage childbearing, the trends and their implications.* Washington, DC: Urban Institute.

Sorensen, E., & Turner, M. (1996). *Barriers in child support enforcement: A literature review* (LR-SB-96-04). Philadelphia: University of Pennsylvania, National Center on Fathers and Families.

Sorrentino, C. (1990). The changing family in international perspective. *Monthly Labor Review, 113,* 41-58.

Spain, D. (1992). *Gendered spaces.* Chapel Hill: University of North Carolina Press.

Spence, J. T., Deaux, K., & Helmreich, R. L. (1985). Sex roles in contemporary American society. In G. Lindzey & E. Aronson (Eds.), *Handbook of social psychology* (pp. 149-178). New York: Random House.

Speth, L. E. (1982). The married women's property acts, 1839-1965: Reform, reaction, or revolution? In D. K. Weisberg (Ed.), *Women and the law* (Vol. 2, pp. 69-92). Cambridge, MA: Schenkmen.

Spickard, P. R. (1989). *Mixed blood: Intermarriage and ethnic identity in twentieth century America.* Madison: University of Wisconsin Press.

Spitze, G. (1988). Women's employment and family relations. *Journal of Marriage and the Family, 50,* 595-618.

Stacey, J. (1996). *In the name of the family: Rethinking family values in the postmodern age.* Boston: Beacon.

Stacey, J., & Thorne, B. (1985). The missing feminist revolution in sociology. *Social Problems, 32,* 301-316.

Stack, C. (1974). *All our kin.* New York: Harper & Row.

Stack, C. B., & Burton, L. M. (1994). Kinscripts: Reflections of family, generation, and culture. In E. N. Glenn, G. Chang, & L. R. Forcey (Eds.), *Mothering: Ideology, experience, and agency* (pp. 33-44). New York: Routledge.

Starrels, M. E., Bould, S., & Nicholas, L. J. (1994). The feminization of poverty in the United States: Gender, race, ethnicity, and family factors. *Journal of Family Issues, 15,* 590-607.

Stein, L., & Baxter, A. K. (Eds.). (1974). A note about this volume. In D. Dix, *How to win and hold a husband.* New York: Arno.

Stern, M., & Karraker, K. H. (1989). Sex stereotyping of infants: A review of gender labeling studies. *Sex Roles, 20,* 501-522.

Stone, L. (1977). *The family, sex and marriage in England, 1500-1800.* New York: Harper & Row.

Straus, M. A. (1991). Physical violence in American families: Incidence, rates, causes, and trends. In D. Knudsen & J. Miller (Eds.), *Abused and battered* (pp. 17-34). New York: Aldine de Gruyter.

Surra, C. A. (1991). Research and theory on mate selection and premarital relationships in the 1980s. In A. Booth (Ed.), *Contemporary families* (pp. 54-75). Minneapolis, MN: National Council on Family Relations.

Sweet, J. A., & Bumpass, L. L. (1987). *American families and households.* New York: Russell Sage.

Synnott, A. (1983). Little angels, little devils: A sociology of children. *Canadian Review of Sociology and Anthropology, 20,* 79-95.

Taylor, E. (1989). *Prime-time families: Television culture in postwar America.* Berkeley: University of California Press.

Taylor, R. L. (Ed.). (1994). *Minority families in the United States: A multicultural perspective.* Englewood Cliffs, NJ: Prentice Hall.

Thompson, L. (1993). Conceptualizing gender in marriage: The case of marital care. *Journal of Marriage and the Family, 55,* 557-569.

Thompson, L., & Walker, A. J. (1989). Gender in families: Women and men in marriage, work, and parenthood. *Journal of Marriage and the Family, 51,* 845-871.

Thorne, B. (1993). *Gender play: Girls and boys in school.* New Brunswick, NJ: Rutgers University Press.

Thorne, B. (with Yalom, M., Eds.). (1992). *Rethinking the family: Some feminist questions* (Rev. ed.). Boston: Northeastern University Press.

Thornton, A. (1989). Changing attitudes toward family issues in the United States. *Journal of Marriage and the Family, 51,* 873-893.

Tiffany, S. (1982). *Women, work, and motherhood.* Englewood Cliffs, NJ: Prentice Hall.

Tittle, C. K. (1981). *Careers and family: Sex roles and adolescent life plans.* Beverly Hills, CA: Sage.

Tong, R. (1989). *Feminist thought.* Boulder, CO: Westview.

Too late for Prince Charming. (1986, June 2). *Newsweek, 107*(22), 54-57, 61.

Towler, J., & Bramall, J. (1986). *Midwives in history and society.* London: Croom Helm.

Traube, E. G. (1992). *Dreaming identities: Class, gender, and generation in 1980s Hollywood movies.* Boulder, CO: Westview.

Trost, J. (1990). Do we mean the same by the concept of family? *Communication Research, 17,* 431-443.

Tucker, R. (1978). *The Marx-Engels reader* (2nd ed.). New York: Norton.

Uhlenberg, P. (1980). Death and the family. *Journal of Family History, 5,* 313-320.

Ullian, D. (1984). "Why girls are good": A constructivist view. *Sex Roles, 11,* 241-256.

Umberson, D., Chen, M. D., House, J. S., Hopkins, K., & Slaten, E. (1996). The effects of social relationships on psychological well-being: Are men and women really so different? *American Sociological Review, 61,* 837-857.

Ungerson, C. (Ed.). (1990). *Gender and caring: Work and welfare in Britain and Scandinavia.* New York: Harvester Wheatsheaf.

U.S. Bureau of the Census. (1975). *Historical statistics of the United States: Colonial times to 1970.* Washington, DC: Government Printing Office.

U.S. Bureau of the Census. (1989). *Studies in marriage and the family* (Current Population Reports, Series P-23, No. 162). Washington, DC: Government Printing Office.

U.S. Bureau of the Census. (1990). *Work and family patterns of American women* (Current Population Reports, Series P-23, No. 165). Washington, DC: Government Printing Office.

U.S. Bureau of the Census. (1991a). *Fertility of American women* (Current Population Reports, Series P-20, No. 454). Washington, DC: Government Printing Office.

U.S. Bureau of the Census. (1991b). *Late expectations: Childbearing patterns of American women for the 1990s* (Current Population Reports, Series P-23, No. 176). Washington, DC: Government Printing Office.

U.S. Bureau of the Census. (1992a). *Marital status and living arrangements* (Current Population Reports, Series P-20, No. 468). Washington, DC: Government Printing Office.

U.S. Bureau of the Census. (1992b). *Marriage, divorce, and remarriage in the 1990s* (Current Population Reports, Series P-23, No. 180). Washington, DC: Government Printing Office.

U.S. Bureau of the Census. (1993a). *The Hispanic population of the United States* (Current Population Reports, Series P-20, No. 475). Washington, DC: Government Printing Office.

U.S. Bureau of the Census. (1993b). *Population projections of the United States, by age, sex, race, and Hispanic origin: 1993-2050* (Current Population Reports, Series P-25, No. 1104: Middle Series). Washington, DC: Government Printing Office.

U.S. Bureau of the Census. (1994a). *Fertility of American women* (Current Population Reports, Series P-20, No. 482). Washington, DC: Government Printing Office.

U.S. Bureau of the Census. (1994b). *Household and family characteristics* (Current Population Reports, Series P-20, No. 483). Washington, DC: Government Printing Office.

U.S. Bureau of the Census. (1994c). *Marital status and living arrangements* (Current Population Reports, Series P-20, No. 484). Washington, DC: Government Printing Office.

U.S. Bureau of the Census. (1995a). *Population profile of the United States* (Current Population Reports, Series P-23, No. 189). Washington, DC: Government Printing Office.

U.S. Bureau of the Census. (1995b). *Statistical abstract of the United States: 1995* (115th ed.). Washington, DC: Government Printing Office.

U.S. Bureau of the Census. (1996a). *Income, poverty, and the valuation on noncash benefits: 1994* (Current Population Reports, Series P-60, No. 189). Washington, DC: Government Printing Office.

U.S. Bureau of the Census. (1996b). *Who's minding our preschoolers?* (Current Population Reports: Household Economic Studies, Series P-70, No. 53). Washington, DC: Government Printing Office.

U.S. Department of Health and Human Services. (1990). *Vital statistics of the United States: Vol. 1. Natality.* Washington, DC: Government Printing Office.

U.S. Department of Health and Human Services, National Center for Health Statistics. (1995). *Births to unmarried mothers: United States, 1980-92* (Vital Health Statistics, Vol. 21, No. 53). Washington, DC: Author.

U.S. Department of Health and Human Services, National Center for Health Statistics. (1996). *Monthly vital statistics report* (Vol. 45, No. 3, Suppl. 2). Washington, DC: Author.

U.S. Department of Labor. (1993). *The Family and Medical Leave Act of 1993 (FMLA)* (Employment Standards Administration Fact Sheet No. ESA 93-24). Washington, DC: Author.

U.S. Department of Labor, Bureau of Labor Statistics. (1994, May). *Women's labor force commitment remains firm* (Issues in Labor Statistics). Washington, DC: Government Printing Office.

U.S. Office of Management and Budget. *Budget of the United States Government: FY 1997.* Washington, DC: Government Printing Office.

Valdivieso, R., & Davis, C. (1988). *U.S. Hispanics: Challenging issues for the 1990s.* Washington, DC: Population Reference Bureau.

Vannoy-Hiller, D. (1984). Power dependence and division of family work. *Sex Roles, 10,* 1003-1019.

Vatsyayana. (1963). *The kama sutra of Vatsyayana* (R. Burton, Trans.). London: Allen & Unwin.

Vega, W. W. (1991). Hispanic families in the 1980s: A decade of research. In A. Booth (Ed.), *Contemporary families: Looking forward, looking back* (pp. 297-306). Minneapolis, MN: National Council on Family Relations.

Voydanoff, P. (1987). *Work and family life.* Newbury Park, CA: Sage.

Walster, E., & Walster, G. W. (1978). *A new look at love.* Reading, MA: Addison-Wesley.

Walter, R. G. (1974). *Primers for prudery: Sexual advice to Victorian America.* Englewood Cliffs, NJ: Prentice Hall.

Warren, C. (1987). *Madwives: Schizophrenic women at mid-century.* New Brunswick, NJ: Rutgers University Press.

Weinberg, D. H. (1996). *A brief look at postwar U.S. income inequality* (Current Population Reports, Household Economic Studies, Series P-60, No. 191). Washington, DC: U.S. Bureau of the Census.

Weitzman, L. (1981). *The marriage contract.* New York: Free Press.

Welter, B. (1966). The cult of true womanhood: 1820-1860. *American Quarterly, 18,* 151-174.

Wertz, R. W., & Wertz, D. C. (1977). *Lying-in: A history of childbirth in America.* New York: Free Press.

West, C., & Fenstermaker, S. (1993). Power and the accomplishment of gender: An ethnomethodological perspective. In P. England (Ed.), *Theory on gender/feminism on theory* (pp. 151-174). New York: Aldine de Gruyter.

West, C., & Iritani, B. (1986). *The male older norm.* Unpublished manuscript, University of California, Santa Cruz.

West, C., & Zimmerman, D. (1987). Doing gender. *Gender & Society, 1,* 125-151.

Westoff, C. F. (1986). Fertility in the United States. *Science, 234,* 554-559.

Whitehead, B. D. (1993, April). Dan Quayle was right. *The Atlantic, 271*(4), 47-84.

Whiting, B. (1965). Sex identity conflict and physical violence: A comparative study. *American Anthropologist, 67,* 123-140.

Whyte, M. K. (1978). *The status of women in preindustrial societies.* Princeton, NJ: Princeton University Press.

Whyte, M. K. (1992). Choosing mates: The American way. *Society, 29,* 71-77.

A wife, too, can say no. (1996, February 1). *Los Angeles Times,* Crimewatch.

Wilkie, J. R. (1993). Changes in U.S. men's attitudes toward the family provider role, 1972-1989. *Gender & Society, 7,* 261-279.

Williams, E., Radin, N., & Allegro, T. (1992). Sex role attitudes of adolescents reared primarily by their fathers: An 11-year follow-up. *Merrill-Palmer Quarterly, 38,* 457-476.

Williams, J. H. (1993). Sexuality in marriage. In B. Wolman & J. Money (Eds.), *Handbook of human sexuality* (pp. 93-122). Northvale, NJ: Jason Aronson.

Williamson, J. (1980). *New people: Miscegenation and mulattoes in the United States.* New York: Free Press.

Willie, C. V. (1981). *A new look at black families.* Bayside, NY: General Hall.

Willie, C. V. (1985). *Black and white families.* Bayside, NY: General Hall.

Wilson, W. J. (1987). *The truly disadvantaged: The inner city, the underclass, and public policy.* Chicago: University of Chicago Press.

Wong, S. C. (1994). Diverted mothering: Representations of caregivers of color in the age of "multiculturalism." In E. N. Glenn, G. Chang, & L.R. Forcey (Eds.), *Mothering: Ideology, experience, and agency* (pp. 67-91). New York: Routledge.

Wood, J. T. (1994a). *Gendered lives: Communication, gender, and culture.* Belmont, CA: Wadsworth.

Wood, J. T. (1994b). *Who cares: Women, care, and culture.* Carbondale: Southern Illinois University Press.

Wood, J. T. (1996). She says/he says: Communication, caring, and conflict in heterosexual relationships. In J. T. Wood (Ed.), *Gendered relationships* (pp. 149-162). Mountain View, CA: Mayfield.

Wood, S. (1989). *The transformation of work.* London: Unwin Hyman.

Wright, M. J. (1979). Reproductive hazards and "protective" discrimination. *Feminist Studies, 5,* 302-309.

Yellowbird, M., & Snipp, C. W. (1994). American Indian families. In R. L. Taylor (Ed.), *Minority families in the United States: A multicultural perspective* (pp. 179-201). Englewood Cliffs, NJ: Prentice Hall.

Zaretsky, E. (1976). *Capitalism, the family, and personal life.* New York: Harper & Row.

Zavella, P. (1987). *Women's work and Chicano families.* Ithaca, NY: Cornell University Press.

Zelizer, V. (1985). *Pricing the priceless child: The changing social value of children.* New York: Basic Books.

Zimmerman, S. L. (1988). *Understanding family policy: Theoretical approaches* (pp. 126-144). Newbury Park, CA: Sage.

Zimmerman, S. L. (1992). *Family policies and family well-being: The role of political culture.* Newbury Park, CA: Sage.

Zinn, M. B. (1989). Family, race, and poverty in the eighties. *Signs, 14,* 856-874.

A

Abel, E. K., 78, 82, 83, 95
Abuse. *See* Physical abuse
Acker, J., 164, 165
Acs, G., 94
Adams, M., 123
Adolescents. *See* Teenagers
Adoption, 85
Advertisements, personal, 46-47
African Americans. *See* Blacks
Agger, B., 142
Agrarian societies, 41, 58-59, 59 (figure), 87, 142
Ahlburg, D. A., 48, 162, 163, 169, 170
Aid to Families with Dependent Children (AFDC), 138-139, 140, 152, 152 (figure), 173
Albert, A. A., 127
Albiston, C., 154
Aldous, J., 67, 136
Allan, K., 12, 102
Allegro, T., 128
Allgeier, E. R., 29, 32
Alwin, D. F., 167
Amato, P. R., 101
American Indians. *See* Native Americans
Amott, T. L., 60
Andelin, H. B., 27, 30, 31
Anderson, M. L., 23, 84
Anthony, Susan B., 146
Archer, W. G., 36
Arendell, T., 152
Ariès, P., 84
Asians:
    birthrates, 91
    employment of, 60, 88, 89
    family composition, 22
    interracial marriage rates, 50
    marriage rates for, 169
    percent of U. S. population, 5, 6 (figure)
Associated Press, 132

B

Baehr v. Lewin, 148
Baehr v. Miike, 148
Bailey, B. L., 42
Balbus, I., 119
Bane, M. J., 136
Baran, S. J., 13
Bardewell, J. R., 127
Barnett, R. C., 68, 70, 98
Baron, A., 144, 157
Barthel, D., 13
Bartko, W. T., 126, 129
Baruch, G. K., 68, 70, 98
Basch, N., 143
Baxter, A. K., 27
Baxter, J., 16, 59, 60
Becker, G., 16
Bem, S. L., 82, 83, 112, 113, 114, 120, 121, 122, 125, 126, 127, 128, 129
Benería, L., 23
Benjamin, J., 119
Berch, B., 164
Berger, P., 3, 15, 113
Bernard, J., 56, 67, 75, 78-81, 89
Bersheid, E., 31, 32, 45
Bianchi, S. M., 100
Bielby, D. D., 67, 69, 73
Bielby, W., 69, 73
Bigler, R. S., 122
Bilateral sexual possession, 41

About the Author

Scott Coltrane is Associate Professor of Sociology at the University of California, Riverside. His research on families, gender, and the changing role of fathers has appeared in various scholarly journals and book chapters. He is coauthor with Randall Collins of *Sociology of Marriage and the Family: Gender, Love and Property*. His book *Family Man: Fatherhood, Housework, and Gender Equity* received the American Library Association CHOICE award as one of the outstanding academic books of 1996.